Sixth Edition

San Francisco On a Shoestring

The Intelligent Traveler's and Native's
Guide to Budget Living in San Francisco.

Includes: Over 500 restaurant listings, over 200 hotels & Inns,
including Bed & Breakfast, Apartments & Hotels With Kitchens,
and Residential Clubs/Hotels. *New*: *Prime rib restaurants*

Louis E. Madison

Published by A.M. Zimmermann & Company, 2210 Jackson
Street, Suite 404, San Francisco, CA 94115, Tel. (415) 929-7577

ISBN Number 0-912125-04-7

Cover design by Maureen Martin

Computer typography by Matthew Holtz,
author of *Mastering Microsoft Word*

Printed and bound by BookCrafters

Printed in the United States of America

Once again –
to Annemarie and Mike
with love

Contents

SAN FRANCISCO

Ratings and Locations

Note: There are only two basic ratings, *Very Good* and *Excellent*. The reason for this is that *all* restaurants and hotels chosen for this book were considered at least *Very Good*. Fortunately, the large choice in San Francisco makes this possible.

Ratings

*** very good
**** excellent, BEST BUY

Note: an asterisk (*) in front of a BEST BUY means "especially recommended". Hotels & restaurants so noted are put at the top of the listings.

Locations

(1) Union Square area to Van Ness, including Post, Sutter, Bush
(2) Chinatown
(3) North Beach
(4) Fisherman's Wharf, Ghirardelli
(5) Union Street area
(6) Marina, including Chestnut, Lombard
(7) Lower Market (incl. South of Market)
(8) Financial District, Embarcadero
(9) Geary Street, south to Market
(9a) Nob Hill area
(9b) Russian Hill area
(10) Upper Polk Street, Van Ness, including Opera area
(11) Pacific Heights, Laurel Heights, Presidio Heights
(12) Japantown
(13) Geary Boulevard
(14) Haight-Ashbury, Western Addition, Panhandle
(15) Upper Market, Castro area
(16) Mission and Valencia areas
(17) Potrero
(18) UC, Parnassus areas
(19) Inner Sunset, lower Irving Street
(20) Outer Sunset, upper Irving Street
(21) West Portal, Lake Merced
(22) Inner Richmond, lower Clement
(23) Outer Richmond, upper Clement

Introduction

This is the Sixth Edition of *San Francisco on a Shoestring*, which first came to light in 1982. It is a guide book written by a practising economist (myself), and is devoted to finding the best values in hotels and lodgings, restaurants, transportation etc. It is designed not only for travellers to San Francisco, but also as a natives' guide to budget living in this city. It lists over 200 lodgings and over 500 eating places, in all categories from "economical" to "big splurge", and contains economic information on other subjects as well (transportation, museums, entertainment etc). It is now available in Hawaii, Canada, the United Kingdom, and in European countries, as well as in all corners of the U.S.

Despite creeping inflation, I have been able to keep almost the same reasonable price levels as in previous editions, with only slight changes. Some prices have gone up unreasonably, and, as a result, some good hotels and restaurants have been dropped. But there is no need to worry, since many new ones have been added. It is still true that *the cost of the book is very often recaptured the first time used.*

New Categories. This Edition continues the three new categories added to the Lodgings section of the Fifth Edition, namely, *Bed & Breakfast*, *Apartments & Hotels With Kitchens*, and *Residential Clubs/Hotels*. The restaurant listings have been expanded--more than 500 in all--and a number of restaurants serving the American specialty of prime rib have been added as a separate category.

Hotel and restaurant prices. Most hotel prices quoted in this edition are *summer season prices*. Some hotels will hike their prices even higher during this period. Hotel prices should come down after the tourist season, and stay down until the following May or June. So, be sure to check carefully. In the off-season, you can bargain for better rates than those quoted.

All restaurant prices are quoted *before* tax (6.5%) or hotel tax (11%), and tip, are added. (Note: a temporary "earthquake tax" of 1/2% has been added). This often confuses foreign visitors, since prices in many countries include *all* taxes and services. They are sometimes unpleasantly surprised when they get the bill. So, be sure to include tax and tip in your calculations *before* making decisions. Also, check prices by phone if you plan to eat a special menu.

Some restaurant and hotel prices have gone up as much as 30-40% in 1989. Some think nothing of adding $1-2 to a $7.95 restaurant entree (12.5%-25%), or $15 to a $40 room (37.5%), if they think the customer will take it. Fortunately, the competition is so keen in this city that good values can always be found to replace those hotels and restaurants that become pricey.

<u>"Shoestring"="value"</u>. For new readers, I must repeat that "shoestring" does not mean "cheap", but "value". This is relative to the price level one chooses. You do not expect white tablecloths and cloth napkins at a $2.75 Chinese lunch (although sometimes they're there). But you should get a tasty lunch, in pleasant and clean surroundings. And that's what you will find in the 50 or so lunch restaurants I recommend, where the lunch usually consists of soup, entree, and tea for $2.75-$3.95. In fact, some are of gourmet quality. By the same token, some (who can afford it) will consider a gourmet French meal for $45--which would cost twice as much in Paris--as very acceptable. And they will find it in this book.

<u>Tipping</u>. Tipping is always a bone of contention. Some suggest 15%, some even 20%. Most Europeans consider 10% adequate (if it is not already included in the price of the meal). One down-to-earth restaurant critic whom I respect suggests 10-15% on the food and drink, but not on the tax, and only if you're satisfied with the service and the food. I agree.

<u>Checking prices</u>. As always, all entries are checked and double-checked, but errors still creep in. Restaurants go out of business, hotels and eating places are often full when you want to go there, or have raised their prices. Hence, be sure to telephone first to confirm availability and price. This is also a good time to get exact instructions about how to get there.

<u>A request</u>. Should you run into a very good restaurant or hotel that fits my philosophy and is not mentioned in *San Francisco on a Shoestring*, please let me know. And if you run into a real stinker, let me know, too, so that I can keep it out of future editions.

Have fun!

Louis E. Madison

1. Transportation

To and from San Francisco and Oakland Airports

By taxi

This is the easiest but most expensive route, unless you are 4 or more-- $25-$30 between the S.F. airport and downtown, and around $35-40 to and from the Oakland Airport.

Airporter Bus to SF Airport

Except for public transportation, this is still the cheapest way to get to and from a downtown hotel-$5 one way, $8 round-trip; children under 2 free; teenagers 13-16 with an adult $3 one-way, $5 round-trip, but if alone they are considered as adults and pay full fare. This bus leaves from downtown hotels in the City every 20 minutes, beginning 5:05am from the Meridian, and stops for pick-ups at the Hyatt Union Square, St. Francis, Hilton, Nikko, Park 55 (formerly Ramada). Last bus leaves Hyatt Union Square at 10:45pm and arrives at SFO at about 11:30pm. The first bus leaves the Airport for the City at 6:20am, and thereafter every 20 minutes until 12 midnight. Call 673-2433 or one of the above hotels for information.

SamTrans to SF Airport

The San Mateo County Transit is the cheapest way to go. The 7B bus, which permits you to take as much luggage as you can carry on your lap (not in the aisle), costs $1.15 (less for seniors and students). It leaves the Terminal at 1st & Mission from 5:30am-12:50am every quarter-hour, half-hour or hour, depending on the time of day. This bus can also be boarded at 3rd, 5th, 7th and 9th & Mission.

The 7F Express bus, which permits only 1 carry-on piece of luggage, also costs $1.25 and makes the trip in about 36 minutes as compared to 55 minutes via the 7B. Phone 761-7000 for exact schedule for both buses.

Mini Buses and limousines to SF Airport

A number of small buses now provide service to and from the SF Airport They used to be $7-8 per person, but now charge $9-

10 (up to 40% inflation!), but still less than a taxi for two. They will pick you up at your hotel or home and drop you at your departing airline. Or you can board them at the Airport and they will drop you at your home or hotel. The first buses arrive at the Airport at about 6:15am and the last ones leave the Airport at about 10pm. You can find these buses in the upper (Departure) level of the Airport, center traffic island, at the Courtesy Vehicle sign. Here are some:

Airport Express, or California Minibus, 775-5121, $8.

Good Neighbors, 777-4899, $9, $7 for seniors over 60, $4 for children 2-12.

Lorrie, 334-9000. This is the oldest service and very reliable, $9.

Super Shuttle, 558-8500, $10.

Yellow Airport and Tour Service, 282-7433, $8, $5 for children over 4, under 4 free. Oakland $27 for 2, $13,50 each additional person.

Airport Connection, (Limo), 885-2666, $15 per person to a neighborhood residence, to hotels $8 per person.

AC Transit to Oakland Airport

To get to the Oakland Airport, take Bus N from the East Bay Terminal at 1st & Mission to Fruitvale & MacArthur Blvd stop, then transfer to a 57 bus to the Airport. Ride, including transfer, costs $1.50 (seniors and students $0.70). The amount of luggage you can take is more or less up to the discretion of the bus driver, but cannot exceed what you can carry, e.g., one large suitcase or 2 small bags. The N bus runs from 6:09am-12:23am. The entire trip, including the 57 bus, takes about an hour. The last bus leaves the Airport for S.F. at 12:47am. Phone 839-2882 for details.

BART to Oakland Airport

Take BART (Bay Area Rapid Transit) to the Coliseum Station in Oakland (Fremont Line) and transfer to the AIR-BART shuttle which runs every 10 minutes, 6am-midnight Mon-Sat, Sun 9am to midnight. The last bus returns from the Oakland Airport at 11:50pm. The transfer to the Shuttle costs $1.00. Phone 788-2278 for information.

Other Services to Oakland Airport

Lorrie. $39, 1-5 persons. Call at least 6 hours before flight time for home or hotel pickup. 334-9000.

Yellow Airport & Tour Service. $27 for 2, $13.50 each additonal person. 282-7433.

S.F. Airport to Oakland Airport

The Bay Area Bus Service runs buses from the San Francisco Airport to the Oakland Airport every hour on the hour, from 7am-midnight and from Oakland Airport to S.F. Airport from 6am-11 pm. Also. on holidays. The fare is $7 per person either way. Phone 632-5506.

MUNI Buses, Street Cars, Metro

Adult fare is 85 cents, 15 cents for seniors over 65 and disabled persons, 25 cents for students 5-17, and free for children under 5. *Be sure to have coins, since they do not accept bills.* Monthly fast passes are $28 for adults, $5 for youths 5-17, $4.50 for seniors and disabled. Fast passes are good on all MUNI lines, including the cable cars. Two transfers are free and can be used in all directions for the time shown (about 2 hours). There is also an *all-day pass* for $6, and a 3-day pass for $10, good on all Muni lines and on the cable cars, valid from midnight to midnight. These can be purchased from machines at the end of the cable-car lines, e.g., at Powell & Market Sts, at the STBS ticket booth at Union Square, at the Visitors Bureau at 5th & Market Sts, and weekdays at the MUNI office. Most buses run from 7am-1am. They allow unlimited trips on all regularly scheduled service, including cable cars, without paying additional fare.

Phone 673-6864 for transit information. Tell them where you are and where you want to go. They're often busy, so be patient.

Other Transit

Cable Cars

Probably San Francisco's single most popular attraction, $2 for adults 18-64, $1 for youths 5-17, 15 cents for seniors 65 and over and disabled persons, children under 5 free. For a transfer from a Muni bus, add $1 for adults and 75 cents for youths 5-17. An adult all-day pass for the whole MUNI system, including cable cars, is $6, and a 3-day pass for $10. See paragraph above on MUNI for further details.

SamTrans

The San Mateo Transit buses run from downtown San Francisco to a number of cities along the Peninsula, e.g., San Mateo, Burlingame, Redwood City, San Carlos, and Palo Alto, as well as to the S.F. Airport (see above) and Daly City. For details and schedule phone 761-7000.

San Francisco Ferry-to Sausalito & Larkspur

Used widely by residents of the two areas, these ferries are also popular tourist rides, about 30 minutes to Sausalito, and about 50 minutes to Larkspur. Prices for Sausalito or return, each way: adults age 13 & over $3.50, age 6-12 $2.60, seniors & disabled $1.75, up to 2 children 5 or under, with parent, free. Prices for Larkspur or return, each way: adults 13 & over $2.20, 6-12 $1.65, seniors or disabled $1.10, 2 children 5 & under, with parent, free. The Larkspur ferry travels between Alcatraz and Treasure Island, past Angel Island and Tiburon. *The ferries do not run New Year's Day, Thanksgiving, and Christmas Day.* For time schedules on weekdays, weekends, & holidays, phone 332-6600. You'll get a detailed recording.

Train Service

AMTRAK runs from the *AMTRAK* Oakland Station, but can be reached by a free bus shuttle from East Bay Terminal at 1st and Mission. From there you can go by train to points East and South, to Valley cities, national parks and clear across the country. Many Reno casinos run special trips at highly reduced fares and offer freebies. For information phone 982-8512. See the phone book for further telephone numbers.

The Southern Pacific Transportation Company runs commuter trains many times daily between San Francisco and San Jose, as well as points in-between. For information phone 495-4546.

Car rentals

The airline terminals and downtown San Francisco (Hilton Hotel area and Mason Street) abound in rental offices. Information on car rentals can be found in the free tourist publications that are available at all large hotel lobbies; they often include discount coupons. Also, be sure to check the larger companies such as *Hertz* (433 Mason St, phone 771-2200) for their weekend or weekly specials which may include *unlimited mileage*.

Other companies worth trying, with *unlimited mileage*: *A-1 Rent-A-Car*, 434 O'Farrell St, 771-3977; *RPM*, 410 S. Airport

Blvd, 775-5900; *Continental*, 404 O'Farrell St, 441-1771; *Thrifty*, 435 Taylor St, 673-6675; *Payless,* 415 Taylor St, 771-7711; *Flat Rate*, 583-9234 (Used Toyotas, low rates, 50-150 free miles daily, limited to S.F. radius only). An interesting car rental for use in the Bay Area is Bob Leech's Car Rental, 435 South Airport Blvd, South San Francisco, 583-3844; they'll pick you up at the Airport, $19.95 per day, 150 free miles, 7th day *free*, new Toyotas.

Overseas travelers are advised to order rental cars from overseas since this gets them *unlimited mileage* and better rates.

Golden Gate Transit

This service runs to points across the Golden Gate Bridge, to Mt. Tamalpais, Stinson Beach and points en route, but only on Saturdays and Government holidays, not weekdays. Phone 332-6600 for information on routes and prices.

Greyhound-Trailways Lines

These buses run to all parts of California, and to much of the United States. They often advertise specials which they do not volunteer over the phone-ask. Phone 558-6789 for information. See telephone book for additional numbers.

Alternative Bus Travel-Green Tortoise

This is an interesting and cheap means of transportation and holiday touring for "young" people from 15 to 75 who have a leisurely attitude toward life. The buses are stripped down, foam mattresses and overhanging bunks are added. There are firm rules: no smoking, no drugs, and no shoes on the mattresses. The company has 8 buses and the owner, Gardner Kent, often drives one himself. *Green Tortoise* has trips every Friday to Los Angeles and return Mondays ($25 each way), and every Monday and Friday night to and from Seattle ($59 each way), as well as cross-country USA (S.F. to N.Y. or Boston) 10-day camping and cookout trips. Also, trips to Yosemite, Grand Canyon, Mexico, Alaska and other destinations. Highly recommended for individualists and the adventuresome. Phone 821-0803 or 285-2441 for schedules and rates.

City and Other Tours

A number of bus companies run City tours as well as tours to outlying areas of San Francisco, e.g., Sausalito, Muir Woods, Mt. Tamalpais, the Wine Country, Carmel, Monterey. Some are: *Dolphin Tour Company,* 441-6810; *Maxi-Tours,* 441-8294; *Great Pacific Tour Company,* 626-4499; *Gray Lines* 558-9400.

Excursions to Reno, Lake Tahoe, and Las Vegas

A number of companies, including Greyhound, run bus trips–one day, overnight or 2 nights–to Lake Tahoe and Reno (some combine both cities) at very low rates. The one-day trip, from early morning until late evening, is about $30 and includes freebies, even cash when you arrive at the casinos. Their overnight trips are around $40 ($50 to Lake Tahoe), and slightly more on a weekend, or if you stay at a first-class hotel like the MGM or the Hilton. These trips are strictly promotional and are subsidized by the casinos who expect you to leave some cash there. But that is up to you. Food and drinks are practically given away.

Some of the companies offering these trips are: *Hee Chan Tours,* 397-2830; *Lucky Reno Tours,* 864-1133; *Betty's Tours,* 495-8430; *Richard Lee*'s Tours, 442-1928. I highly recommend the *Hee Chan Tours* to Reno, with stay at the Hilton or MGM. Consult the last pages of the *Sunday Examiner* pink section for advertisements of such tours. Some of the above also offer tours to other parts of the State. Some airlines offer package tours to Reno, beginning at about $139.

The excursions to Las Vegas are usually in conjunction with a local airline and begin at about $165, including airfare and 1-2 night's lodging. These are also advertised in the *Examiner's* Sunday pink section.

Driveaway Cars

If you are prepared to deliver a car to another city and have a valid driver's license, good references, and a minimum deposit ($75-$100), this is a good way to get there. You can get from and to almost any large city, e.g., from New York City to San Francisco, if you shop around. But it is getting more difficult. Sometimes the large auto rental companies, e.g., Hertz or Avis, have cars to be delivered to other parts of California. Here are two companies in this area:

Auto Caravan Corp. 64 Golden Gate Ave., 567-6029.

Auto Driveaway, 330 Townsend, 777-3740.

A Able Transport Co., 864-8800.

2. Lodging

San Francisco has the undeserved reputation of being one of the most expensive hotel cities in the U.S. It gets this from business travelers who stay in the $100-$200 rooms in the large, deluxe hotels, and from journalists who interview them, as well as from travel agents who book their customers into the bigger hotels. Once you know your way around, you'll find that hotels in San Francisco don't have to be prohibitively expensive. San Francisco is overbuilt with hotels and is still building more, especially in the deluxe category. Deluxe smaller hotels (up to 100 rooms), and deluxe Bed & Breakfast Inns, up to $100 per day for double, are also expanding, as alternatives to the large, more expensive deluxe hotels.

The prices in this Edition are tourist-season prices. Still, you should be able to get a first-class hotel room for, say, $50-$60 (double) that will compare favorably with a $100+ room in a plush hotel. You can also get a room with bath for as little as $35 (double), or a bed-and-breakfast room for less. Good, clean accommodations are also to be found in the $9-$15 per person category, and even less. Prices are lower when there are 3 or 4 to a room. If possible, correspond in advance, especially in season, and reserve, enclosing one-night's deposit.

Most hotels that include breakfast in the room rate will appear in detail in the *Bed & Breakfast* category, but will also be mentioned in this section. Apartment hotels and hotels that provide kitchens appear in detail in the category, *Apartments & Hotels With Kitchens*.

An asterisk (*) before a name denotes "especially recommended". Those so noted will be placed at the top of the listings in order to make a choice easier.

Hostels, Hostel-Type, $9-$15 Per Person

Hostels

SAN FRANCISCO INTERNATIONAL YOUTH HOSTEL, (127 beds), Bldg 240, Box A, Fort Mason, San Francisco, CA 94123, 771-7277. Opens at 4:30pm daily. (You can also register from 7am until 2pm, but admission only from 4:30pm). Hostel price is $10 per night, no age limit, *3-day maximum stay.* To get there, take bus 30, 42, or 47 to Bay and Van Ness Avenue, walk one block on Bay to the entrance to Fort Mason. Restrictions: must be out of the room by 10am, out of the hostel from 2-4pm, and in by midnight (curfew). Advantages: cooking in *communal kitchen*, hiking around piers, excellent site. For general information on hostels in the Marin Headlands, phone 331-2777 and Point Reyes, phone 663-8811.

Hostel-Type Hotels

These are lodgings intended for young people, often dormitory-type. They are very simple but clean and adequate. Young people will often find the same spirit of camaraderie which they find in hostels. An asterisk (*) in front of a name denotes "especially recommended".

*NETWORK HOSTEL (142 beds, 4 to a room, with shower, toilet, refrigerator), 10 Hallam Place (between Folsom & Harrison, 7th & 8th Sts), 431-0540. Also known as Interclub or Globe Hostel. $12 day, including tax; some, smaller, rooms for $10 per person. No curfew, 24-hour desk attendant, security. Available to genuine travellers only, either foreigners with passport or Americans who are travelling. Simple breakfast $2.50. Laundry facility, 2 common rooms, sauna. Best to reserve in writing, with 1 night's deposit (cashier's check or traveller's check preferred), made payable to "Interclub" and sent to 8 Dudley Avenue, Venice, CA 90291, USA, 2 weeks in advance. Network accommodations also in Los Angeles, Hawaii, Canada, Australia, New Zealand, Indonesia. ***(7)

UNIVERSITY OF CALIFORNIA, S.F., Housing Office, 510 Parnassus, 476-2231. Limited dormitory housing during summer months only. Pool, gym. ***(18)

SAN FRANCISCO STATE U., Housing Office, 800 Font Blvd, 338-1067. Twin-bedded room with shared-bath and dormitory housing for students during summer months. ***(18)

EUROPEAN GUEST HOUSE (15 rooms), 763 Minna (between 8th and 9th, just south of Mission), 861-6634. $9 per night per person, dormitory style, 3-6 in a room. Communal kitchen, social room with TV, showers. Has large European clientele. They organize wine-country trips, beach parties, and serve as communications center for youth travel. Well-located, near Holiday-Inn and the Greyhound bus terminal. Just off the Tenderloin, patronized by men and women. ***(7)

Y's

YMCA CENTRAL BRANCH (109 rooms), 220 Golden Gate

(Hyde), 885-0460. For men and women. Rates include use of pool and gym facilities, laundry room. Singles without bath $25, no doubles without bath. Single/double with bath $33.50. No membership required. ****(9)

YMCA CHINATOWN (47 rooms), 855 Sacramento (Stockton), 982-4412. Men only, 16 and older. Rates include tax, also use of pool, gym, and weight room. Single without bath $23.75, double $30.50. Single with bath $30.50, no double with bath. Weekly rates on request. No membership required.****(2)

Economical Hotels, $15-$25 Per Person

This listing is based on the lowest rate per person for double occupancy without tax (11%). Hotels including breakfast in the room rate are also listed in detail under *Bed & Breakfast* later in this Edition.

Note: An asterisk (*) before a name means "especially recommended". I am placing those at the top of the list in order to facilitate a choice.

BEST BUY****

*SHEEHAN (65 rooms, 20 with bath), 620 Sutter (Mason), 775-6500. This is the former YWCA, refurbished in 1988. *New rates include continental breakfast.* Single without bath $35, with private bath $50; double without bath but with sink in room $45, with private bath $65. Extra bed $10. Suites for 4-5 $85. Use of pool free for guests, $6 for the public or $60 per month. ****(1)

*OLYMPIC (85 rooms, 1/2 with bath), 140 Mason (Ellis), 982-5010. Single or double without bath $28; single with bath $35, double $42, extra bed $9. This hotel is used by German and other tour groups. It is right next to the new Park 55 (formerly Ramada), across from the Hilton. Clean and well-run, good value. ****(1)

*ADELAIDE INN (16 rooms, hall baths), 5 Isadora Duncan Lane (formerly Adelaide Place, off Taylor, near Post), 441-2261. *Rates include hot rolls and coffee for breakfast.* Single $32, double or twin beds $42. A *kitchenette and microwave are available* for light food preparation, e.g. sandwiches, salads, soups. European character. ****(1)

*THE AMSTERDAM (26 rooms, most with bath), 749 Taylor (Sutter) 673-3277. See under Bed & Breakfast, Economical

Hotels. ****(1)

*VERONA (65 rooms, 50 with bath), 317 Leavenworth (Eddy), 771-4242. Formerly, Burbank, completely refurbished, color TV in all rooms. Single without bath (double bed) $28, with bath $32. Double without bath $35, with bath $42. Extra person $10. Adjoining rooms with a bath are available. Area is a bit questionable, especially at night. ****(9)

*TEMPLE (120 rooms, 20 with bath), 469 Pine (Kearny/Montgomery), 781-2565. Single without bath $30, double $35, rollaway $5 extra. Single with bath $40, double $45. Weekly rates on request. This is a clean, well-run hotel, in the heart of the business area, ****(8).

*OBRERO, 1208 Stockton (Pacific), 989-3960. See under Bed & Breakfast, Economical Hotels. ****(2)

*GRANT PLAZA (72 rooms with bath, color TV, phone), 465 Grant Avenue (Pine). 434-3883. Single $34, double $42, twin beds $47, family suite, up to 5 persons, $82. Rooms are small but clean and comfortable. ****(2)

*HILL POINT GUEST HOUSES (9 guest homes in the area, 47 rooms, 10 with bath, plus 12 apartments with kitchen & bath), 15 Hillpoint Ave. (Parnassus Ave/Irving), 753-0393. Caters to students and guests visiting nearby University of California Medical Center on Parnassus Avenue. Single with share-bath and share kitchen $25, plus $5 for extra person; double $35 plus $5 for extra person, twin $32. Single with private bath & use of kitchen $50, extra person $5; double $60. Weekly rates are basically the same rates for 6 days and one day free. *All rooms with private bath, apartments, and some shared-bath rooms receive continental breakfast daily.* Coin-operated laundry. ****(18)

THE ANSONIA-CAMBRIDGE, 711 Post (Jones), 673-2670. See under Bed & Breakfast, Economical Hotels. ****(1)

METRO (23 rooms, all with private showers, color TV, cable), 319 Divisadero (Page/Oak), 861-5364. Single $37-43, double $43-51, twin beds $51, 2 double beds (up to 4 persons) $69. Victorian style, European character. Neighborhood is somewhat depressed but safe, 2 blocks from Haight. ****(14)

VERY GOOD***

Listed roughly in order of distance from Union Square.

ALL SEASONS (89 rooms, about half with bath), 417 Stockton (Union Square), 986-8737. Single without bath $30, with private bath $45; double without bath $35, with private bath

$50. Extra bed $7.***(1)

VIRGINIA (120 rooms, about 50 with bath), 312 Mason (O'Farrell), 397-9255. Single without bath $30, double $35; single with bath $35, double $40. About half the rooms have color TV. Hotel is old but well-kept. Good location near Union Square. ***(1)

WINDSOR (125 rooms, 1/2 with bath), 238 Eddy (Taylor/Jones), just behind the old Airporter Terminal), 885-0101. Single/double without bath $30, with bath $40. Area is a bit seedy but hotel is very good, same management as the Olympic (see above). ***(7)

GEARY (120 rooms, 100 with bath), 610 Geary (Jones/Leavenworth), 673-9221. Single without bath $24, double $26; single with bath $36, double $40, twin beds $50, 3-4 persons $55. Students receive $4 discount on room rates. European style, very popular. ****(1)

GOLDEN GATE (23 rooms, 14 with bath), 775 Bush (Stockton/Grant), 392-3702. Single without bath $45-50, double $50-55, single with bath $69, double $79. *Rates now include continental breakfast.* Building is 1913 Edwardian, decor is turn-of-the-century, many antiques, charming. ****(1).

BEL AIR (70 rooms, 35 with bath), 344 Jones (Ellis), 771-3460. Single without bath $29, with bath $32; double without bath $32, with bath $36. Extra bed $10. Refurbished in 1986. ***(9)

HOTEL ONE OF SAN FRANCISCO (175 rooms, 1/2 with baths), 108/ Market (7th St.), 861-4946. Single without bath $26.50, with bath $31.50; double without bath $34.50, with bath $39.50. Suite with bath $41.50. Extra person $5. Refurbished in 1988. ***(7)

GRAND CENTRAL (100 rooms, 10 with bath) 1412 Market (10th St), 431-9190. Single without bath $25, double $35. Single with bath $35, double $40. Weekly rates on request. ***(7)

ATHERTON (70 rooms, all with bath, 12 in guest house, share bath), 685 Ellis (Larkin), 474-5720. Single or double with shared bath $29 & $39. Single or double with private bath $49-79, extra bed $10. ***(9)

GRANT (76 rooms, all with bath, shower, TV), 753 Bush (Powell), 421-7540. Single $38, double $42, twin $50, extra person $5. Hotel is older but clean, refurbished in 1984. Two blocks north of Union Square. ***(2)

SAM WONG (62 rooms, 1/2 with bath), 615 Broadway (Grant Av), 781-6836. Single without bath, from $22, double from $24.

Single with bath $27-34, double $29-38. Is on busy corner, ask for room in rear.

PENSION INTERNATIONAL, 875 Post (Hyde/Leavenworth), 775-3344. See under Bed & Breakfast, Economical Hotels.

BALDWIN (63 rooms, all with bath), 321 Grant Ave (Sutter/Bush), 781-2220. Rent mostly by the week but will rent by the day if rooms are available. Single $35, double $45 day. Phone for weekly & monthly rates. ***(1)

ESSEX (105 rooms, 56 with bath), 684 Ellis (Larkin), 474-4664. Single without bath $38, double $42; single with bath $46, double $64; suites for 3-4, 2 rooms, $80. ***(9)

GOUGH-HAYES (70 rooms, hall baths), 417 Gough (Hayes), 431-9131. Hotel has 7 kitchens for sharing. Single $30, double $55, depending on size and location). Phone for weekly rates. Hotel consists of four 3-story Victorians, most rooms furnished with antiques. Facilities: sauna, washer and dryer, color TV, BBQ patio, sundeck. Hotel is gay-oriented. Being renovated in 1990. ***(10)

GAYLORD. See under Apartments & Hotels.

EMBASSY (48 rooms, all with bath & color TV), 610 Polk (Turk), 673-1404. Single $36, double $42, 2 beds $48. ***(9)

LELAND (107 rooms, 80 with bath), 1315 Polk (Bush), 441-5141. Single/double $35 without bath, $40-44 with bath. 10 rooms have kitchenette and bath, $58. Phone for weekly rates. Hotel is gay-oriented. ***(10)

SHANGRI-LA. See under Bed & Breakfast, Economical Hotels.

EUROPA (79 rooms, all without bath), 310 Columbus (Broadway), 391-5779. Single $20, no doubles.Phone for weekly rates.***(3)

JACK'S HOUSE (5 rooms, hall bath), 311 Steiner (Haight), 863-0947. Single $30, double $40. German-run, large, clean rooms. Use of *com*munity *kitchen*, garden for sunning, information center, group discussions, family atmosphere. Rates are high for rooms without private bath but worth it for those who wish to explore the Haight-Ashbury scene. The neighborhood is safe during the day but the approach is questionable, although several buses (Nos. 6,7,66,71) run almost to the door. ***(14)

Intermediate Hotels, $25-$35 Per Person

This listing is based on the lowest rate per person for double occupancy, without tax (11%). Those hotels which include breakfast in the room rate are now listed in detail in the *Bed & Breakfast* section later in this guide. Unless otherwise noted, all rooms have private baths, color TVs and inroom phones. Listed in order of distance from Union Square.

Note: An asterisk (*) in front of a hotel name indicates "especially recommended". I am placing those so noted at the top of the list in order to facilitate a choice.

BEST BUY****

*CORNELL. See under Bed & Breakfast, Intermediate Hotels.

*LOTUS (70 rooms, 45 with bath). 580 O'Farrell (Leavenworth), 885-8008. Single without bath $45, with bath $55. Double without bath $55, with bath $65. Extra bed $10. In-out parking $12 day. Completely refurbished in 1988. ****(9)

PENSION SAN FRANCISCO, 1668 Market (Van Ness/Haight), 864-1271. See under Bed & Breakfast, Intermediate Hotels. ****(15)

THE GROVE INN, 890 Grove (Fillmore), 929-0780. See under Bed & Breakfast, Intermedite Hotels.

THE RED VICTORIAN. See under Intermediate Hotels (B&B).

*STANYAN PARK. See under Bed & Breakfast, Intermediate Hotels (B&B).

*MONTE CRISTO. See under Bed & Breakfast, Intermediate Hotels (B&B).

SAN REMO (62 rooms, hall baths), 2237 Mason (Francisco/Chestnut), 776-8688. Single $35-45, double $55, triple $65. Phone for weekly rates. Cheapest rates for the Fisherman's Wharf area. ***(4)

VERY GOOD***

ALEXANDER INN (70 rooms, all with bath), 415 O'Farrell (Taylor), 928-6800. Single $60, double $69; 2 connecting rooms and bath for 2 $89, for 3 $99, for 4 $109. Hotel was refurbished completely in 1986. ***(9)

MOSSER'S VICTORIAN (166 rooms), 54 4th St. (Market/Mission), 986-4400. Single/double $59, weekly rate on request. ***(7)

OXFORD. See under Bed & Breakfast, Intermediate Hotels (B&B).

UN PLAZA. See under Bed & Breakfast, Intermediate Hotels (B&B).

WILLOWS BED & BREAKFAST INN. See under Bed & Breakfast, Intermediate Hotels (B&B).

MAYFLOWER APTS (100 units, 90 with kitchenette), 975 Bush (Jones), 673-7010. Daily rates are with bath but without kitchenette-single $50, double $60. Phone for weekly and monthly rates. ***(1)

COMMODORE (113 rooms), 825 Sutter (Jones), 923-6800. Single $60-70, double $65-75, extra person $10. ***(1)

BRITTON (79 rooms), 112 7th St. (Mission/Market), 621-7001. Single $52-61, double $59-68. ***(7)

CASA ARGUELLO. See under Bed & Breakfast.

Motels

Unless otherwise noted, all have private baths, color TV, free parking. Those including breakfast in the room rate are also listed in the *Bed & Breakfast* section later on.

The rates quoted in this section are *summer rates*, i.e., for the *tourist season*. If the season is good and the motels are full, they will even hike these rates, so be sure to check carefully. During the off-season, these rates will drop and you can even bargain for rates lower than the posted ones.

An asterisk (*) before a name means "especially recommended". I am listing those at the head of the list in order to facilitate a choice.

Economical Motels ($15-25 Per Person)

BUDGET (23 rooms), 111 Page (Gough), 626-4155. Single $45, double $50, 2 beds $60. Near Opera, Davies Hall etc. Free covered parking. ****(10)

*BENTLEY MOTOR INN (39 rooms), 465 Grove (Octavia), 864-4040. Single $40, double $45, triple $50, quad $55, 2-room suite, up to 4 persons, $65. Refurbished 1986. ****(10)

SUNSET (10 rooms), 821 Taraval (off Highway 1, between 18th & 19th Avs), 681-3306. Single/double $45, 3-4 persons $55.***(19)

MARINA (44 rooms, 18 with kitchen), 2576 Lombard (Broderick/Divisadero), 921-9406. Single $40, double $50, 2 double beds $60 .$5 extra for kitchen. ****(6)

OCEANVIEW (23 rooms, all with bath, color TV), 4340 Judah (Great Highway, Pacific Beach), 661-2300. Single/double $40/45, triple $52, quad $55. Satellite TV, free ***(23)

Intermediate Motels ($25-35 Per Person)

Note: During the season, motels are more apt to raise their prices than regular hotels, especially on Lombard Street. If they're not full, you can bargain.

VAN NESS, 2850 Van Ness Av, 776-3220. Single/double $55, 2 beds $55. ****(10)

RODEWAY (73 rooms), 895 Geary (Larkin), 441-8220. Single $65, double $70, 2 beds $75. ****(1)

BAYWOOD (20 rooms, all with shower & toilet), 365 Ninth Street (Harrison/Folsom), 431-5131. Refurbished in 1988. All rooms with TVs & HBO. Free ice. Single $55, double $65, water bed (king size) $75. Extra bed $10. The 19 Polk bus goes by the door.****(7)

RED COACH (45 rooms), 825 Polk (Eddy), 771-2100. Single $55, double $59, triple $65, quad $75. ***(10)

AIR TRAVEL (100 rooms), 655 Ellis (Polk), 771-3000. Single $39-$50, double $59-64, extra person $6. Covered parking. ***(9)

FLAMINGO BEST WESTERN, (38 rooms), 114 7th St. (Mission), 621-0701. Single $62-68, double $68-75, 3 persons $80. ***(7)

BECK (57 rooms), 2222 Market (15 St), 621-8212. Single $62-84, double $67-89, extra person $5. ***(15)

Splurge Hotels, $35-$40 Per Person

Based on the lowest rate per person for double occupancy, without tax (11%). Unless otherwise indicated, all listings include private bath, color TV and room phone. Those including breakfast in the room rate are listed in detail under Bed & Breakfast later on in this guide.

Note: An asterisk(*) in front of a name means "especially

recommended". I am putting these at the head of the list in order to facilitate a choice. The rest will be listed roughly in order of distance from Union Square.

BEST BUY****

*THE ANDREWS. See under Bed & Breakfast, Splurge Hotels (B&B).

*BERESFORD ARMS (95 rooms, half with kitchenette, some with jacuzzi), 701 Post (Jones), 673-2600. *Rates include free donuts and coffee for breakfast.* Single $65, double $75. Room with jacuzzi & kitchenette, double, $90, additional person $10. One of my favorites. ****(1)

*BERESFORD (112 rooms), 635 Sutter (Mason), 673-9900. Single $65, double $75, triple 75. ****(1)

DAVID. See under Bed & Breakfast, Splurge Hotels (B&B).

MARK TWAIN (115 rooms), 345 Taylor (O'Farrell/Ellis), 673-2332. Single $65, double $75, triple add $12. ****(9)

PACIFIC BAY HOTEL. See under Bed & Breakfast, Splurge Hotels (B&B).

LAUREL MOTOR INN (49 rooms, 18 with kitchenette), corner Presidio Avenue & California St., 567-8467. *Rates include coffee & Danish for breakfast.* Single $67-77, double $74-84. ****(11)

THE INN SAN FRANCISCO. See under Bed & Breakfast, Splurge Hotels (B&B).

THE QUEEN ANNE, see under Bed & Breakfast, Splurge Hotels (B&B)

VERY GOOD

BEVERLY PLAZA (150 rooms), 342 Grant (Bush, at gate to Chinatown), 781-3566. Single $65, double $72-76, extra bed $6. In-out parking $5 day. Renovated in 1986. ***(2)

EDWARD II. See under Bed & Breakfast.

Big Splurge Hotels, $40-50+ Per Person

This is for double occupancy, excluding tax (11%). This category is for the one-time special occasion, or for well-heeled travelers. These accommodations rival the luxury of the deluxe hotels which charge up to $200 (double). Some are the result of expensive renovations of larger, older hotels, each at a cost of as much as $7 million. Most of these remodeled hotels have rates just under $100. All hotels in this category are considered ****BEST BUY. Those including complimentary breakfast (some also offer tea or wine in the afternoon) are listed in detail under Bed & Breakfast.

An asterisk (*) in front of a name means "especially recommended". I am putting these at the top of the list in order to facilitate a choice. The remainder are listed roughly in order of their distance from Union Square.

*CHANCELLOR (148 rooms), 433 Powell (facing Union Square), 362-2004. This hotel recently received a $2.3 million face-lift which included double-paned windows. Single $85, double $95, extra person $15. Weekends slightly higher. ****(1)

*VILLA FLORENCE, 225 Powell (Geary/O'Farrell), 397-7700. This was the old Manx Hotel which was refurbished at a cost of some millions. Single or double $119, suites $139. Close to Union Square and cable-car turntable. ****(9)

*POWELL WEST (65 rooms), 771-7185, 111 Mason (Eddy). Brand-new luxury hotel, same ownership as the Powell Hotel. Single $75, double $85, double-double $105. Senior citizen discounts. ****(9)

*KENSINGTON PARK. See under Big Splurge, Bed & Breakfast (B&B).

*RAPHAEL (151 rooms), 386 Geary (Mason/Powell), 986-2000. Single $79, double $92. Extra person $10. Coffee & tea in lobby each morning. One block from Union Square, often called the "Poor Man's St. Francis". ****(1)

*DIVA. See under Bed & Breakfast, Big Splurge Hotels (B&B).

UNION SQUARE. See under Bed & Breakfast, Big Splurge Hotels (B&B).

KING GEORGE, (144 rooms), 334 Mason (Geary/ O'Farrell), 781-5050. Single $85, double $93, extra bed $10. Hotel completely renovated in 1987-88, and in 1989 the entire front lobby and desk area are being refurbished. ****(9)

CANTERBURY HOTEL & WHITEHALL INN (250 rooms), 750 Sutter (Taylor/Jones), 474-6464. Single $79, double $89-95. Complimentary HBO, coffeemaker in room. ****(1)

THE MAJESTIC (59 rooms), 1500 Sutter (Gough), 441-1100. Single $95, double $110, extra bed $15. On bus route, near

Japantown. Ask for room in back. Has prestigious restaurant on premises, which is above our price level. ****(12)

MILLEFIORI INN. See under Bed & Breakfast, Big Splurge Hotels (B&B).

EL DRISCO (40 rooms), 2901 Pacific Ave. (Baker), 346-2880. Elegant, remodeled hotel in prestigious Pacific Heights, 20-30 minutes by bus to downtown San Francisco. Single $85-95, double $95-105. ****(11)

*ORCHARD (96 rooms), 562 Sutter (Mason/Powell), 433-4434. This is part of a prestigious chain which has hotels in Australia and Singapore. Hotel was opened in 1985 and shows Asian influence, including oriental prints in rooms. Single or double $96-115. ****(1)

*INN ON CASTRO. See under Bed & Breakfast, Big Splurge.

*THE ARCHBISHOP'S MANSION. See under Big Splurge, Bed & Breakfast.

*THE SPRECKELS MANSION. See under Bed & Breakfast, Big Splurge.

JULIANA, see under Bed & Breakfast, Big Splurge Hotels (B&B).

YORK. See under Bed & Breakfast, Big Splurge Hotels (B&B).

LA PETITE AUBERGE. See under Bed & Breakfast, Big Splurge Hotels (B&B).

HANDLERY UNION SQUARE (378 rooms), 351 Geary Street (Powell/Mason), 781-7800. Single $80-100, double $90-110. Refurbished in 1987 for about $5 million. ****(1)

SHANNON COURT (173 rooms), 550 Geary (Taylor/Jones), 775-5000. This is the old El Cortez remodeled into a super-luxurious hotel at cost of about $10 million. Extra-large rooms. Single $90, double $110. Since this hotel is new, they have "promotional rates", so ask for them. ****(1)

VINTAGE COURT (106 rooms), 650 Bush (Powell), 392-4666 or 800-654-7266. *Rates include complimentary coffee in the morning.* Single/double $107, extra person $10. ****(1)

THE QUEEN ANNE. See under Bed & Breakfast, Big Splurge Hotels (B&B).

Bed & Breakfast

This listing contains smaller Bed & Breakfast locations that are more like the kind one finds in Europe and which are referred to as "B & Bs", as well as hotels that include breakfast in the room rate. (Hotels will be shown separately in this section after the strictly B&B listings). All in this listing are subject to the 11% hotel tax, since they are considered commercial. (Only those B&Bs in private homes are not taxed-see Referral Services below).

All listed below provide continental breakfast or more. If more, it will be noted. All are considered BEST BUYS.

Note: An asterisk (*) shows it's a favorite. I am placing those so noted at the top of the list to facilitate a choice.

Economical B&Bs, $15-$25 Per Person

*MOFFAT HOUSE (14 rooms, in 3 separate houses in same area, all with shared baths), 431 Hugo Street (near 5th & Irving and Golden Gate Park), 753-9279. *Extended continental breakfast.* Single/double $37-52. There is an unusual arrangement for joggers, runners, even walkers, in the Golden Gate Park: for every mile covered in one day, 25 cents is deducted from the bill (honor system) In other words, an "exercise discount". ****(14)

Intermediate B&Bs, $25-$35 Per Person

*CARL STREET UNICORN HOUSE (2 rooms, shared bath), 156 Carl (Stanyan/Cole), 753-5194. Single $40 for one night, $35 for 2 or more nights. Double $50 for one night, $45 for 2 or more nights. 7 nights 10% discount. No smoking. 1895 Victorian. Good bus connections, near Golden Gate park..****(14)

*TWENTY FOUR HENRY (5 rooms, 1 with private bath, others with shared bath), 24 Henry Street (Sanchez), 864-5686. *Full breakfast.* Victorian (1887). Single $30, double $45, 2 double beds $50, queen with private bath $65. ****(15)

MAISON TU (3 rooms), 3663 17th Street (Church/Dolores), 864-3574. Single $45-60, double $55-70. *Extended continental breakfast.* Remodeled Victorian (Queen Anne, 1903) with antique furnishings and modern art. Near Dolores Park & Castro areas. Good transportation. ****(15)

DOLORES PARK INN (5 rooms, shared bath), 3641 17th St

(Church/Dolores), 861-9335 . *Extended continental breakfast.* Single/double $50-85 (latter with kitchen, sun deck & color TV). Sunny patio & garden. Also, carriage house with fireplace, 16' ceilings, full kitchen, bath with jacuzzi, 1700 square feet, $150.****(16)

CASA ARGUELLO (6 units, all with bath), 225 Arguello Blvd (California/Sacramento), 752-9482. Single/double $63, apartment for 2-3 $83, 2-room suite for 4 $93. *Extended continental breakfast.* Apartment for 2-3 $58-68, 2-room suite with bath for 4 $78. In residential area, near busy Geary Blvd and its shops & restaurants, good transportation. ****(13)

BOCKS B&B (2 rooms with private baths), 1448 Willard (Parnassus), 664-6842. 1906 Edwardian with view of the City. No smoking. Single $37, double $52. Good bus connections. ****(18)

Splurge B&Bs, $35-$40 Per Person

*ALAMO SQUARE INN (12 rooms, 10 with bath), 719 Scott, San Francisco, CA 94117 (Fulton), 922-2055. Double with shared bath $70, with private bath $85. No smoking. *Full American breakfast.* Historic Victorian mansion. Free parking. ****(14)

*EDWARD II (29 rooms, 13 with bath, 4 suites), 3155 Scott (Lombard), 922-3000. Elegant bed-and-breakfast inn. Also, complimentary sherry on arrival. Single-double without bath $75, single-double with bath $80 (up to 3 persons), suite with jacuzzi $135. ****(6)

HERMITAGE HOUSE (6 rooms), 2224 Sacramento Street (Laguna/Buchanan), 921-5515. Buffet breakfast & complimentary wine in evening. Single/double with private bath $70-110, $110 with open fireplace. Restored 1901 Victorian in prestigious Pacific Heights residential area, featured in Country House magazine. Good bus connections. ****(11)

Big Splurge B&Bs, $40-$50+ Per Person

*MILLEFIORI INN (17 rooms), 444 Columbus (Vallejo), 433-9111. Single $75, double $95, 2 double beds for up to 4 persons $130. ****(3)

*ALBION HOUSE (8 rooms, all with bath), 135 Gough Street

(Oak/Page), 621-0896. Single/double $89 (1 room is $110). ****(14)

*WASHINGTON SQUARE INN (15 rooms, 10 with bath), 1660 Stockton (Filbert/Washington Square), 981-4220. Single without bath

$65-$75, with bath from $80. Double without bath $75-85, with bath from $85. *Full breakfast–in bed, on request–and tea in the afternoon with hors d'oeuvres.* Rooms have French & English antiques, half-canopied beds. ****(3)

*INN ON CASTRO (7 rooms), 321 Castro (17 St/Market), 861-0321. Single from $75, double from $95. There is a suite with sitting area, jacuzzi and a sun deck, $125. Owner is an interior decorator; he restored this Victorian in modern luxurious decor. ****(15)

JACKSON COURT B&B INN (10 rooms, all with private bath), 2190 Jackson Street (Buchanan), 929-7670. *Extended continental breakfast, sherry in the afternoon.* Single from $78-88, double from $98. Located in prestigious Pacific Heights residential area. Excellent bus connection to downtown & all parts of the City. ****(11)

*THE ARCHBISHOP'S MANSION (15 rooms), 1000 Fulton Street (Steiner, Alamo Square), 563-7872. Built in 1904 for the Archbishop himself, now a historic landmark, carefully & liberally rebuilt and refurbished in 1980. Each room is named after an opera. Two rooms at $100 (La Boheme, and Daughter of the Regiment), 5 rooms at $139 (Manon, Aida, Italian Girl in Algiers), with sitting areas & fireplaces, 2 rooms at $159 (Rosenkavalier & Romeo & Juliet), with jacuzzi tubs, 3 rooms at $159 (La Traviata, Carmen, & Cosi Fan Tutti Suites), with sitting areas, park views. Rates include continental breakfast in room, and complimentary wine in the afternoon. 2 nights minimum stay on weekends. Limited parking available at no cost. One critic called this "arguably the most elegant in-city small hotel on the West Coast, if not the USA." Expensive? Yes. But if you can afford it, it is cheap compared to the luxury hotels at $175-200. ****

*THE SPRECKELS MANSION (10 rooms in 2 houses adjacent to each other), 861-3008, 737 Buena Vista West (just above the park, above Haight Street). Built in 1887 & 1898, completely rebuilt & refurbished in 1980. All rooms have private baths. Rates start at $98, a few at $110 & $138. 2 nights minimum on weekends. Included in rate: continental breakfast in room, wine in the afternoon. Same management & ownership as the Archbishop's Mansion. One reviewer called this "merely the

most elegant bed and breakfast establishment I have seen in my eight years of researching inns." Same comment on price as for The Archbishop's Mansion above. ****(14)

Economical Hotels (B&B), $15-$25 Per Person

*OBRERO & BASQUE RESTAURANT (12 rooms, hall baths), 1208 Stockton (Pacific), 989-3960. *Rates include a huge breakfast consisting of fruit, egg, ham, cheese, hot sourdough bread, honey, jam coffee, or tea.* Single $35, double $42, triple $57. An excellent value, considering the breakfast. Located in the heart of Chinatown shopping area. Also has an interesting Basque restaurant which serves a 7-course meal with 2 entrees for $13 (including tax & tip). See under Basque Restaurants. ****(2)

*Sheehan (65 rooms, 20 with bath), 620 Sutter (Mason), 775-6500. Single without bath $35, double $45; single with bath $50, double $65; suites (for 4-5) $85. Extra bed $10. Includes use of pool & gym. ****(1)

*ADELAIDE INN, 5 Isadora Duncan Lane (formerly Adelaide Place, off Taylor, near Post), 441-2261. See under Economical Hotels.

*THE ANSONIA (123 rooms, 1/3 with bath), 711 Post (Jones), 673-2670. *Rates include full American breakfast and dinner, on daily basis, as well as breakfast and dinner on weekly basis (6 days).* Single with hall bath $30 day, double $40. Single with private bath $40 day, double $50 day. Weekly rates on request. ****(1)

*THE AMSTERDAM (26 rooms, most with bath), 749 Taylor (Sutter), 673-3277. Single without bath $37, double $42. Single with bath $52, double $60, 3 in room $67. Old wortld charm, clean. ****(1)

GOLDEN GATE, 775 Bush (Powell/Stockton), 392-3702. See under Economical Hotels. ****(1)

PENSIONE INTERNATIONAL (46 rooms, 12 with bath), 875 Post (Hyde/Leavenworth), 775-3344. Single without bath $30-40, double $45. Single with bath $40, double $50. *Extended continental breakfast is served every day except Thursday.* ***(1)

SHANGRI LA (30 rooms, all with bath, color TV), 1485 Van Ness (Bush), 776-9300. Single $40, double $50, twin $55, 3-4 persons-2 double beds-$65. ***(10)

Intermediate Hotels (B&B), $25-$35 Per Person

*CORNELL (58 rooms, 40 with bath), 715 Bush (Stockton), 421-3154. Single with bath $50, double $55-70. Weekly rates, *including breakfast and dinner 5 days a week, only breakfast on weekends*--single with bath $350, double with bath $425. French management with large French clientele. Remodeled in 1988, now more French than ever. Excellent food. ****(1)

*PENSION SAN FRANCISCO (32 rooms, 16 hall baths), 1668 Market (Van Ness Ave), 864-1271. Single $40, double $50, twin beds $55, suite (2 rooms) for 2 $70. Each room has individual decor. ****(15)

*THE RED VICTORIAN (16 rooms, 3 with bath), 1665 Haight (Cole), 864-1978. Single without bath $45, double $60; Single with bath $69, double $79. *Rates include extended continental breakfast*. Near Golden Gate Park, in the heart of the Haight-Ashbury scene. Each room has a special character, some with canopied beds, 60s posters on the wall, and other memorabilia. It was once called "world's most unique hotel". ****(14)

OXFORD (115 rooms), Mason at Market, 775-4600. Single $55, double $60, triple $66, 2 double beds for up to 4 persons $72. ****(7)

UN PLAZA (135 rooms), 1112 Market at 7th, 626-5200. Single/double $55. Same management as Oxford Hotel. ***(7)

PACIFIC BAY HOTEL (84 rooms, all with bath), 520 Jones (O'Farrell), 673-0234. *Rates include continental breakfast*. Reasonably-priced Italian restaurant on premises. Single $55, double $65. Weekly rates on request. Parking available. ****(9)

STANYAN PARK (36 rooms), 750 Stanyan (Walnut), 751-1000. Single/double $68-88, extra bed $20. ****(14)

MONTE CRISTO (14 rooms, 12 with bath), 600 Presidio Ave. (Pine), 931-1875. *Expanded continental breakfast*. Single/double, shared bath, $53-63, private bath $68-98. All rooms with antique furniture. ****(11)

ALBION, 135 Gough, 621-0896. Single/double $55-85, 2-room suite (up to 4 persons) $110. *Full breakfast*. Renovated in 1988. ****(10)

THE GROVE INN (18 rooms, 5 with bath), 890 Grove

(Fillmore), 929-0780. *Rates include extended continental breakfast.* Single-double, shared bath, $55-65. Extra person $5. Parking $2 day. Weekly rates on request. Extremely well-run, clean hotel. The immediate area is safe but at night the approach-including the 22 Fillmore bus-calls for caution. ***(14)

Splurge Hotels (B&B), $35-$40 Per Person

*ANDREWS (48 rooms), 624 Post (Taylor), 563-6877. *Also, wine in the afternoon.* Single/double $72-99. Extra bed $10. ****(1)

*BERESFORD ARMS, 701 Post (Jones), 673-2600. See under Intermediate Hotels. ****(1)

WILLOWS INN (11 rooms, shared baths), 710 14 St. (Market), 431-4770. Single $56-72, double $66-82. 2-room suite $90 for 2, $110 for 3-4. *Also, afternoon apple juice, cheese and crackers, and a port night-cap.* Busy Market Street area, good transportation, restaurants etc. Gay-oriented. ***(15)

THE INN SAN FRANCISCO (20 rooms, 14 with bath), 943 South Van Ness (20/21 Sts), 641-0188. *Rates include buffet breakfast, use of hot tub, sun deck, and garden.* Single-double with shared bath from $68, with jacuzzi or hot tub and private bath, some with fireplace, up to $180. Garage parking $7.50 day. Beautifully restored Victorian. ****(16)

LAUREL MOTOR INN, corner Presidio Ave. & California, 567-8467. See under Motels. ***(11)

Big Splurge Hotels (B&B), $40-$50+ Per Person

Many of the hotels listed below have been restored at costs up to $7 million, and offer even more luxury than the $150-200 deluxe hotels, while remaining more intimate in character. Since rates include breakfast and, often, other amenities, they represent excellent value and a good alternative to the much more expensive deluxe hotels.

*KENSINGTON PARK (96 rooms), 450 Post (Powell/Stockton), 788-6400. *Rates include coffee and croissants in the morning, tea and sherry in the afternoon, and a newspaper in front of the door.* Single/double $110-120. The upper corner rooms have stunning views of Nob Hill & Union Square at no extra price. ****(1)

*DIVA (100 rooms), 440 Geary (Mason/Taylor), 885-0200. Single/double $119-130. Combination of modern & baroque decor. VCR in every room. Coffee & croissants in the morning. ****(1)

*LA PETITE AUBERGE (28 rooms), 863 Bush (Mason/Taylor), 928-6000. *Full American breakfast. Also, complimentary tea in the afternoon.* Decorated in antique French furnishings. Single/double $105-155. ****(1)

*UNION SQUARE (131 rooms), 114 Powell (Ellis), 397-3000. Single/double $92-119, extra person $10. ****(9)

DAVID (50 rooms, most with bath), 474 Geary (Mason/Taylor), 771-1600. *Rates include full breakfast, 10% discount in restaurant to hotel guests, free transportation from S.F. Airport if 2 nights or more.* Single without bath $58, with bath $69; double with bath $89, 2 connecting rooms with bath, up to 4 persons, $116. ****(1)

JULIANA (107 rooms), 590 Bush (Stockton), 392-2540. *Extended continental breakfast, and complimentary wine in the afternoon.* Single/double $98. One block from Union Square. ****(1)

YORK (100 rooms), 940 Sutter (Hyde/Leavenworth), 885-6800. *Rate includes free limousine service to Fisherman's Wharf, 4 times during the morning.* Single/double $95-110, extra person $10. Use of gym. ****(1)

GRIFFON (53 rooms), 155 Steuart (Mission/Howard), 495-2100. Recently completely remodeled. $105 single, $115 single/double with king or queen bed. Tea & muffins in the morning. Fitness center next door free to guests from 6-10pm. ****(8)

THE QUEEN ANNE (49 rooms), 1590 Sutter (Octavia), 441-2828. From $94-$125. All rooms with queen or king bed and bath. Rates include continental breakfast & tea & sherry in the afternoon. Parking $6 day. ****(12)

Referral Services

Bed & Breakfast (B&B) in private homes in San Francisco (as is common in England, for example) is relatively expensive, but for a reason. The hosts are carefully vetted, they supply a room with bath and breakfast, and are located in good areas not too far from the city. In calculating the price, you must remember that breakfast is included, and that *no tax is added.*

AMERICAN FAMILY INN BED & BREAKFAST SAN FRANCISCO, P.O. Box 349, San Francisco, CA 94101, 931-3083. This is a reservation service for bed-and-breakfast facilities in private homes in San Francisco, ranging from simple shared-bath to deluxe private-bath arrangement with hot tubs etc. Singles start at $45 for shared-bath and $65 for private bath. Doubles are from $55 shared bath, $75 private bath. More luxurious accommodations--e.g., with jacuzzi, fireplace, view--can go up to $155. At time of making the reservation, a one-night deposit, or a credit-card guarantee, is required.

BED & BREAKFAST INTERNATIONAL, 525-4569. 1181-B Solano Ave., Albany, CA 94706. Covers Bay Area, California, and other parts of the U.S. and Hawaii. In San Francisco and the Bay Area singles with shared-bath start at $40, doubles at $48; singles with private bath start at $44, doubles at $50. Most doubles with private bath are in the $50-70 range, but luxury accomodations can go up to $100 per night. A special attraction are houseboats in Sausalito which offer doubles with private bath--sometimes the whole boat--for $60-125 a night, some including breakfast. Also, in-law apartments for 2 are available from $60-125 per night, with or without breakfast. Longer stays are negotiable.

Apartments & Hotels with Kitchenettes or Kitchen Facilities

Hotels & apartments with kitchen facilities, which were listed in previous Editions under *Hotels*, are now listed in this section. A few hotels which rent most of their rooms without kitchen facilities continue to appear under *Hotels* but are also mentioned in this section.

An asterisk (*) before the name denotes "especially recommended". I am putting those at the top of the list in order to facilitate a choice.

Economical, $15-$25 Per Person

*HOSTELS. All have kitchen facilities. See under Hostels.

*ADELAIDE INN (16 rooms, hall baths), 5 Isadora Duncan Place, 441-2261. See under Economical Hotels. ****(1)

*HILL POINT GUEST HOUSES, 15 Hillpoint Ave, 753-0393. See

under Economical Hotels. ****(18)

JACK'S HOUSE, 311 Steiner (Haight), 863-0947, has a community kitchen. See under Economical Hotels. ***(14)

GAYLORD (156 rooms with kitchenettes), 620 Jones (Geary/Post), 673-8445. Single $150-175 week, $575-610 month; double $175 week, $610-650 month. ***(1)

MAYFLOWER APTS (100 units, 90 with kitchenette), 975 Bush (Jones/Taylor), 673-7010. Weekly rates--single $240, double $300, triple $370. Monthly--single $675, double $875. ***(1)

JAMES COURT (35 rooms, 3 studios with kitchens), 1353 Bush (Polk/Larkin), 771-2409. $125-150 week with daily maid service, & $500-550 month without maid service. ***(1)

Intermediate, $25-$35 Per Person

*CLASSIC SUITES (22 1-bedroom, 1 2-bedroom, & 1 3-bedroom suite), 60 Leavenworth (McAllister/Golden Gate), 626-3662. Each suite has a living room & fully equipped kitchen. There is no maid service but cleaning gear, including vacuum, is made available. Cleaning service can be hired for $15 each cleaning. Minimum 3 days. One-bedroom suites are $49.86 per day for 1 and $10 additional person; 2-bedroom is $79.86 for 2, additional persons $10 each up to 4; 3-bedroom $99.86 per day for 3, plus $10 per person up to 6. Weekly & monthly rates on request. Public parking nearby $4 day. This suite-hotel opened in 1988. ****(9)

*HOTEL ALTERNATIVE (50 apartment suites), 725 Pine (Bush) 578-1366. Minimum stay 3 days. 3 locations. 1 St. Francis Place (near 3rd & Folsom, Moscone Center), $54-94, depending on size and length of stay; has pool, spa, gym, 24-hour security, parking $5 day. La Galleria, 900 Bush, $89-114 day, depending on size & length of stay; has spa, sauna, pool, exercise room, 24-hour security, covered parking free. At 725 Pine (Bush), studio or 1-bedroom apt, $40-73 day. Limit 3 persons in 1-bedroom apt and up to 6 in 2-bedroom apts. All have fully-equipped kitchens, color TV with cable & HBO. ****(7)(1)

*EXECUTIVE SUITES, 567-5151 (reservations). Suite locations: 900 Bush (Taylor) & 737 Post (Jones). Studio, with kitchen, for 1 or 2, $65-84 daily; 1 bedroom with living-dining and kitchen $90-119. Maid service Mon-Fri. Complimentary newspaper, fitness center. Parking included in 1-bedroom suite, otherwise $10 day. Special rates for extended stays. ****(1)

ALFA INN (22 rooms with kitchenette), corner Divisadero &

Lombard, 921-2505. See under Motels. ****(6)

MARINA MOTEL (44 rooms, 18 with kitchen), 2576 Lombard (Broderick/Divisadero), 921-9406. Single/double from $55. ***(6)

OCEAN PARK, 2690 46th Ave (Wawona), 566-7020. See under Motels. ***(21)

Splurge, $35-$40 Per Person

*BERESFORD ARMS (95 rooms, about 1/2 with kitchenette), some with jacuzzi), 701 Post (Jones), 673-2600. See under Intermediate Hotels. ****(1)

LAUREL INN (18 rooms with kitchenette), corner Presidio Ave. & California, 567-8467. See under Splurge Motels. ***(11)

Residential Clubs/Hotels

These listings should interest travelers who come to San Francisco for longer stays, and/or those who would welcome having breakfast and dinner included in the room rate. Stays of at least 1 week are usually required, but some rent by the day.

*MARY ELIZABETH INN (80 rooms, shared baths), 1040 Bush (Jones/Leavenworth), 673-6768. $35 day, $110-150 week depending on size and location of room. Includes American breakfast & dinner 6 days except Sundays. Towels & linen supplied. Run by Methodist Mission. Guests from all over the world. ****(1)

*GUM MOON WOMEN'S RESIDENCE (22 rooms), 940 Washington (Stockton/Powell), 421-8827. Women only. Run by United Methodist Church. Single $83 week, double $67 each per week. House has 4 levels: 1st level is kitchen, laundry, dining, recreation; 2nd is 2 living rooms; 3rd & 4th sleeping accommodations. Language classes, employment & training program. ****(2)

*BERESFORD MANOR (89 rooms, only a few with bath), 860 Sutter (Leavenworth/Jones), 673-3330. Formerly Sutter Manor, now in same group as Beresford & Beresford Arms. Completely renovated in 1988. Single without bath $45 day, double $40-65, single with bath $55, double $55-65. American breakfast & dinner 6 days, no Sunday, 5-day maid service. In-house laundry, TV lounge. Weekly on request. ****(1)

MARINE VIEW RESIDENCE (42 rooms, 9 with bath), 2820 Scott

(Union/Green), 346-3717. This is a converted mansion in prestigious Pacific Heights. Single without bath $125-195 week, with bath $220-225. Double without bath $225-295 week for 2, with bath $300-350 for 2. American breakfast & dinner Mon-Fri, no Sat-Sun. ****(11)

BAKER ACRES (30 rooms, 1/2 with bath), 2201 Baker (Jackson), 921-3088. Located in prestigious Pacific Heights residential area. Single without bath $140-190 week, with private bath from $175; double without bath $220-280, with private bath $250 per week for 2. Breakfast & dinner Mon-Fri, no meals or maid service on weekends. ****(11)

SAN FRANCISCO RESIDENCE CLUB (90 rooms, only few with bath), 851 California (Powell), 421-2220. Single without bath $225-275 week, with bath $400. Double without bath $350 week, $950-1200 month; double with bath $400 week, $1200-1400 month. Breakfast & dinner Mon-Sat.***(1)

MONROE RESIDENCE CLUB (100 rooms), 1870 Sacramento (Van Ness/Franklin), 474-6200. Single without bath $155 week, $600 month; double without bath $115 week, $440 month each person. Double with private bath $130 week, $500 month each. American breakfast & dinner Mon-Sat, Sunday brunch. Recreation room, pool table, ping-pong, sun deck. ***(10)

KENMORE RESIDENCE CLUB (100 rooms), 1570 Sutter (Octavia/Gough), 776-5815. Single without bath $155 week, $600 month; with bath $185 week, $720 month. Double without bath $115 week, $440 month per person; double with private bath $130 week, $500 month per person. American breakfast & dinner daily, breakfast & brunch on Sunday. Many foreign visitors. ***(11)

HARCOURT RESIDENCE CLUB (92 rooms), 1105 Larkin (Sutter), 673-7720. Single without bath $155 week, $600 month; with private bath $185 week, $750 month. Double without bath $115 week, $440 month per person; with private bath $130 & $500, respectively. American breakfast & dinner Mon-Sat, breakfast & brunch Sunday. Sun deck, TV room, maid service 5 days week. ***(1)

3. Low-Priced Restaurants

Note: for menu terms of *Asian & Mexican* restaurants, see Glossary at end of book.

Buffets

The restaurants with all-you-can-eat salad bars are listed separately under *Salad Bars*. You will also find a few sushi buffets in the *Sushi* section.

Note: An asterisk (*) before the name of the restaurant means *especially recommended*. I am putting these at the top of the section in order to make the choice easier.

Buffets Up to $5

TOWNHOUSE (Chinese), 1169 Market (8 St), 626-8333, lunch buffet Mon-Fri $3.95. ****(7)

KUBLAI KHAN'S MONGOLIAN BBQ (Korean), 1160 Polk (Sutter), 885-1378. ll:30am-11pm, Fri-Sat to lam. Lunch $3.50, Includes soup of day, pot-stickers and 1 serving of sliced raw meats and raw vegetables which are cooked on a stainless-steel stove, Japanese-style; $1.50 for each additional serving. Dinner $6.95, return as often as you wish, no extra charge. ****(10)

UNIVERSITY OF SAN FRANCISCO, University Center (between Fulton Street & Golden Gate Avenue, off Masonic), 666-6294. A student cafeteria-buffet that is open to the public, which has hot & cold sections, salads, hamburgers, sandwiches, desserts, a choice of drinks. Breakfast $2.75, 7-9:30am; lunch $3.60 11am-12:30pm; dinner $4.70, 4:30-6:30pm; Sunday brunch, 10:30am-12:30pm, $4.15. These are semester prices; they go up during Summer Session. Quality is surprisingly good for student-cafeteria dining. ****(14)

GOLDEN PALACE (Chinese), 1830 Irving (19th Ave.), 566-5370. ll:30-2pm, Mon-Fr. $3.49. ***(19)

NEW GOLDEN PALACE (Chinese), 250 West Portal Ave., 665-1193. 11:30am-2pm Mon-Sat, $3.75. Varies daily but usually consists of soup, chicken dish, beef dish, fried rice, fried noodles, tea. ***(21)

Buffets, $5-$10

---

*DEWEY'S, Powell & Geary (in St. Francis Hotel), 397-7000. 11am-3pm Mon-Fri, 11am-4pm Sat-Sun. Sandwich, soup, or salad bar, all-you-can-eat. Sandwich only $6.95 (cheese, roast beef, ham, corned beef etc, 9-grain, French bread & foccacio roll), salad bar only $6.95, soup only $3.50 (bean, clam chowder), cracked crab only $8.90, cracked crab & soup or sandwich bar $8.90, sandwich & salad bar (both unlimited) $8.95, plus cracked crab $10.50. Of course, they expect yo uto buy a drink or two at the bar, and they are fairly expensive.

****(1)

*S.F. COMMUNITY COLLEGE, 4th & Mission, 239-3685. During school semesters only, from mid-February to mid-May and then from mid-September. Lunch buffet, Fridays only during school session, $7.50, 11:30am-1:30pm. This elegant buffet is prepared by the students of the "Hospitality Training Program"--which trains students in Dining Service & Food Preparation--and served in the "Educated Palate" dining room. This Program prepares students for entry-level jobs in leading restaurants in San Francisco. They serve a complete lunch on other days, consisting of soup or salad, choice of entree, and dessert for $4.95-7.95. Also, a la carte dishes at low prices, e.g., fettucine alfredo $2.75, escargot in puff pastry shell $2.95, pasta $3.25. The students serve, and there is a big sign "No Tipping, Please".
****(7)

*CHARLEY'S COUPE & CONSERVATORY, 2750 Leavenworth (Holiday Inn at Fisherman's Wharf), 776-8511. Price includes validated parking, glass of champagne. Lunch buffet $7.50, 11:30am-2:30pm, Mon-Fri, includes a hot fish entree, prawns, crab, seafood salads, and salad bar. Dinner buffet $17.95, 5:30-9:30pm, consists of hot and cold seafood items, including oysters, smoked salmon, crab, seafood salads, salad bar, cheese, desserts. Sunday brunch buffet is only $12.95 and includes a hot entree plus the cold seafood evening items--an unusual value in an elegant restaurant setting. **** (4)

MAHARANI (Indian), 1115 Polk (Post), 775-1988, 11:30am-2:30pm, Mon-Fri. $6.95. Vegetables, curries, tandoori chicken etc. ****(10)

BRANDI'S, 2775 Van Ness Ave (Lombard, in Quality Hotel), 928-5000, 5-9pm. $7.95, seafood buffet & salad bar, including clam chowder. ****(4)

NEW DELHI (Indian), 160 Ellis Street (Cyril Magnin/Mason), 397-8470, 11:30am-2:30pm. Lunch buffet $7.50 includes tandooris, curries, nam, saffron rice, vegetables, salads. ****(9)

DARBAR (Indian), 48 - 5th Street (Market/Mission), 957-0140. Lunch buffet, 7 days—with salad, tandfoori, curries, rice, etc.-- $5.99. ***(7)

GITA'S (Indian), 1048 Market Street (6/7 Sts), 864-4306. Indian buffet dinner $9.95. ***(7)

GAYLORD (Indian), Embarcadero One, 397-7775, 11:30am-3pm Mon-Fri, $9.95. Large selection of Indian curries, tandoori etc. ***(8)

GOVINDA'S (natural foods), 86 Carl Street (Cole), 753-9703. All you can eat--$8.50--salad bar, vege or pakoras, dahl or soup, rice or chapatis, Daily Special or lasagna. ***(14)

SHABU SHABU (Chinese), 1375 9th Ave (Irving/Judah), 661-2086, 11am-10pm, Sun 4-10pm. BBQ & Shabu Shabu only, all-you-can-eat, $8.99. You cook in soup (like fondue) or on a grill. They supply raw vegetables, meat (pork, beef, chicken) and seafood. ***(19)

GOVINDA'S, 86 Carl Street (Cole), 753-9703, 11:30am-9pm, closed Sun. Dinner buffet, including organic salad bar, $9. ***(14)

Buffets over $10

*FAIRMONT HOTEL, CROWN ROOM, California & Mason, 772-5131, lunch $17.50 11:30am-2:30pm, dinner $25 6:30-9:30pm. Elegant buffet, over 40 items, fantastic views. A worthwhile Big-Splurge.

*CARNELIAN ROOM, 52nd floor in Bank of America Bldg, 555 California (California/Montgomery), 433-7500. Big splurge Sunday brunch, $19.50, children under 10 $9.75. 10am-2:30pm. Includes parking and unlimited champagne. Highest spot in town, spectacular. Big Splurge value. ****(8)

FERRY PLAZA, 1 Ferry Plaza (behind Ferry Bldg), 391-8403. $16.95. Unlimited champagne. ****(8)

LEHR'S GREENHOUSE, 740 Sutter (Taylor), 474-6478. Sunday brunch. $14.95, includes Ramos gin fizz or other drink, a sumptuous buffet which features a number of cajun dishes. Garden setting. ***(1)

GAYLORD (Indian), Ghiradelli Square, 771-8822, Sunday only

12 noon-2:45pm, $13.95. Curries, tandooris, salads, coffee, tea. ***(4)

Salad Bars, All You Can Eat

BEST BUY****

Note: An asterisk (*) before a name denotes "especially recommended". I am putting those so noted at the top of the list in order to facilitate choice.

Some salad bars are over $5 but are listed in this section because it is probably where you would look.

*LEHR'S GREENHOUSE PATIO CAFE', 740 Sutter (Taylor), 474-5047, 6am-10pm. Soup & salad bar with more than 50 items. Salad bar only $5.95, soup only (vegetarian, French onion, & soup of day) $4.95, soup & salad bar $6.95. Salad bar includes--cottage cheese, cheddar cheese, curried rice with chicken, pasta salad, waldorf salad, pineapple & peanut coleslaw, pickled herring, seasonal fruit, Thai seafood salad, Chinese chicken salad. ****(1)

*SIZZLER, Eddy & Leavenworth, in the Tenderloin, 775-1393. Salad bar is $5.29 at lunch ($2 with meal) and $6.99 after 5pm ($3.49 with meal). Discount for seniors. This is the best buy in the Bay Area. It includes a pasta bar and a taco bar, as well as soup, avocado, various fruits, diverse salads and vegetables, cottage cheese, etc. This franchise is run by a non-profit organization which uses the profits for the benefit of the jobless in the Tenderloin, for drug-counselling and for aiding needy Seniors. ****(7)

DEWEY'S, Powell & Geary (in St. Francis Hotel), 397-7000. 11am-3pm Mon-Fri, 11am-4pm Sat. Salad bar $6.95. See Buffets above for more details. ***(1)

THE WHITE HORSE, 637 Sutter (Mason/Taylor, in Beresford Hotel), 673-9900. 11am-2pm, Mon-Fri. Lunch. Salad cart alone is $4.50 but it is included in the price of the entree, and that is a better deal. ***(1)

GOVINDA'S, 86 Carl (Cole), 753-9703, 11am-9pm, closed Sun. Organic salad bar $5, soup & salad bar $6.50. ***(14)

VERY GOOD***

FISHERMAN'S COTTAGE, 1040 Columbus Avenue (Taylor, former site of Sirloin & Brew), 885-4910. Unlimited soup & salad bar $4.95. ***(4)

BRANDI'S, (in Quality Hotel), 2775 Van Ness Ave (Lombard), 928-5000, 6:30am-9pm. Salad bar at lunch only Mon-Fri 11:30am-1:30pm, $4.95. Seafood & salad bar at dinner 5-9pm, 7 days, $7.95. ***(4)

BURGER KING, see phonebook for locations, 6am-9pm daily, 8am-6pm Sunday. Around $3. Salad bar has 18-20 items. 819 Van Ness Ave (Eddy) and Civic Center branches especially recommended. Not all Burger Kings have salad bars (at this writing, Powell St at Market have suspended it). ***

CARL'S JR., see phonebook for locations. Around $3. ***

WENDY'S, see phone book for locations, $3.50.

BULLSHEAD, 840 Ulloa (West Portal), 665-4350. Noon to 10pm except Sun 4-10pm. $4.25, with hamburger or sandwich $2.25 additional; included with steak entree. ***(13)

Cafeterias

Note: An asterisk (*) in front of a name denotes "especially recommended". I am putting those so noted at the top of the list in order to facilitate choice.

BEST BUY****

*BROTHER JUNIPER'S BREADBOX, 1065 Sutter (Larkin), 771-8929. Breakfast only, counter service. 7am-11am, Mon-Fri, 11am-2:30pm espresso drinks & pastries, Sat breakfast 7am-12:30pm. See under Breakfast below. ****(1)

*LA CUMBRE (Mexican), 515 Valencia (16th St), 863-8205. 11am-9pm daily. Tacos $1.60, burritos $2.15, vegetarian burrito $1.70, rice & bean burrito $1.20, super burrito $3-4.20, Mexican beer $1.75, 1/2 pint rice or beans 85 cents. Huge dinner plates with rice, beans, salad & tortillas $3.45 (vegetarian), $4.50 (chicken, beef or pork), $5.75 (combination). Most popular taqueria in the Mission. ****(16)

*PANCHO VILLA TAQUERIA (Mexican), 3071 16th (Valencia), 864-8840. 11am-10pm. Burritos (soft tortillas filled with meat, rice, beans)--$3.25, also with cheese & guacamole $3.35, also sour cream $4.25. Dinners--with rice, beans, salad, tortillas--pork, chicken steak etc. $4.35-6.25, Super Combos $6.95-7.95. Tacos $1.65-2.65. Flautas (tortillas stuffed with meat, guacamole, sour cream) $3.75, garlic prawns $5.95, guacamole & chips $2.35. Portions are large. ****(16)

*TAQUERIA EL TORO (Mexican), 17th & Valencia Sts, 431-

3351. 11am-10pm. Same owners, same menu as Pancho Villa just above. ****(16)

NEW CHINESE TEA GARDEN, 713 Market (Third), 777-2970, 11am-6pm, closed Sun. Very large cafeteria, always jammed for lunch (good sign). Large portions. Won ton & noodle soups--with pork $2.75, beef $3.45. Rice plates with pork, chicken or beef $3.20. Combination plates from the steam table 1 item $1.85, 2 items $2.75, 3 items $3.60. Highly recommended is the Big Bowl, with won tons, chicken, ham, noodles $2.85. Also, very reasonable breakfasts. ****(7)

PAPA JOE'S, 1412 Polk (Pine), 441-2115. 7am-4pm, Mon-Sat. Breakfast: 2 eggs, bacon, hash browns, toast $2.95; hot cakes $1.85, hamburger special (1/3 lb) with fries and salad $2.25. Deluxe hamburger with fries and salad $2.65. Joe's Special with fries or salad $3.25, chef salad $2.65. Tuna or chicken salad sandwich with soup and salad $2.95, soup, salad & large roll $2.95. ****(10)

CHABELA (Mexican), 1803 Haight (Shrader), 751-6204, 11am-3am. Simple. Very large & good burritos etc. Burritos $2.50, super-burritos, with guacamole $3.80, chile verde plate with salad $2.90, chile relleno with salad $3, quesadillo with sour cream & guacamole $2.90, tamale plate $2.50, taco $2.20. ****(14)

TAQUERIA EL FAROLITO, 2092 Mission (17 St), 621-6971 & 2770 Mission (24th St), 824-7877, 9am-2am, Sat to 4am. Burritos $2.30 & $3.50, tacos $1.50, tortas $2.10, quesadillos $2.10. Plates, with beans, salsa, tortillas, $3.75-4. Simple decor, large portions, always crowded. ****(16)

LA PARRILLA SUIZA, 1188 Mission (19 St), 861-5736, 9am-3am. Burritos $2.40, super burritos $3.50, tacos $1.50, plates (with rice, beans, tortillas) $3.85-4. ****(16)

TAQUERIA SAN JOSE, 2830 Mission (24/25 Sts), 282-0203, 8am-1am, to 4am Fri-Sun. Tacos $1.50, burritos $2.90, super burritos $3.50, plates (with rice, beans, avocado, sour cream, tortillas) $5. ****(16)

ALIDO'S (Philippine), 2186 Mission (18 St), 863-9144 & 2729 Mission (23/24 Sts), 647-9361, 10am-7pm. Native dishes from $3.45 (shrimp with rice noodles, pork rind & tofu, beef stew with rice. Desserts $1, jack-fruit bowl $1.50. Good Filipino food at fast-food prices. ****(16)

SUAD'S (Mid-Eastern), 500 Divisadero (Fell), 553-8817, 8:30am-7pm. Plates, with pita bread & mid-east salads--Humous $4.79, shawarma $4.89. Gyros with humous $3.49. Double hamburger

(2x1/3) with fries $4.18, 1/3 lb burger on pita bread, with fries $3.49, falafel sandwich with humous $2.99. ****(14)

CAFE' NIDAL (Mid-Eastern), 2491 Mission (21 St), 285-4334, 7am-7pm Mon-Fri, Sat 8am-7pm, closed Sun. Bowl soup $2.25, with salad $3.25. Falafel $4.25 (in pita bread, with tahini salad, tomatoes, humous); shawarma $3.95 (marinated beef in pita bread, tomato, onion, side order of humous); Mid-East Plate $4.25 (3 falafel, tahina salad, tabuleh, feta cheese, humous, cucumber, Greek olives, pita bread), Greek salad $4.25 (avocado, tomatoes, cucumbers, onion, feta cheese, olives, pita bread); French brie & fruit plate $3.75. ****(16)

VERY GOOD***

Note: There are a number of cafeteria-style food stalls on Market Street, for several blocks between 5th & 9th Streets, which are worth checking out. The food is on display and often looks very attractive. Prices are unusually low, from as little as $2.

TAD'S, 120 Powell (Ellis), 982-1718, 7am-11:30pm. With salad, baked potato & sourdough bread--hamburger $2.99, hamburger steak $3.95, steak $4.99. ***(9)

BUSH & KEARNY FOOD CENTER, 380 Bush (Kearny), 11am-3pm, Mon-Fri. A series of clean ethnic stalls, all with tasty food at low prices ($3 will buy a good lunch)--Filipino, Japanese, Mexican, pizza. ***(8)

P & E (Chinese), 1441 Polk (California), 775-3679, 11am-10pm. Entrees with rice, $2.99, including tea. Entrees with egg roll, country salad, & chicken or pork dish $3.75. Hot & sour or won ton soup $1, imperial egg roll 75 cents, 6 potstickers $1.95. All dishes cooked to order, will omit MSG on request. ***(10)

THE BAGEL (Jewish), 1300 Polk (Bush St), 441-2212, 8am-9pm. Hungarian goulasch $6.50, brisket of beef $6, stuffed cabbage $5.10, bockwurst & beans or sauerkraut $3.95, borscht with sour cream, cup $1.35, bowl $2.15, 1/2 BBQ chicken $2.85, knockwurst & beans or sauerkraut $3.95. Resembles a lower middle class cafeteria in New York. ***(10)

HAHN'S HIBACHI II (Korean), 1710 Polk Street (Clay), 776-1095 & 3318 Steiner (Lombard/Chestnut), 931-6284, 11:30am-10pm, closed Sun. Fast-food Korean BBQ. With salad, rice, kimchee--beef or short ribs $4.50, pork spareribs $4.50, chicken $4.50. Udon noodles with beef $2.95, with pork $2.80, with shrimp $3.20. ***(10)

CHONG'S BBQ, 3091 16th St (Valencia), 431-4232, 7am-midnight. With rice, beans, sprout salad, kimchee--beef, pork or chicken BBQ $4.50; beef ribs, spareribs, or beef short ribs $4.95; BBQ shrimp $5.95. BBQ sandwiches $3.25. Also, Chinese & Korean dishes, and American breakfasts. ***(16)

CHICKEN AND COOP, 3036 16 St (Mission/Valencia), 864-1748, 11am-8pm. With salad or vegetables, potato--1/2 chicken $4.67, spareribs $5.69, choice of roast beef, turkey, ham or pastrami $5.49. Takeout--1-lb spareribs $4.99, 1/2 chicken $2.59, 1/2-lb beef, pastrami, corned beef, turkey, or ham $3.39. ***(16)

PETE'S BAR B Q, 2399 Mission (20 St), 826-1009, 10:30am-8pm. Counter service. Dinners with baked potato, salad, & bread--1/4 chicken $3.60, 1/2 chicken $5.29, choice of ham, turkey or roast beef $5.69, spareribs (10-12 ozs) $5.69. Spaghetti $1.70, baked potato & butter 65 cents. Takeout--1-lb spareribs $4.79. ***(16)

EL POLLO SUPREMO (Mexican), 3150 24th Street (Shotwell/South Van Ness), 550-1193. Whole chicken (8 pieces) $7.60, 1/2 chicken (4 pieces) $4.09, 3 pieces $3.09. all served with tortillas and Mexican salsa. Corn on the cob 85 cents. Chicken is flattened and charbroiled, with Spanish sauce. ***(16)

FOOD FAIR, 2729 Mission (23/24 Sts). An arcade of a number of food restaurants, including pizza (Mamma Mia), Philippine (Alido's, see above), Chinese, Latin American, bakery. You can get a substantial meal in any one of them for under $3. They are open from about 8am to 8pm. ***(16)

EL POLLO LOCO (Mexican), 2813 Mission (24th/25 Sts), 695-9203. Marinated, charbroiled chicken Mexican-style, served with corn or flour tortillas & salsa--2 pieces $2.25, 3 pieces $3.99, 4 pieces $4.99, 10 pieces $10.69. 10% off for persons over 55, discount coupon card with 20% off. ***(16)

TOKYO STOP (Japanese), 6050 Geary (25th Av) 387-8088, 11am-10pm daily. Take-out and eat-in, parking, Japanese fast food, e.g., tempura $3.25, udon (noodle soup) with vegetables, egg and crab $2.85-3.25, teriyaki burger $1.85, teriyaki dinner $3.75, French fries $1, miso soup 60 cents, .green tea ice cream $1. ***(15)

PSGHETTI (Italian), 2304 Market (Noe/Castro), 621-0503, 11:30am-10pm. Choice of angel-hair, fettucine, lasagna, and choice of sauces--regular $3.49, grande $5.49, all-you-can-eat $6.99. Meatballs 3 for 99 cents, green salad $0.59-1.19. Pasta salad & bread $2.99. ***(15)

Hofbraus

These are the typical beer and carved-meat cafeterias, with adjoining bars. All are clean and have a distinctive atmosphere.

BEST BUY****

*LEFTY O'DOULS, 333 Geary (Powell), 982-8900. 7am-11pm daily. Large sandwiches, large servings. Carved sandwiches $3.95. Regular dinner plates, including salad, potatoes & or vegetable–$6.99. Daily special e.g., spaghetti & green salad $3.99. ****(1)

*TOMMY'S JOYNT, corner Van Ness and Geary, 775-4216. 10am-2am daily. Very picturesque, very popular, beers from all over the world. Carved sandwich on sourdough roll $3.24, buffalo stew (specialty) $4.95, buffalo stew sandwich $3.50, buffalo chili $3.50, meat balls and spaghetti $3.95, meat plate with potatoes and vegetables $4.75, beer'n soup (specialty) $1.75, pasta & meatsauce $1.25. large stein beer $1, Heineken's $1.50. Sandwiches are getting skimpy, so stick to the dinner plates which are enormous. ****(10)

Sandwiches

Sandwiches are America's favorite lunch. Almost every neighborhood deli and many grocery stores make sandwiches to order at their deli counters. Prices and quality vary considerably. This section lists some which I have found to be good buys, some unusually good, both for quality and for price. Most cafeterias listed previously sell sandwiches, as do some restaurants. Most of the hamburger, steak and rib restaurants listed in subsequent chapters also serve sandwiches.

Note: An asterisk (*) before the name denotes "especially recommended". To make the choice easier, I am placing these at the top of the list.

BEST BUY****

*THE SANDWICH PLACE, 2029 Mission (16th-17th Sts), 431-3811. Take-out only. Lunch only, closed Sat-Sun. Giant sandwiches on extra-wide French bread, 9"-9 1/2" (equivalent in volume to 12" of other sandwich places), with lettuce, tomatoes, chili peppers–Combination with 4 meats and 2 cheeses, $3.10; roast beef, ham or turkey breast $3.20; bologna or cheese $2.70; egg salad $2.85; hot pastrami $3.85; shrimp $4.35. Also, overstuffed 24" party loaf $9.95. Bowl of chili $1.60, soup 80 cents. Steamed hot dogs on tasty roll, with trimmings, $1.50, double $2.40. One of the best sandwich values in the City and a favorite. ****(16)

*DEWEY'S, Powell & Geary (in St. Francis Hotel), 397-7000. 11am-3pm Mon-Fri, 11am-4pm Sat. Soup $3.50. Create-your-own sandwich $6.95; sandwich & salad $8.95. Roast beef, ham, pastrami, cheese, choice of breads, including 9-grain and foccacio rolls. Return as often as you wish. ****(1)

*PANELLI BROS. (Italian), 1419 Stockton (Vallejo/Green), 421-2541. Italian sub with 5-6 meats and cheese $3.25, prosciutto $3.95. Very good value. ****(3)

*MOLINARI (Italian), 373 Columbus (Vallejo/Broadway), 421-2337. Combo with 3-4 meats & cheese $2.75, prosciutto $2.95. One of the best. ****(3)

*FLORENCE RAVIOLI COMPANY (Italian), 1412 Stockton (Vallejo/Green), 421-6170. Combo (1/4 lb meat & cheese) $3.25, prosciutto $3.75. Very good. ****(3)

FETTUCCINE BROS (Italian), 2100 Larkin (Vallejo), 441-2281, lunch 11:30am-2:30pm Mon-Sat. With soup or salad, on Italian roll--whole breast of chicken $4.50, turkey $2.95, cheese & nuts $2.95. ****(10)

SCANDINAVIAN DELI, 2215 Market (Noe/Sanchez), 861-9913, closed Sat-Sun. Ham, pastrami or roast beef $1.70, smoked salmon $3.25. Coffee, tea, or milk 50 cents. ****(15)

ROSSI'S DELI, 426 Castro (Market/18 Sts), 863-4533, 10am-7pm Mon-Sat. Large combination on French roll $2.75. Limited number each day, so come early or phone. Also, Italian specialities at reasonable prices. ****(15)

SUNRISE DELI (Armenian), 2115 Irving (22 Av), 664-8210, 9am-8:30pm, Sun to 6:30pm. With pita bread & tahini--falafel $3.09, humous $2.85. Also, generous plates of humous $2.95 & 3.95, souvlaki $5.25 & $7.50 (enough for 2-3), shawarma $5.25 and $7.50 (for 2-3). ****(20)

LUCCA RAVIOLI CO. (Italian), 1100 Valencia (22 St), 647-5581, closed Sun. Torpedo on French roll (4-5 meats) with mustard & mayonaisse $1.30; other deli sandwiches $2-3, prosciutto $2.75. Very busy Italian deli, discount cheese specialties. ****(16)

VERY GOOD***

BON MUA, 611 Geary (Jones), 775-4898. Vietnamese hole-in-the-wall. French submarine (ham, cheese, pate) $2. ***(1)

NGOC VIEN (Vietnamese), 668 Larkin (Ellis), 775-2314, 6am-9pm. Sub with meats on French bread $1.50, meat balls with French bread $1.50. ***(7)

PAPA JOE'S, 1412 Polk (Pine), 441-2115, lunch only. Tuna or chicken salad, with soup *and* salad $2.95. ***(10)

SUBWAY, 1500 Fillmore (Geary, Fillmore Center), 771-5583, 11am-2am. First of a chain in S.F., 5 more to follow. Foot-long sub on soft narrow-width French bread with many toppings--combination $3.19 & $4.19 (depending on meats), ham & cheese $3.79, pastrami $3.89; 6" $1.99 & $2.99. Super-combo (twice the meat) $4.89 & $5.99. Hot foot-long--meatball $3.59, steak & cheese $4.19. Also available as salad plates, with lettuce, tomato, dill pickle, green pepper. olives--cold-cut combo $3.99, antipasto $4.19, chef $4.39. Chips 69 cents, dessert 40 cents. ***(13)

BREAKFAST

Breakfast at many restaurants--especially in large hotels--can cost as much as lunch or dinner. Most of the cafeterias listed in a previous section serve economical breakfasts. This section also contains a number of good restaurants that serve good breakfasts at reasonable prices. A few will exceed the $5 limit, but they are included in this section because I assume you will look for breakfast here.

Note: An asterisk (*) before a name denotes "especially recommended". I am putting these at the top of the list in order to facilitate a choice.

BEST BUY****

*BROTHER JUNIPER'S, 1065 Sutter (Hyde/Larkin), 771-8929, 7am-11am, espresso beverages & pastries to 2:30pm, Sat 7am-12:30pm. Counter service. With hash browns, toast--2 eggs $2.65; 1 egg, bacon or ham $3.50; 2 eggs, bacon or ham $3.90; 3-egg omelette $3.75, corned beef hash & 1 egg $4.40; tofu hash with mushrooms, green onions & tomatoes, & 1 egg $4.75; Parson's Plate--2 scrambled eggs with diced ham $3.90; 3 scrambled eggs with chopped sausage, mushrooms, green onions, tomatoes, melted cheese $4.90. With whipped butter & real maple syrup--special pancakes $2.75-3.25, blueberry pancakes (specialty) $3.25-3.90, French toast $3.75. Hot cereal $1, cold cereal or granola $1.60, yoghourt $1, 2 pieces toast 85 cents, prunes 75 cents. They bake their own bread (which is also for sale by the loaf). Run by Raphael House, a charity organization that provides shelter to needy families. Good place for a scrumptious breakfast. ****(1)

*SEARS, 439 Powell (Union Square), 986-1160, 7am-2:30pm. Famous for its tiny pancakes, 18 for $3.95, with Canadian bacon $5.95. French toast of sourdough bread $4.95, coffee or tea with meal 45 cents. Usually, a long wait. ****(1)

*WHITE HORSE TAVERNE, 637 Sutter (Mason/Taylor), 673-9900. Breakfast 7:30-10:30am Mon-Fri. Continental breakfast with large juice, choice of muffin, toast or Danish, coffee $2.50. ****(1)

*SALLY'S, 320 De Haro (16th St), 626-6006, 7:30-10:30am Mon-Thurs, 8am-2:30pm Sat-Sun. They bake their own bread & muffins. With home-fried red potatoes & choice of 4 kinds of toast--eggs with link sausages or Black Forest ham $4.75; choice of 5 omelettes, e.g., Denver or spinach $4.75-5.75, whole grain pancakes, small stack $2.95, blueberry pancakes $3.95. Large portions of beautiful breakfast food. A little higher than many of my "specials", but worth it. ****(17)

*PAT O'SHEA'S, 3848 Geary Blvd (3rd Av), 752-3148. Serves fabulous, bountiful Irish Sunday brunches. With fresh fruit, potatoes, bread--cheese omelette $4.95, green chili omelette with sour cream or jack cheese $4.95, applewood smoked ham & eggs $5, eggs benedict $6.25, Welsh eggs & Canadian bacon on an English muffin with cheese sauce $6.25, 10-oz N.Y. steak & eggs $8.25. ****(13)

*IRELAND'S 32 BAR & GRILL, 3920 Geary Blvd (3 Av), 386-6173. Sat & Sun only, huge Irish breakfasts--Leinster Waffles: waffles & seasonal fruit $3.50; Munster Omelette: mashed potatoes, ham, onion $4.50; Connaught Fry: eggs, rasher, sausage, black & white pudding, home fries $6.50. French toast $3.50, 3-egg omelette (ham, mushroom, cheese or tomato) $4.95, pork chops & eggs $5.95, steak & eggs $5.95, eggs benedict $5.95, eggs with bacon, ham or sausage $4.95. All egg breakfast served with Irish bread, home fries, and fruit. Sausages & bacon are imported from Ireland. ****(13)

TU LAN, 8 Sixth Street (Market/Mission), 626-0927. Two eggs, hash-browns, toast, jam $1.75, with ham $2.25. Also, great lunches and dinners. ****(7)

PACIFIC COURT CAFE', 728 Pacific Ave (Grant/Stockton, Miriwa Center, ground floor), 781-8312, 8am-10:30am only--2 eggs, ham, bacon or sausage, hash browns, toast, butter, & jelly $2.50; eggs benedict, English muffin, Canadian bacon, hash browns $2.75; 3 pancakes or French toast 2.50, hot oatmeal & cream $1.25, toast & jelly 75 cents. ****(2)

LE CAFE' DU COIN, 696 Geary (Leavenworth), 441-6770, 7am-10pm. Breakfast special: 2 eggs, bacon, ham or sausage, hash browns or toast $2.50. ****(1)

COMMODORE COFFEE SHOP, 817 Sutter (Jones), 771-4999, 7am-2pm. With hash browns, jam, toast & butter--1 egg $1.95, 2 eggs $2.20, 1 egg & bacon or sausage or ham $3, with 2 eggs $3.20. 3 pancakes $2.25, with 1 egg $2.60, with 2 eggs $2.85. 3-egg omelette $2.50, with cheese $2.90, Denver omelette $3.90.

THE SNACK FACTORY, 2226 Polk St (Vallejo), 441-6730, 7:30am-6:30pm Mon-Fri, from 8am Sat, closed Sun. $1.99--orange juice, hard-boiled egg with toast or donut, coffee; 2 steamed eggs with 2 sausages, patties & toast $2.29; western omelette with bacon, toast & jelly $2.49; 2 steamed eggs & smoked salmon, toasted bagel, tomatoes, red onion, cream cheese & fruit $4.49. ***(10)

COMMUNITY BLEND CAFE', 233 Fillmore (Haight), 626-1482, 8am-9:30pm. Steamed eggs served with a bagel--3 eggs topped with a herb sauce $3.25; 3 eggs topped with cheese & a Spanish sauce $3.95; 3 steamed eggs topped with cheese & grilled lamb merguez $4.95; 3 eggs with boudin blanc sausage, topped with cheese $4.95. Omelettes (3-egg) with potatoes & a bagel-- with grated Jack cheese $4.95; stuffed with Greek feta cheese, tomatoes & onions $5.25; mushroom, spinach & jack cheese $5.35. Continental breakfast $2.95--coffee, orange juice, choice of a scone, a large bran muffin, or croissant. ****(14)

AUNT MARY'S, 3122 16th St (Valencia), 626-5523, 7am-2pm. Specials up to 10am--2 pancakes, 2 bacon, 1 egg $1.99; 2 eggs, hash browns, toast, jelly $1.99. After 10am both items are $2.75. ****(16)

BLUE MUSE, 1101 Valencia (22 St), 647-7497, 7am-3pm. Lite Breakfast--sausages, scrambled eggs, English muffin $2.25; 2 pancakes & eggs $2.50, buttermilk pancakes $2.50, 2 French toast, bacon or sausage $2.50, buttermilk pancakes with strawberries & sour cream $3.50, NY steak & eggs $6.95, huevos rancheros with avocado & sour cream $4.95. ****(16)

VERY GOOD(***)

TAD'S, 120 Powell (Ellis), 982-1718. Breakfast 7am-noon. Cafeteria. With hash browns & toast--2 eggs $2.49; 2 hot cakes, 2 eggs $2.79; 3 hot cakes $2.10, hamburger steak & eggs $4.25, steak & eggs $4.95, breakfast cereal $1.20. ***(9)

TINA'S, 83 Eddy (Mason), 982-3451, 6am-6pm. Breakfast (to 11am), with hash browns, toast & jelly–2 eggs $2.05; 2 hot cakes, 2 bacon, 1 egg, juice $3.25; 2 eggs, 2 hot cakes, 2 sausages, coffee $3.50. ***(9)

LITTLE SWEET CAFE', 597 Post (Taylor), 673-3454. 2 eggs, hash browns, toast $1.65, with bacon $2.35. ***(1)

FIVE BROTHERS, 522 Jones Street (O'Farrell), 775-5414, 10am-10pm. With potatoes, toast & butter–2 eggs $2.25, 2 eggs & sausage, ham or bacon $2.95, hot cakes or French toast (made with French bread) $2.95, eggs benedict $3.25, herb omelette $3.25. ***(9)

LITTLE HENRY'S, 955 Larkin (Geary/Post) 776-1757, and 280 Golden Gate Ave. (Hyde/Larkin), 776-0327, 9am-9pm, Sun 11am-9pm. With potatoes, toast, butter–2 eggs, ham, sausage or bacon $2.50; 2 eggs, toast $1.85; hot cakes or French toast $1.85; Joe's Special (ground beef, spinach, eggs) $2.95; sirloin steak & eggs $4.25. ***(1)

ALL YOU KNEAD, 1466 Haight (Masonic/Ashbury), 552-4550. To 10am–2 eggs, home fries, toast $1.99, with ham, bacon or sausage $2.99, banana or blueberry pancakes $2.99. ***(14)

AUNT MARY'S, 3122 16th Street (Valencia), 626-5523. Breakfast Specials, 10am-2pm: 2 pancakes, 2 strips bacon, 1 egg $1.99; 2 eggs, hash browns, toast, jelly $1.99. ***(16)

CHANG'S BBQ, 3091 16th St (Valencia), 431-4232, from 7am. With hashbrowns, toast & jelly–2 large eggs $1.99, with bacon or sausage $2.95. With syrup & butter–pancakes with 2 eggs $2.95, pancakes with sausage or bacon $2.95. Denver omelette (with ham, onion, bell pepper) $3.25. Coffee or tea 65 cents, milk 99 cents. ***(16)

PSGHETTI, 2304 Market (Noe/Castro), 621-0503, Fresh-squeezed orange juice, coffee, muffin $1.75, bagel & cream cheese $1, muffin 50 cents. ***(15)

MARY'S, 5524 Geary Blvd (19 Av), 751-5508. With coffee–waffle with butter & syrup $1.85, French toast with butter & syrup $2.25, 2 eggs, toast & hash browns $2.25. ***(13)

TOM'S PLACE, 5716 Geary Blvd (21 Av), 221-9890. 2 sausages, 2 eggs, muffin $2.50; 2 pancakes, 2 eggs $2.50. ***(13)

HAMBURGER HAVEN, 800 Clement (9 Av), 387-3260, 7-11am. 2 eggs, bacon or sausage, pancake or toast $1.79. ***(22)

DE WINDMOLEN, 1220 9th Avenue (Irving/Lincoln), 753-0557, from 8am. 2 bacon, 2 pancakes, 2 eggs $2.22. ***(19)

YAS CAFE', 822 Irving (9/10 Avs), 664-5113, 7-11am. Special: 2eggs, 2 bacon, 2 hotcakes or toast $2.25. ***(19)

Lunch up to $5

A large number of first-class Chinese restaurants offer special lunches, usually from 11am to 2:30 or 3pm, at prices ranging from $2.50-$3.95, a few a little higher (the higher price is usually for shrimp dishes). Most are for weekdays only, not holidays, but some include weekends as well--and these are noted. The lunch usually consists of soup, a main dish over rice, and the ubiquitous tea; some even include an appetizer or dessert. Often there is a choice of 10 or more entrees; others keep the list short. Most are also suited for evening and weekend dining. Be sure to ask for the Special lunch menu, since the restaurants often give tourists the regular menu first.

Note: An asterisk (*) in front of the name indicates "especially recommended". I am putting those at the top of the list in order to facilitate choice. In view of the large number, my 6 top favorites lead the list.

Chinese lunches

BEST BUY****

*TSING TAO, 3107 Clement (32 Av), 387-2344, Mon-Sat. $3.25-$3.75. A longtime favorite. ****(23)

*TAI CHI, 2031 Polk (Broadway/Vallejo), 441-6758. $3.50. I especially like the sweet-sour shrimp and tomatobeef. ****(10)

*BRANDY HO'S, 217 Columbus Ave (Jackson), 788-7527, 11:30am-3pm. $4.25, including onion cake; $5.25, including noodles salad & dim sum. A little higher than most Chinese lunches, but worth it. ****(2)

*LOTUS GARDEN, 532 Grant (Pine), 397-0707. ll:30-2:30pm. $3.45-$3.75. Includes soup, appetizer, salad, entree, cookies, & tea. See also under Vegetarian. ****(2)

*GOLDEN DRAGON, 833 Washington Street (Grant/Stockton), 398-3920, $2.75. ****(2)

*POT STICKER, 150 Waverly Place (Grant/Stockton, off Washington), 397-9985,   335 Noe (17/Castro), 861-6868, 11:30am-4pm, also Sat-Sun, $3.50-4.65 (prawns). ****(2)

*CHUNG KING, 606 Jackson (Kearny/Grant), 968-3899. $3.25-

$3.75 (shrimp). ****(2)

*RED CRANE, 1115 Clement (12 Av), 751-7226. $2.85. Vegetarian or fish entrees. ****(22)

*FOUNTAIN COURT, 354 Clement (4th Av), 668-1100, $3.25 & $4.25 (shrimp). Elegant, gourmet quality. ****(22)

*BEIJING ON IRVING, 1030 Irving (11/12 Avs), 731-8110, $3.50. Also, Sat. Includes soup *and* appetizer. ****(19)

TAIWAN, 289 Columbus Ave (Grant), 989-6789, $2.95 ($2.25 without soup). ****(2)

GOLDEN PAGODA, 960 Grant Ave (Jackson), 397-1411, $3.95. ****(2)

OCEAN KING, 684 Broadway (Stockton), 989-8821, $2.39-4. ****(2)

HUNAN VILLAGE, 839 Kearny, 956-7868. Vegetarian lunch special, $4.50, with spring roll, hot & sour soup, choice of 12 entrees. ****(2)

WOK SHOP CAFE', 1307 Sutter Street (Franklin/Van Ness), 771-2142. 11am-4pm, includes soup, fried rice, dessert $4.50-4.95 (shrimp). ****(10)

HUNAN SHAOLIN ON POLK, 1150 Polk (Sutter), 771-6888. $3.50-3.95 (shrimp). ****(10)

SZECHUAN TASTE, 1545 Polk (Pine), 928-1379, Mon-Sat. $3.25-4.25. Served all day. ****(10)

SZECHUAN, 2209 Polk (Green/Vallejo), 474-8282, Mon-Sat. $3.30. Lunch includes egg roll and soup. ****(10)

HUNAN COURT, 2227 Polk (Green/Vallejo), 928-6688, $3.55-4.75 (shrimp). Elegant. ****(10)

SAN WANG, 1682 Post (Buchanan/Japantown), 921-1453, & 2239 Clement (23/24 Avs), 221-1870. $3.50. ****(12)

SZECHUAN VILLAGE, 3317 Steiner (Lombard/Chestnut), 567-9989, $3.95, including soup, salad, entree. ****(6)

HAPPY VALLEY, 2346 Lombard Avenue (Pierce/Scott), 922-9179, $3.75-4.50 (shrimp, scallops). ****(6)

TIEN FU, 1395 Noriega (21 Av), 665-1064, $3.25 (also for shrimp). Includes egg roll. See telephone book for other locations. ****(20)

VERY GOOD***

JER MAY, 696 Sutter (Taylor), 771-9331, $3.99. Includes egg

roll. ***(1)

JOE JUNG'S (Chinese-American), 1098 Sutter (Larkin), 673-1818. American or Chinese lunch, including soup and coffee or tea $3.95. ***(1)

WORLD OF PASTRY, 712 Grant Ave (Sacramento), 982-4893, 11:30am-9:30pm, $3.25. Dinner, with soup, rice & tea, $4.95. ***(2)

CIVIC CENTER HUNAN, 600 Polk (Turk), 885-2882, 11am-3pm Mon-Fri, $3.25-3.50 (shrimp). In additon to soup & entree, lunch includes egg roll & fruit. ***(10)

CHEF YEE, 1695 Polk (Clay), 771-8989. $3.50-4.50 (shrimp). Lunch includes soup & salad. ***(10)

MAY SUN, 1748 Fillmore (Sutter), 567-7789. $3.50-3.95. ***(11)

FIRST HUNAN, 1828 Divisadero (Pine/Bush), 346-8235. $2.95. ***(11)

HUNAN ON HAIGHT (corner Masonic), 621-0580. $4.45 & $4.75. On the high side for a Chinese lunch, but good. Dinner prices are also on the high side. ***(14)

JOY, 3258 Scott (Chestnut), 922-0270, $3.25-3.75 (prawns). ***(6)

CHAN'S CHINESE KITCHEN, 336 Clement (4 Av), 387-8370. $2.65. ***(22)

ST HONORE' CAFE', 634 Clement (7/8 Avs), 221-4686. $3.99-$4.25. ***(22)

GOLDEN HUNAN, 736 Clement (8/9 Avs), 386-3388. With soup, egg roll, & tea $3.25-3.75. ***(22)

HAPPY FAMILY, 3727 Geary Blvd (2/3 Avs), 221-5095. $3.50-3.95. ***(13)

5 HAPPINESS, 4142 Geary Blvd (6 Av), 387-2666, $3.25 & $3.75 (shrimp). Lunch includes chicken salad and won ton, no soup. ***(13)

DRAGON HOUSE, 5344 Geary Blvd (17/18 Avs), 751-6545. $2.95-3.45 (prawns). ***(13)

TAIWAN, 307 Church (15 St), 863-7121. Vegetarian $3.35, seafood $3.65. ***(15)

TAIWAN, 445 Clement (5th Av), 387-1789. Choice of vegetarian lunch $3.95, or seafood lunch $4.25. ***(22)

CANTON WINTER GARDEN, 1125 Clement (12 Av), 668-8368,

$3.75, vegetable or seafood lunch. ***(22)

SEA GULL, 535 Irving (6/7 Avs), 681-4373, $3.25-3.45 (prawns). Very simple. ***(19).

MARY'S, 5524 Geary Blvd (19 Av), 751-5508, $3.35, also Sat & Sun. ***(13)

PEKING, 1375 Noriega Street (21st Av), 665-2199. With soup, rice, tea & a fruit, dessert $3.25 & $3.55 (shrimp). ***(20)

Other ethnic lunches

Vietnamese

*AUX DELICES, 2327 Polk (Green), 928-4977 & 1022 Potrero (22 Av),285-3196. Also Sat-Sun. $4.25 ****(10)(17)

*101 RESTAURANT, 1091 Eddy (Mason), 928-4490, $4.95, includes soup, salad, imperial roll, entree, & soft drink or coffee. One of best Vietnamese. ****(9)

*MEKONG, 730 Larkin (Ellis), 928-8989. $3.75. ****(9)

ROSE GARDEN, 509 Haight Street (Fillmore), 621-1500, 12 noon-10pm. $4.25--soup, salad, imperial roll, choice of BBQ chicken, beef or pork with sauteed rice, & soft drink or coffee. Elegant setting, cloth napkins etc. ****(14)

ROSE, 791 O'Farrell (Larkin), 441-5635, $2.95, also Sat-Sun. ***(9)

Japanese

*SAN RAKU, 704 Sutter (Taylor), 771-0803. With tea, rice, soup, & salad--$4.50 (e.g., sesame chicken), $6.05 (salmon teriyaki), $7.50 (assorted sushi). ****(1)

*AZUMA, 3520 20th Street (Mission/Valencia), 282-1952, $3.50 & $3.95. With vegetable appetizer, salad, rice & tea, e.g., udon $3.25 (noodle soup with beef, vegetables, fish cake, egg); beef teriyaki or tempura $4.25. ****(16)

OSOME, 1923 Fillmore (Bush/Pine), 346-2311. With tsukemono soup & tea--udon noodles cooked in broth, plain $3.50, with raw egg $4.50, with sliced beef $4.75, with shrimp & vegetables $5.75. ****(11)

TAKEYA, 5850 Geary Blvd (22/23 Avs), 386-2777, $3.55, Mon-Sat. ***(13)

HANA, 408 Irving (5/6 Avs), 665-3952, $3.95. ****(19)

SAGAMI-YA, 1525 Irving Street (16/17 Avs), 661-2434. $3.95, includes entree (e.g., pork spareribs teriyaki or deep-fried fish), miso soup, salad, rice, green tea. ****(20)

SUSHI-TO-GO, 2126 Irving (22/23 Avs), 564-1122. $4.95-5.50. ***(20)

Thai

*FRANTHAI, 939 Kearny (Pacific), 397-3543. $3.50-4.50 (prawns). ****(2)

SIAMESE GARDEN, 3751 Geary Blvd (2 Av), 668-8763, $2.95-3.75. ****(13)

RAMA THAI, 3242 Scott (Lombard/Chestnut), 922-1599. $3.95, with salad and tea. ***(6)

Burmese

*BURMA'S HOUSE, 720 Post (Jones), 775-1156. Includes soup & dessert–$2.75-4 (prawns). ****(1)

MANDALAY, 4344 California (6 Av), 386-3895, $3.50-3.95.

ON LOK YUEN, 3721 Geary Blvd (Arguello/2 Av), 386-6208. With soup & salad $3.35-4.35 (Shrimp). ***(13)

Korean

BROTHER'S, 4128 Geary Blvd (5/6 Avs), 387-7991. Includes soup, rice, vegetables & entree $4.50. ***(13)

Indonesian

JAVA, 417 Clement (5 Av), 752-1541, $2.95. ***(22)

Cambodian

*CAMBODIA HOUSE, 5625 Geary Blvd (20/21 Avs), 668-5888, $3.95. With soup, spring roll, entree, rice & tea or coffee. ****(13)

Russian

IRVING INTERNATIONAL FOODS, 1920 Irving St (20 Av), 753-0401. Russian deli & cafe'. $3.99. ****(20)

Peruvian

FRANCESCA, 2909 Mission (25 St), 648-3368, 11am-3pm. Entrees served with salad, French fries or rice & beans–fried fish (with fries & salad) $4, fried beefsteak (with rice & beans), shrimp (rice & beans) $4.25, veal parmigiana with spaghetti

$4.95. ****(16)

Continental & American

PIZZERA UNO, Lombard & Steiner, 563-3144 & Bay & Powell, 788-4055, Express Lunch Mon-Fri, 11am-3pm, $4.25, consisting of soup or salad & personal style deep-dish pizza. ****(6)

DISH, corner Masonic & Haight, 431-3534, 7 days. With salad & fries–$3.95. ****(14)

SHANGRI-LA (vegetarian), 2026 Irving (21/22 Avs), 731-2548. With soup, egg roll, rice & tea $3.25. ****(20)

Chinese-American lunches and dinners

Chinese-American is a good sign to look for if you want a full-course meal for under $5. The meal usually consists of soup or salad, entree with potatoes and vegetable, dessert and coffee or tea, for–believe it or not–$2.50-4.95, or a dollar or two more if you order prime rib or steak. The restaurants are often cafeterias, with plain tables, some even a bit rundown or seedy-looking but very often serving good, wholesome food. If the place is new to you, check the decor, take a good look at the diners–more often than not seniors with low income or local Chinese–and make your decision. The prices shown below are for a complete meal, or as described

BEST BUY****

*PING YUEN BAKERY, 650 Jackson (Grant), 986-6830. 7am-7pm daily. Entrees, with soup, dessert, coffee or tea, e.g., calves liver $4, veal, wienerschnitzel or lamb curry $4.95, prime rib $7.95. This is about as close as you can get to "gourmet" in a low-priced Chinese-American restaurant. ****(2)

VALLEY CAFE', 1089 Sutter (Larkin), 885-4412. Entrees, with soup or salad & dessert, $3.95-6.50–grilled liver & bacon $3.95, filet sole & tartar sauce $4.25, market or filet steak (8 ozs) $6.50. A Seniors' favorite. ****(1)

VERY GOOD***

EASTERN BAKERY & RESTAURANT, 720 Grant (Sacramento), 392-4497. 8am-7pm daily. With soup & dessert, $3.15-3.55. ***(2)

SUN WAH KUE, 848 Washington St. (Stockton/Grant), 982-3519, 7am-7pm, closed Tues. With soup, vegetables, potatoes, dessert (pie, jello or ice cream), hot rolls or bread--fried beef liver & bacon or onions $3.95, breaded veal cutlets $4, breaded pork $4, veal stew $4.10, hamburger steak $4.15, beef pot roast & spaghetti $4.20, fried chicken $4.25, beef meat loaf $4.20, grilled halibut steak $5.25, prime rib of beef au jus $6.35, grilled rib steak $6.75. Very simple, hearty food, jammed with Chinese clientele. ***(2)

NEW LUN TING CAFE', 670 Jackson (Grant/Kearny), 362-5667, 11am-10pm, closed Wed. With vegetable, coffee or tea--beef stew $3.55, corned beef & cabbage $3.55, pork spareribs (Sat) $3.90, rib steak $5.75. Apple pie 50 cents, coffee or tea 50 cents. ***(2)

Other Low-Priced Restaurants Under $5

Since there are so many restaurants in this section, I am listing them by ethnic origin. beginning with *Chinese* and ending with *Continental & American*. Almost all Chinese restaurants include tea at no extra cost.

An asterisk (*) in front of the name denotes "especially recommended". I am putting those at the top of the list in order to facilitate a choice.

Chinese

*SAM WOH, 813 Washington (Grant/Stockton), 982-0596. 11am-3am, closed Sun. Probably most famous bare-bones restaurant in Chinatown. You walk alongside kitchen up narrow stairs to 2 more levels. Food is good and cheap. Stick to simple dishes like won ton soup with pork or chicken (enough for 4 as first course) $2.75, chicken with greens $3.75, roast pork with noodles $3.25, chow fun (fried rice noodles) with chicken $3.25, porridge (thick rice soup) $2.50-2.75. ****(2)

*GOLDEN DRAGON, 833 Washington (Grant/Stockton), 398-3920. 8am-lam, Fri-Sat to 2am. Don't confuse this bustling restaurant and take-out place with the large restaurant of the same name across the street, which has the same ownership but is more expensive. Wonton soup with noodles $2.75, braised noodles with beef stew $4.10, spare ribs with rice $4, beef chow mein $4.50. Large choice of rice-porridge dishes $3-4.90. ****(2)

*FRANTHAI (Chinese, Thai), 939 Kearny (Pacific), 397-3543,

11:30am-10pm. Thai & Hunan cuisine. Vegetarian Thai salad $3.95, hot-sour soup $3.95, Hunan eggplant $4.95, seafood chow mein $4.50, Thai noodles with shrimp, chicken, peanuts $4.95. One of the best low-priced restaurants in the area. ****(2)

CAPITAL, 839 Clay (Grant/Stockton), 397-6269. Lunch or dinner--$3.99--choice of beef liver & onions, veal parmigiana, filet sole, fried chicken. Daily special $4.25, e.g., beef stew, fish & chips. Fried jumbo shrimp $5.95. ***(2)

HON'S WUN TUN HOUSE, 648 Kearny (Clay), 433-3966. This restaurant serves won ton in various forms and a few dishes over rice or noodles (made on premises). Noodle soup $1.80, won ton & noodle soup $2.45, brisket of beef & noodle soup $2.55, shrimp dumpling soup $2.65. BBQ pork over rice $3. ***(8)

SILVER RESTAURANT, 737 Washington (Grant/Kearny), 433-8888. *Open 24 hours.* Specialize in rice and noodle combinations. Porridge dishes $2.60-4.95, noodles in soup $2.25-4.10, chow mein & chow fun (noodles) $4.25-4.95, ***(2)

A-1 CAFE', 779 Clay (Grant/Kearny), 421-1666, 10:30am-11:30pm. Most dishes served with rice or noodles, $2.25-3, e.g., shrimp with black bean sauce over rice $3. BBQ dishes $3.75, e.g., roast pork, spareribs, roast duck, soy sauce chicken. Rice soups $2.25-3.50, won ton soups $1.90-2.50. Busy place, Chinese clientele. ***(2)

CHAU'S, 2234 Mission (19 St), 863-5710, 11:30am-10pm. Attractive, clean, very reasonable prices. Egg rolls (2) $1.95, potstickers (6) $2.95, hot & sour soup $3.25, westlake beef soup $3.50. Hot braised chicken $4.50, garlic chicken $4.25, mu shu pork $4.25, ginger beef $4.50, cashew prawns $4.50, vegetables deluxe $3.80. ***(16)

CHAN'S, 3367 Clement (4 Av), 387-8370, 11am-8:45pm. Westlake minced beef soup $4.25, almond chicken $4.95, curry lamb $5.95, pressed duck with sweet-sour sauce $3.95, beef with plum sauce $4.50, prawns with greens $5.95, sweet-sour spareribs $3.95, mixed vegetables $3.75. A put-together meal for 4 (1 soup & 1 dish per person) can remain under $6 per person. ***(22)

ST. HONORE' CAFE', 634 Clement (7/8 Avs), 221-4686, 7am-9pm. Porridge $0.90 (plain porridge)-$2.75 (beef porridge). Rice plates $3.25 (e.g., with beef & tender greens)-3.95 (with prawns & scrambled egg). Won ton & noodle soups $2.25-2.50.

Steamed chicken $3.50, roast duck $3.50. Ice cream $1. ***(22)

SEA WU WONTON HOUSE, 5830 Geary Blvd (22/23 Sts), 668-8080, 11:30am-3:30pm & 5-10:30pm, Sat-Sun no break. Noodle soup $1.95, with meats or fish $2.45-3.75; chicken, beef & pork dishes $4.95-5.95, seafood $4.95-6.95. Family dinners are unusually attractive. A dinner for 4 includes 8 dishes at $7.50 per person (6 dishes for 2 persons, 7 for 3). ***(13).

CANTON, 524 Castro (18 St), 626-3604, 11:30am-11pm, 2:30-11pm Sun. Popular Castro take-out and eat-in, large portions, low prices. Combination plates including chicken chow mein, fried won ton, pork fried rice and 1 dish--e.g., almond chicken, sweet & sour pork, ribs in black bean sauce--$3.75. ***(15)

WON TON HOUSE, 1325 Noriega, 753-5065. Noodle soups--won ton $2.30, shrimp dumpling $2.55, beef brisket $2.55, spicy beef $3.50. Braised noodles with pork or beef or duck $2.65-4.65. Rice soups $2.65-3.75. ***(20)

Vietnamese

*BANH MI BAHLE, 511 Jones (Geary/O'Farrell), 5am-midnight. Grocery-restaurant, deli, with large variety of goodies. Soups, served with bean-sprout salad, $3-3.75; noodle & rice combinations $3.50-3.75; catfish stew in clay pot $3.75, pork sparerib stew $3.75, shrimp & pork stew $3.75. Shrimp rolls (4) $2.25, egg rolls (4) $2.50, Vietnamese desserts $1.20. Sandwiches on French roll $2. Also, very interesting Vietnamese take-out grocery. ****(9)

*TU LAN, 8 Sixth St (Market/Mission), 626-0927. Looks sleazy, 1 row of tables & counter, but great food. Note on menu: "any appetizer, noodle soup, noodle dish, or a la carte dish is enough for lunch". Dinner for 1: soup, salad, steamed rice, and 1 dish from a la carte menu, add $2.25. Noodle soups (8 choices) $3.75, noodle dishes with choice of pork, beef, shrimp or combinations $4.25. Chicken, beef, or pork dishes $4.25-4.95, seafood dishes $5.15 & $5.45. 11 vegetarian dishes $3.45-4.25. Fried bananas or pineapple $1.25, tea or coffee 60 cents. ****(7)

*MEKONG, 730 Larkin (Ellis/O'Farrell), 9am-9pm, 928-8989. Crab & asparagus soup $2.95, beef noodle soup $2.95, fried prawns sweet-sour $4.75, chicken in lemon-grass & coconut sauce $3.95, 5-spice BBQ beef $4.25, sauteed pork & vegetables $4.25. Beef Dinner Special--7 beef dishes, including beef fire-pot, BBQ beef, grilled beef--$14.95 for 2. ****(9)

NHU'S, 581 Eddy (Larkin), 474-6487, 8am-9pm. Appetizers--imperial rolls, with rice noodles & salad $3.95,. Soups--crab meat & asparagus $3.15; escargots $3.75. Beef BBQ at table $7.50, firepot (fondue) with prawns, pork vegetables in beef broth $9, Imperial Seven of Beef (7 beef dishes), for 2, $15.95. ***(9)

ROSE, 791 O'Farrell (Larkin), 441-5635, 11am-10pm. Beef noodle soup or noodles in chicken broth with beef, pork, or seafood $2.75-3.25. Seafood soups $3.50-5.25 (hot & sour shrimp). Rice or noodle plates with chicken, pork, beef, or shrimp $2.95-3.95. Beef, pork or chicken dishes $4.25-5.25; prawn or shrimp dishes $4.95-5.75. Beef 7-Ways $16 for 2 persons. Seafood & beef fondue, $16 for 2 persons. Vietnamese desserts $0.75-1.50. ***(9).

PHO GOLDEN FLOWER, 667 Jackson (Grant/Kearny), 433-6469, 10am-10pm. Very crowded new restaurant. Most dishes under $5--beef noodles soups $3.25-3.95, seafood soups $3.50-3.95, chicken salad $3.25, sizzling chicken $4, lemon grass chicken $4, curry beef $4.25. ****(2)

LITTLE PARIS, 939 Stockton (Clay/Washington), 982-6111. Sandwiches on French roll $1.50. No menu for the almost 100% Vietnamese clientele. Simple. Good food around $3 per dish. ***(2)

NEW SAIGON, 915 Kearny, 982-3853, 9am-10pm. Simple, small restaurant which keeps very busy serving good food at low prices. Imperial roll (2) $2.95, chicken salad $3.50, crabmeat soup $2.95, won ton & noodle dishes (each is a meal in itself) $3.50, e.g., shrimp & pork with noodles, beef & noodles. Chicken dishes $3.50-4.50, e.g., coconut chicken sauteed in lemon grass; pork & beef dishes $4.50, e.g., sauteed pork with vegetables; beef dishes $4.50, e.g., lemon grass BBQ beef; seafood $4.50-4.95, e.g., prawns with black mushrooms. Also, 12 vegetarian dishes $2.95-3.75. ***(2)

PHUONG, 925 Kearny, 398-1626. Simple. Very busy at lunch & dinner. With noodles or rice, large portions--Charbroiled chicken $3.25, charbroiled chicken & pork $3.95, shrimp $4.95, chicken with vegetables $3.75, seafood with vegetables $3.75. Beef soup with rice noodles $3.25, seafood combination soup with noodles $3.50. Egg rolls (2) $2.95, (1) $1.50. ***(2)

Mexican

*NEW CENTRAL (Mexican, Peruvian), 301 S. Van Ness (14 St), 431-8587. 8am-4pm. Lunch, $4.50--served with refried beans,

Spanish rice, homemade tortillas & butter--choice of flauta, tostada, burrito, enchilada, chile relleno, or Taco. Chips & salsa 85 cents, guacamole & chips $2.50, nachos & chips $2.75. Tacos $1.60, burritos $3.25-3.75, vegetarian burrito $3.25. ****(16)

*LOS JARRITOS (Mexican/Peruvian), 901 S. Van Ness Ave (20 St), 648-8383, 9am-11pm. Same management as New Central, also similar menu. ****(16)

*CHAVA, 18th & Shotwell, 552-9387. (also CHAVA No. 2 at 570 4th St. 11am-6pm. Machaca $5.50, huevos rancheros or Mexicana $5, birria (lamb or goat stew) $4.50, tacos carne asada $3.25, burritos carne asada $3.50, chile rellenos $5, tripe soup (menudo grande) $5.50, galena mole (chicken with chocolate mole sauce) $5, tortas de camarones $5. Some experts say "best tortillas in town". Menudo & birria Sat-Sun only. ****(16)

*EL TAZUMAL (Mexican/Salvadoran), 3522 20 St (Mission/Valencia) 550-0935. Lunch, 10am-4pm, Mon-Fri. Beef soup $4.25. Also $4.25--liver & onions, shredded plank steak, pork chops, tongue in sauce, eggs & sausage, Spanish omelette, chicken in red sauce. $3.25 dishes--enchilada, rice & beans; chile relleno, rice & beans; 1 tostado, beef or chicken; 1 burrito, beef or chicken, chicken salad with cheese or dressing. ****(16)

*ROOSEVELT TAMALE PARLOR, 2817 24th St (York), 550-9213, 10am-10pm, closed Mon. Barebones-looking but one of best Mexican restaurants in the Mission, good food, tastefully presented. With rice and beans (large portions)--enchiladas $3.95-5.95, tamale $4.25, tostada $4.20-4.75, chile relleno $4.45, quesadillo $3.95, combinations $6.45-6.95. ****(16)

LA CABANA, 2931 16th St (S. Van Ness), 863-7528, 11:30am-2pm Mon-Fri, & 5-10pm 7 days. With rice, beans, salad (salsa & chips on all tables)--birria (goat stew, specialty) $5.25, chicken mole (with chocolate sauce) $5.75, chicken Michoacan-style (with green peas, tomatoes, bell peppers, onions) $5.50, meatballs Mexican-style $4.50, prawns rancheros $7.95, eggs rancheros with cheese $4.50, menudo (tripe soup) $4.50, Spanish omelette $3.50. Paella for 1 $9.95 (very large portion). Flan $1.50. Wine $1 glass. ***(16)

Japanese

*SAKURA DEL SOL (Japanese, Salvadoran), formerly Beef Express, 324 S. Van Ness (14/15 Sts), 863-8184. 11:30am-3:30pm, Mon-Fri, lunch $3.75--chicken teriyaki over rice, &

salad; chicken curry with vegetables, over rice; beef in teriyaki sauce over rice, & salad; combination of sliced beef & boneless chicken with vegetables, in teriyaki sauce, over rice. Green salad $1.50, miso soup 75 cents. Salvadoran menu, served with rice, beans, tortillas, & salad, $4.50--grilled, marinated beef; deep-fried whole perch; 6 prawns braised in the shell, with tomato sauce; chicken in tomato sauce. ****(16)

*YOKOSO NIPPON, 314 Church Street (15 St), no phone. Jammed each lunch & dinner, so come early. In addition to sushi at low prices, they serve a number of cooked fish dishes, e.g., donburi (cooked fish over rice, with shredded vegetables) for $3.10-$4.98 (BBQ eel). Worth trying. ****(15)

*OZUMA, 1331 Polk (California), 474-0882, 11:30am-2:30pm & 4:30-9pm, Sat 1-8pm, closed Sun. With soup, rice & salad--chicken teriyaki $4.50, vegetable tempura $4.50, prawns tempura $4.75. Noodle or rice dishes $3.95-4.50, donburi over rice (with beef, chicken or pork, and vegetables $4.25-4.50. ****(10)

SUSHI CAFE' COUNTRY STATION, 2140 Mission (17/18 Sts), 861-0972, 11am-9pm, Fri-Sat to 10pm, closed Sun. Lunch with miso soup & 3 pieces California roll--teriyaki chicken $3.65, deep-fried salmon $4.45. Sushi lunch specials, with miso soup, $3.95-5.55 (shashimi $4.95). Donburi over rice--chicken $3.80, pork $4.25, smoked eel $5.95. ***(16)

Salvadoran

*SAKURA DEL SOL (Japanese/Salvadoran), 324 S. Van Ness Ave (14/15 Sts), 863-8184. See under Japanese above. ****(16)

Mid-Eastern

GREAT CITY DELI, 1801 Divisadero (Bush), 931-5455, 7:30-9pm Mon-Fri, 9am-7pm Sat, 10am-5pm Sun. Beef shish-kebab with humous & tabouli salad $6.99, half-order $4.25; beef souvlaki & humous $4.99; BBQ chicken with bread & salad $4.25; sharama (lamb) plate with humous or tahini $4.99, 1/2-lb hamburger with fries $4.95, falafel sandwich on pita bread $3.95, vegetarian plate with falafel etc. $4.95. ****(11)

THE SNACK FACTORY, 2226 Polk (Vallejo), 441-6730, 7:30am-6:30pm, Sat from 8am, Sun closed. Deli cafe', counter service. Diced lamb meat cooked with spices & cheese, on pita bread $3.50; kebab--ground lamb, spices, tahini sauce, pita bread

$3.50; vegetarian–lentils & rice, yoghourt, cucumber salad, & tabouli $2.99; humous plate with falafel, dolmas, pickles, tomato, pita bread $2.75. Choice of 2 salads and soup of the day $2.75. Meat Special–choice of ham, turkey, or salami, cheese, can of soft drink $3.50. ***(10)

CAFE INTERNATIONAL, 508 Haight (Fillmore), 552-7390, 6:45am-9pm, Sat from 8am, Sun 8am-6pm. Counter service (no tip). Falafel Plate (garbanza-bean patties, onions, garlic & parsley in a pita bread topped with tahini, tomato & cucumber salad $3.95; Mid-Eastern Plate $5.75 (falafel, humous, tabuleh, feta cheese, olives, pita bread), Humous Plate $3.95, Brie & fruit plate $5.95, Greek salad $4.25, croque monsieur (toasted ham & cheese sandwich, topped with melted cheese) with green salad $4.25, couscous with warm vegetable stew $4.50, bowl soup $2.75. ***(14)

Philippine

*ALIDO'S, 2186 Mission (18 St), 863-9144, see under Cafeterias above.

Armenian

VILLAGE DELI CAFE', 495 Castro (18 St), 626-2027, 9am-10pm, Sun 11am-7pm. Specials with soup or salad $4.95, with soup *and* salad $5.95–e.g., quiche, meatloaf, stuffed pepper, Armenian meat pie, spinach & cheese pie, potato pie stuffed with meat. Bowl soup with bread & butter $2.25. Soup & salad $3.50. Vegetarian mid-eastern platter with pita bread $4.95. ***(15)

Peruvian

*NEW CENTRAL, 301 S. Van Ness (14 St), 431-8587. 8am-8:30pm, to 6pm Sun. See above under Mexican. ****(16)

LOS JARRITOS, 901 S. Van Ness Ave (20 St), 648-8383, see under Mexican. above. ****(16)

Indonesian

INDONESIA, 678 Post (Jones), 474-4026. 10am-11pm. Simple, small restaurant (8 tables) with charm, good food and low prices. All dishes with rice, e.g., chicken curry $3.60, coconut beef $3.95, shrimp and egg $4.05, combination (interesting for introduction to Indonesian food), $4.25 Fish curry $3.95, chicken BBQ $4.25. Indonesian meatball soup (spicy) $2.65. Mixed salad with peanut sauce $2.85. ****(1)

Italian

*LITTLE HENRY'S, 995 Larkin (Geary/Post), 776-1757. 7am-9pm Tues-Sun. Joe's Special (ground beef & spinach) $2.95, N.Y. steak with soup or salad $5.95, spaghetti with mushrooms $4.35, fettucini al-pesto $4.35. ****(1)

Scandinavian

*SCANDINAVIAN DELICATESSEN, 2251 Market (Sanchez/Noe), 861-9913. 8am-8:30pm Mon-Fri. Cafeteria-style. Lunches and dinners with vegetables, potatoes, choice of salad, and bread and butter--Danish stew $2.75, Polish sausage $3.50, Swedish meat balls $3.50, stuffed cabbage $3.25, cold plate $4.50, pork roast $4.50, Norwegian beef soup $1.50. Beers, soft drinks at deli prices. No nonsense, counter-service, very large portions of wholesome food at very low prices. ****(15)

Thai

*FRANTHAI (Chinese, Thai), 939 Kearny (Pacific), 397 -3543, 11:30am-10pm. See under Chinese above.

KOREAN

HAHN'S HIBACHI, 3318 Steiner (Lombard), 931-6284, & 1710 Polk (Clay), 776-1095. BBQ chicken, beef, or pork, large portions $4.95, BBQ beef or spareribs $5.25. Udon (noodle) soups with chicken, beef, pork, or shrimp $3.25. ***(6)(10)

English

*PENNY FARTHING PUB, 679 Sutter (Taylor), 771-5155, 11:30-11pm. Lunch--11:30am-4:30pm--beer-battered cod & chips $4.25, steak & kidney pie, topped with puff pastry, $4.95, shepherd's pie $4.95, BBQ beef ribs $4.95, French onion soup $3.95, pork pate' with garlic bread $2.95, spinach salad (spinach, bacon & egg, & musshrooms) $3.75, 1/3-lb burger with cheese, & fries $3.95. Bread pudding with bourbon sauce, or sherry trifle $1.95. ****(1)

Continental & American

*WHITE HORSE TAVERNE, 637 Sutter (Mason/Taylor), 673-9900, 7am-10:45am and 11:30am-2:15pm Mon-Fri. Lunch includes salad cart (seconds), e.g., hamburger 1/2-lb, (charbroiled) and fries $4.75, fish (catch of the day) $5.95, veal cutlet $5.25. Salad cart alone (all-you-can-eat) $4.50. Elegant restaurant. Excellent value, considering salad cart. ****(1)

*CARAVANSARY, 2257 Chestnut (Scott/Divisadero), 922-2707, 6am-midnight. Deli-cafe'. With soup or salad or fruit salad--quiche $4.25, lasagna $4.95, aram (mideast) sandwich & wedge of quiche $5.25, pate', cheese & fruit $5.45. ****(6)

LE CAFE' DU COIN, 696 Geary (Leavenworth), 441-6770, 11:30am-10pm. With soup or salad, vegetables, sourdough bread--meat loaf $4.50, vegetarian lasagna $4.50, spaghetti or ravioli with meat sauce $4.50, center-cut pork chop $5.25, fish & chips $5.75, sauteed or fried prawns $5.95. ****(1)

LA DOLCE VITA, 311 Divisadero (Fell/Oak), 558-9911, 7:15am-6pm, 9am-4pm Sat, closed Sun. Breakfast & lunch only. Pasta marinera with sausage $4.95, hot sausage sandwich on French bread $4.25, burger & pasta salad $4.25; eggplant timbale (layers with cheese, eggs, tomato sauce) $3.95, with soup or salad $5.50; calzone $4.50, with soup or salad $6.50. Very popular meeting place of the young, near Haight. ****(14)

CAFE' MOCONDO, 3161 16th St (Valencias/Guererro), 863-6517, 11am-10pm. Very large, full of young people. A few dishes, served with salad & bread--stuffed peppers $3.50, spinach artichoke $3.50, vegetable lasagna $4.50. Spinach pie $1. ****(16)

PICARO, 3120 16th St (Valencia/Guererro), 431-4089. Large bustling cafe' full of young people, very low prices, large servings. Lunch, with salad & wholewheat bread $2.99-4.50--pastas, quiche, fish ($3.50, mahi mahi $4). Dinners, with potatoes, salad, & bread--seafood platter $7, langustinos $7, halibut swordfish $6.50, shark $5.50. With salad & bread--pastas $5-6.50, N.Y. steak $5, lamb chop $5, chicken breast $5. Bowl soup with bread $2.45. ****(16)

CLARION, 2118 Mission (17/18 Sts), 552-4393, 9am-9pm Tues-Sun, closed Mon. Fruit pancakes $2.50. Spinach quiche $3.75, BBQ rib sandwich $3.75, eggplant parmigiana $3.95, split pea soup 1.25 cup & $1.88 bowl. Soup or salad with dinner $1 extra. Dinner served with French bread & butter--pastas $3.95-4, with pesto $4.50; chicken parmigiana $5.25, chicken with mushrooms $4.50, calamari $4.50, prawns $5.75, T-bone steak (with fries & vegetable) $5.95. ****(16)

TINA'S, 83 Eddy (Mason), 982-3451, 6am-6pm, Sat to 7pm. Soup & sandwich (changes daily) $3.95, 1/2 lb hamburger & salad $3.95. ****(9)

FIVE BROTHERS, 522 Jones (O'Farrell), 775-5414, 10am-10pm. With soup and salad, baked potato or rice, bread & butter--grilled halibut steak, tartar sauce $5.95, seafood combination $6.75, breaded pork chops $5.75, T-bone steak $6.95, N.Y. steak $6.95. ***(9)

NOB HILL, 655 Clay (Montgomery/Kearny), 421-1223. Popular for lunch. With salad & roll--1/4 chicken c$3.49, 1/2 chicken $4.49, turkey $4.99, roast beef $5.79, ham $4.49, ribs $6.75. ****(8)

CHESTNUT CAFE', 2016 Fillmore (California/Pine), 922-6510, 8am-6pm. Soup & salad $2.95, sandwich & soup (lunch special) $3.25, beef teriyaki plate with rice & salad $3.75, 2 poached eggs & toast $2.49. ***(11)

HAMBURGERS

Many restaurants listed in other sections of this book also serve hamburgers, but in this section I concentrate on those that *feature* hamburgers, particularly the 1/2 pounders which, with fries, constitute a meal, for under $5 (a few are just over $5). In ordering, be sure to specify the degree of "doneness", e.g., "medium rare", and try to get one that is charcoal-broiled, although those made on a very hot griddle can be excellent. Also, try to get it on a sourdough or French roll (which you can seldom get in a fast-food place).

Note: An asterisk (*) in front of the name denotes "especially recommended". These are placed at the top of the list to facilitate a choice.

BEST BUY****

*ORIGINAL JOE'S (Italian), 144 Taylor (Eddy) 775-4877, 10:30am-1am. For my money, the best value in town. Chuck is fresh-ground. 12-oz (yes, 3/4-pounder!), served on a scooped-out sourdough roll, with thick fries, $5.70. They are charbroiled after 5pm; before that time they are made on the griddle. For the beef-hungry, 16-oz hamburger steak with vegetables or

pasta $8.75. ****(1)

*WHITE HORSE TAVERNE, 637 Sutter (Mason/Taylor), 673-9900. 7am-2:15pm Mon-Fri. Charbroiled hamburger (1/2-lb) and fries $4.95, available at lunch (11:30-2.15pm), including salad cart. Good quality, good atmosphere, excellent value, considering the salad cart. ****(1)

*POLO'S (Italian), 34 Mason (Market/Eddy), 362-7719, 11am-3pm Mon, 11am-11pm Tues-Sat, closed Sun. 1/2-lb hamburger, fries $4.95; 16-oz. hamburger steak, vegetables and fries, $8.25. Charbroiled after 5pm. ****(1)

*JAY'N BEE'S CLUB, 2736 20th St. (York), 648-0518. Lunch: 11am-2:30pm Mon-Fri. This is also a bar, serving lunch only. The bar is open all hours. The 1/2-lb hamburger comes with soup, pasta or salad, a small bottle of wine & coffee--all for $5.50. There is also 12-oz ribeye steak on the full menu for $6.50 and a 12-oz N.Y.steak for $8.50. Every Fri nite there is a prime rib dinner for $8.50, or a prawn dinner for $8.95, with the same trimmings as for lunch, $8.50. Crowded pub atmosphere, simple setting, good food. Be prepared for a wait. ****(17)

*IRELAND'S, 3920 Geary Blvd (3 Av), 386-6173, Sat-Sun lunch only. 1/2-lb with sauteed mushrooms & cheese, & fries $4.50, cheeseburger with Irish bacon $5. ****(13)

MO'S, 1322 Grant Ave (Green), 788-3779, 11:30am-10:30pm, to 11:30pm Fri-Sat. Although only 6-ozs, Mo's serves one of the best charbroiled hamburgers in town. With fries $4.65. Also good are his cajun sausage with fries $4.25, Polish sauasge with fries $3.85, bowl of homemade chili & French bread $3. ****(3)

HARD ROCK CAFE', 1699 Van Ness Avenue (Sacramento), 885-1699, 11:30am-midnight, Fri-Sat to 9pm. 1/2-lb with fries $4.95. Mecca for teenagers and older, be prepared for a wait, and very loud rock. ****(10)

BOBBY RUBINO'S, 245 Jefferson (Fisherman's Wharf), 673-2266, 11:30am-11pm Sun-Thurs. to midnight Fri-Sat. 1/2-lb, charbroiled, with fries $4.95. ****(4)

COMMUNITY BLEND CAFE', 233 Fillmore (Haight), 626-1482, 8am-9:30pm. Grilled 1/2-lb with home-fried potatoes $3.2, with cheese $4.25. Young people gather here. Indian dishes, e.g., grilled marinated chicken dinner with spiced basmati rice &

vegetables $5.95. Indian restaurant next door is under same ownership. ****(14)

19TH AVENUE DINER, 1201 19th Avenue (Highway 1, corner Lincoln), 759-1517. Charbroiled 1/2-lb with fries $5.95. Made with organic meat. Also, angel hair pasta & fries $7.95, baby back ribs (1/2) & fries $9.50, meatloaf & mashed potatoes $9.50, 10-oz aged N.Y. steak & fries $13.95. ****(20)

BULLSHEAD, 840 Ulloa (West Portal), 665-4350. noon-10pm Mon-Sat, 4-11pm Sun. 1/2-lb & fries $4.95, with salad bar $2.25 additional. ****

VERY GOOD***

TINA'S, 83 Eddy (Mason), 982-3451, 6am-6pm, Sat to 7pm. With green salad, 1/2-lb $3.95. ***(9)

LE CAFE' DU COIN, 696 Geary (Leavenworth), 441-6770, 11:30am-10pm. Charbroiled 1/2-lb with fries $3.75. ***(1)

PAPA JOE'S, 1412 Polk (Pine), 441-2115, 7am-3pm Mon-Fri, to 2pm Sat, closed Sun. Counter-service. 1/3lb with fries or salad $2.95, 1/2lb $3.15. ****(10)

BRUNO'S (Italian), 2389 Mission (19/20 Sts), 641-1144, 11am-2am Mon-Sat, Sun 4pm to midnight. 1/2 lb on quarter loaf of French bread, with fries $5.95. ***(16)

COVE CAFE, 434 Castro (Market/18 St), 626-0462. Charbroiled 1/2 steakburger with fries $4.95. ***(15)

WELCOME HOME, 464 Castro (Market/18 Sts), 626-3600. Charbroiled 1/2 burger with fries, potato salad, or coleslaw $4.95. ****(15)TOM'S PLACE, 5716 Geary Blvd (21 Av), 221-9890. 1/2 lb French burger & fries $4.75. ***(13)

HAMBURGER NANCY'S, 2001 17th Street (Kansas), 863-6777, 11am-10pm, to 7pm Sat, closed Sun. 1/2 lb with cheese and fries $5.50. ***(17)

SUN'S SUPERIOR, 312 8th Avenue (Clement), 221-9165, 7:30am-4pm. 1/2 lb on French roll, with fries, $3.85, French burger with cheese $4. 10-oz hamburger steak with green salad & fries $4.55. ****(22)

BILL'S PLACE, 2315 Clement (9 Av), 221-5262, 7am-11pm. 1/3-lb $3.95, fries $1.25 extra. 10-oz burger with fries & salad at $6.25 is good value. Has great reputation but is overpriced. ***(23)

FUJI COFFEE SHOP, 3420 Geary Blvd (Stanyan), 668-8778, 7am-5pm, Sat to 2pm, closed Sun. Two 1/3-lb patties (they'll put them together, if you ask), with fries $4.29. ***(13)

CAFE' RAIN TREE, 654 Irving (8th Av), 665-3633. 1/2-lb with fries $4.45. ***(19)

KIESER'S, 1833 Irving (19/20 Avs), 681-6100, 4-9pm Mon-Sat. 1/2-lb $4.65, with fries plus 50 cents, with salad plus 75 cents. ***(20)

Pizza

Pizza is an economical meal. 3-4 persons can dine well on an *extra-large* pizza for $12-$14 (some are even cheaper). A few definitions: *Neapolitan* is thin crust, *Sicilian* is thick-crust; some restaurants offer both. *Calzone* is a folded-over or stuffed pizza usually containing cheese and meat (e.g., ham or sausage). *Chicago-style* is a *deep-dish* pizza.

Sizes are usually referred to as *small, medium, large* and *extra-large* and the meaning of these sizes often varies, but *extra-large* is usually 18" in diameter. As a rule, *medium* is often too much for 2, and *extra-large* too much for 3. Most pizza restaurants also serve pastas, some a whole menu of Italian dishes, at reasonable prices.

An asterisk (*) in front of a name denotes "especially recommended". Those are placed at the top of the list to facilitate a choice.

BEST BUY****

*BLONDIE'S, 63 Powell (Ellis), 982-6168. 11am-9pm, Sun to 7pm. Huge slice $1.25 cents, with 1 topping $1.75, with 2 toppings $1,85, with 3 toppings $2.11. 16oz soft drink 56 cents. Whole pizzas–12"-18", cheese & sauce $5.90-9.95; with 1 extra topping $6.90-11.90. You'll see mobs there, a good sign. ****(9)

*VICOLO, 201 Ivy (Franklin), 863-2382 & 900 North Point (Ghiradelli Square), 776-1331, 11:30am-11:30pm, 2-10 Sun, 11:30-am-9pm at North Point. Deep-dish gourmet pizza with freshest ingredients–12" with 4 cheeses $16.50, with sausage $18.50, enough for 4. Slice $2.80-3.15 is on the high side. ****(10)

*GOLDEN BOY, 542 Green (Columbus/Grant), 982-9738, Large square, cheese & sauce, $1.50, pesto, clam,or garlic $2, sheet (16 pieces) $22.50 & $26.50. ****(30

GOLDEN BOY, 637 Clay Street (Montgomery/Kearny), 398-

6044, 9am-6pm, Sat 11:30am-6pm. Slice, cheese & sauce $1.45, others to $2.25. 12"-18", cheese & sauce, $5.35-12.50, 1 extra topping $5.85-13.50. ****(8)

*PIZZERIA UNO, 2200 Lombard (Steiner), 563-3144, and 2323 Powell (Bay), 788-4055. 11:30am-12:30am, FriSat to 1:30am. Chicago-style deep-dish pizza, individual $4.95, *regular*, for 2-3 persons $9.75. House salad--lettuce, green pepper, mushrooms, tomato--$1.95. Express Lunch--house salad or soup & individual pizza of day--$3.95. ****(6)(4)

*VILLAGE PIZZERIA, 3348 Steiner (Chestnut), 931-2470 and Van Ness (Sutter), 673-7771, 11am-11pm   daily. Slices--Neapolitan $1.25, Sicilian $1.50, 45 cents extra for one topping. Neapolitan range from $8.50-14.50; Sicilian range from $9.50-14.50. Slices $1.50-1.60. ****(6)(10)

*ROYAL KITCHEN, 3253 Mission (29 St), 824-4219, 11am-9pm, closed Tues. This a Chinese restaurant that harbored an acclaimed Italian pizza section and then took over when the Italian pizza-maker left. They now make the entire Italian range plus an interesting Chinese version of their own. With cheese & sauce, 12"-18", $5.75-11, with 1 extra topping $6.50-11.75, Chinese or Italian combination $8-14.50. Try the pesto or garlic for Italian, also the Chinese variety. ****(16)

COLUMBUS, 314 Columbus Ave, 398-3555, 4pm-midnight, to 1am Sat-Sun. 12"-18", with cheese & sauce $5.95-9.25, with 1 extra topping $6.25-10. Calzones, $8.25-14.85, depending on size and stuffings. Also, Italian menu. ***(3)

VIVA, 1224 Grant (Columbus), 989-8482, 5-11, Fri to 2am, Sat-Sun 2pm-2am. 12"-18", cheese & sauce, $5.90-9.60, with 1 extra topping $6.75-10.85. Also, complete Italian menu. ***(3)

NORTH BEACH, 1310 Grant Ave (Green), 433-2444, 1499 Grant Av (Union), 433-2444. 11am-1am, Fri-Sat to 3am. 12"-18", cheese & sauce, $5.77-10.05, with 1 extra topping $6.76-10.66. Incudes tax. Entrees with soup or salad, bread & butter--ravioli with meat balls $7.40, fettucine alfredo $7.05, cannelloni $7.70, eggplant parmigiana $7. veal scallopini $8.95, BBQ pork spareribs 1/2 lb $7.50, 1 lb $11.50. ****(3)

CAPRI, 2272 Market (16/Noe), 552-3000, to midnight Sun-Thurs, to 2am Fri-Sat. With cheese & sauce, 12"-18", $5.75-10.75, with 2 extra toppings $7.35-12.45. Calzone $5.75-6.75. Pastas $5.55-6.75.. Very good, light crust. ****(15)

GIORGIO'S, 151 Clement (2 Ave), 668-1266, 11am-11:30pm. 11"-17", with cheese & sauce $6-11.50, with 2 extra toppings $7-13.50. Calzone (stuffed pizza), depending on size and stuffing,

$6.50-12.95. Cannelloni, baked lasagne, or baked rigatoni $6.95. Pasta dishes $5.50-6.50. ****(22)

MONASTERI'S, 1725 Polk (Washington), 673-7174, 11am-11pm Sun-Thurs, to midnight Fri-Sat. Chicago-style pan-pizza. Individual, cheese, $2.75. Others $5.35-10.35, with sausage or pepperoni $6.45-12.50. Pasta with bread & butter, spaghetti or linguini, with meat sauce or pesto $4.95, ravioli $5.50. Meat balls (3) $1.50. Soup, with bread & butter, $1.75. ****(10)

BELLA, 4124 Geary Blvd (5/6 Avs), 668-4150, 11am-2am, Fri-Sat to 3am. Cheese & sauce, 12"-18", $6.85-11.50; with 2 extra toppings $8.75-13.95. ****(13)

PASQUALE'S, 700 Irving (8 Av), 661-2140, 4pm-1am Sun-Thurs, to 2am Fri-Sat. Cheese & sauce, 12"-18", $6.25-10; plus 1 topping $7-11.25. Will prepare with thin or thick (Sicilian) crust on request. Bowl minestrone $2.50, pastas $5.45-7 (with meat balls), cannelloni or gnocchi $7, lasagna $6.45. ****(19)

VERY GOOD***

THE FRONT ROOM, 1500 California (Polk/Larkin), 771-1591, 4am-midnight, Fri-Sat to 2am. Two other locations: 823 Clement (9th Ave), 387-7733 and 1385 9th Ave. (Judah), 665-2900. Cheese & sauce, 7"-16", $3.75-11.65. Deep-dish pizza, small-"colossal", $7.30-18.95. ***(10)(22)(19)

GOLDEN CITY, 1552 Howard (11/12 Sts), 864-1411, 11am-11pm. 12"-18", cheese & sauce, $5.45-9.60, with 1 extra topping $6.35-11.30. Calzones small to-x-large with ricotta & mozzarella only $6.35-11.30, with one extra topping $7.25-11.90. Pastas, with salad & garlic bread, $6.50-8.25. With soup or salad--BBQ ribs $8.75, lasagna $7.70, BBQ chicken half $7.30, whole $9.30. ***(7)

DE PAULA'S, 2114 Fillmore (California), 346-9888, 5-11:30pm, Fri-Sat to 1am. Cheese & sauce, 12"-18", $5.85-9.50; plus 2 toppings $5.90-11.15. Also, Brazilian specialties, which are on the high side, e.g., feijoada (the national dish of black beans & pork stew) $11.35, marinated pork & Brazilian vegetables $11.50, chicken with okra, spices and polenta $10.75. Also, hearts of palm salad $3.95, large salad with salami & cheese (a meal in itself) $6.95. Fettucine specialities $6.50 & $6.85. ***(11)

SPARKY'S, 246 Church (Market), 626-8666. Pizza or calzone with cheese & sauce, 12"-16", $8-10. ***(15)

MARCELLO'S, 420 Castro (Market), 863-3900 (see phone book for other locations), 11am-1am. Cheese & sauce only, 8"-18"

$6.35-10.35, plus 2 toppings $8.50-13.25, calzone $5.60-5.85. ***(15)

MILANO, 1330 9th Avenue (Irving/Judah), 665-3773, 3pm-midnight Sun-Thurs, to 1am Fri-Sat. 12"-18" cheese & sauce $5.95-10.15, with 1 extra topping $6.85-11.05. Pastas $5 (spaghetti with garlic or pesto) to $7.25 (pasta with clams). ***(19)

DIM SUM

Dim Sum includes many Chinese delicacies, a choice of which make for an excellent lunch, e.g., shrimp dumplings, pork buns, meat turnovers, wrapped chicken, spareribs. A waiter or waitress comes by every few minutes, and you can choose a dish, usually with 3 items on it. Later, the plates are tallied up, and you pay according to the number of plates yo have accumulated. Two or three persons can have a good lunch for $3-4 per person, depending on the price per dish. There is a charge for tea, usually around 50 cents per person, unless otherwise indicated. Price shown is for small dish.

Note: An asterisk (*) in front of a name denotes "especially recommended". Those so noted are placed at the top of the list in order to facilitate a choice. Many of these serve a range of Japanese cooked food as well.

BEST BUY****

*TUNG FONG, 808 Pacific (Stockton), 362-7115. 9am-3pm daily, except Wed. $1.60, tea 30 cents. ****(2)

*OCEAN CITY, 644 Broadway (Stockton/Grant), 982-2328. Branch of Hong Kong's famous dim sum restaurant (there are branches in Seattle & Los Angeles). This is arguably the best dim sum in the United States. $1.50, tea 40 cents per person. Also, a variety of good Chinese food at reasonable prices. ****(2)

*GRAND PALACE, 950 Grant (Washington/Jackson), 982-3705, 9am-3pm daily. $1.60 per dish, combination of 6 items $4.25. **** (2)

*KING OF CHINA, 939 Clement (9am-10pm), 668-2618. $1.50-2.25. Also, full Chinese menu. ****(22)

NEW ASIA, 772 Pacific Ave (Grant/Stockton), 391-6666, $1.60, tea 40 cents. ****(2)

YANK SING, 427 Battery (Washington), 362-1640, 11am-3pm,

Mon-Fri, 10am-4pm Sat. $1.80-2.15. Expensive but excellent quality. Some consider it the best in San Francisco. ****(2)

ROYAL KITCHEN, 3253 Mission (229 St), 824-4219, 11am-9pm, 3-9pm Tues & Sun. $1.75. Large portions, tea included. ****(16)

THE FOOK, 332 Clement (4/5 Avs), 668-8070. $1.50. ****(22)

VERY GOOD***

HANG AH TEA ROOM, 1 Hang Ah St. (Off Sacramento near Stockton). 982-5686, 10am-9pm Tues-Sun. $1.55, tea 50 cents. Dim sum plate for one person: 7 items, $4.50. Also, full Chinese menu. ****(2)

LOUIE'S OF GRANT AVENUE, 1014 Grant Ave (Jackson), 982-5762. $1.35, 30-50 cents for tea. ***(2)

CANTON TEA HOUSE, 1108 Stockton (Jackson), 982-1030, 7:30am-4pm, $1.50. ***(2)

MIRIWA, 728 Pacific Ave (Grant/Stockton), 989-9888, $1.60, tea 50 cents. ***(2)

CLEMENT, 621 Clement (7 Av), 752-9520, 9am-9pm. $1.35. ***(22)

TONG PALACE, 933 Clement (10/11 Avs), 668-3988. $1.50. ***(22)

Sushi

Sushi--basically raw fish filets, usually wrapped in a special "vinegar rice" or served over the sushi-rice--has been around for about 100 years but only recently has it exploded into a national pastime. Almost every Japanese restaurant now serves sushi, and sushi bars devoted solely to sushi have sprung up everywhere, some mere holes-in-the-wall.

An asterisk (*) in front of a name means "especially recommended". Those are put at the head of the list in order to facilitate a choice.

BEST BUY****

*ISO BUNE, 1737 Post (Japantown), 563-1030,. 11:30am-10pm daily, The sushi appears on little boats; you take your pick, like choosing dim sum. ****(12)

*MIFUNE, restaurant mall Japantown, 922-0337, 11am-9pm. ****(12)

*ISUZU, 1581 Webster (Japantown), 922-2290, 10am-2pm & 5-9:30pm, closed Wed. ****(12)

*SANPPO, 1702 Post (Buchanan/Japantown), 346-3486. 11:45am-3pm and 5:30pm-10.30pm Tues-Sat, 3-10pm Sun. ****(12)

TEMPURA HOUSE, 529 Powell (Bush/Sutter), 392-3269, 5:30-10pm. Attractive decor. Sushi assortments $9-13.50. ****(1)

SAN RAKU, 704 Sutter (Taylor), 771-0803. 11am-10pm, Sat 4-10pm. ****(1)

SUSHI ON THE ROCKS, 1475 Polk (California), 441-6854. All-you-can-eat Special--lunch 11:30-2pm $8.95, dinner $10.95 5-9pm. ****(10)

OSOME, 1923 Fillmore (Pine), 346-2311. 11:45am-2:45pm Mon-Fri & 5:30-11pm 7 days. ****(11)

WASABI, 553 Haight (Fillmore/Steiner), 626-4632. ****(14)

MIYABI, 253 Church (Market/15 Sts), 861-0447, noon-3pm Mon-Fri & 5-10:30pm 7 days. ****(15)

NIPPON, 314 Church (15 St). See Low-Priced Japanese Restaurants above. ****(15)

COUNTRY STATION SUSHI, 2140 Mission (17/18 Sts), 861-0972. ****(16)

LADY SEIKKO'S, 2154 Mission (18th/19th Sts.), 558-8246, 11:30am-10pm, Sat.4:30-10pm, closed Sun. ****(16)

HANA, 408 Irving (5/6 Avs), 665-3952. ****(19)

VERY GOOD***

INO SUSHI, Japantown, 1620 Webster, 922-3121. 5:30-10.30pm Tues-Sat. Very small bar with only 8 seats at counter and 2 small tables. ***(12)

SUSHI GEN, 4248 18th St (Diamond), 864-2197, 5:30-10pm. ***(15)

*KABUTO, 5116 Geary Blvd (15 Av), 752-5652 ***(13).

Fish & Chips

San Francisco is running out of genuine fish-&-chips-only restaurants. As a result, I am listing restaurants in this section that include fish & chips in their menus. Some are every bit as good as the genuine thing.

Note: An asterisk (*) denotes "especially recommended". Those are put at the top of list in order to facilitate a choice.

BEST BUY****

*PICADILLY, 1348 POLK (Pine), 771-6477. 11am-11pm Mon-Fri, to 1am Sat-Sun. English-style. Special: 1 large piece fish with fries & onion rings $1.89 (incredible value). Two pieces & chips $3.19, 3 pieces $4.12. Also chicken and chips $4.12, crab & chips $4.87, prawns & chips $5.35. Large ,excellent fries. ****(10)

THE OLD CHELSEA, 932 Larkin (Post/Geary), 474-5015. 4-10pm daily. English type fish and chips 2 pieces $3.40, 1/2 order $2.30, prawns & chips $5.70, chips only $1.50. ****(1)

PENNY FARTHING PUB, 679 Sutter (Taylor), 771-5155, 11:30am-midnight. Deep-fried beer-battered cod & chips $4.25. ****(1)

LONDON FISH & CHIPS, 225 Clement (3rd Ave), 752-8481. 11:30am-10pm Mon-Sat and 3-9pm Sun. Full order (2 pieces fish and chips) $3.40, 1/2 order (1 piece) $2.40; full order prawns and chips $4.35, half-order $2.99; clams and chips $2.65. ****(22)

EXPO FAMILY, 160 Jefferson (Wharf 45), 673-9400, 7:30am-10pm. All-you-can-eat fish fry, including French fries, coleslaw, sourdough roll & butter $7.995 adults, $4.25 children 12 and under. ****(4)

LEHR'S GREENHOUSE PATIO CAFE', 740 Sutter (Taylor), 474-5047, 6am-10pm. Beer-battered rockfish with choice of French fries or sweet potato fries $6.50. With 50-item salad bar $3 extra. ****(1)

LIVERPOOL LIL'S, 2942 Lyon (off Lombard), 921-6664, 11am-4pm & 5pm-midnight. At dinner, with soup or salad, fish & chips $8.95. ****(6)

FUJI COFFEE SHOP (Japanese), 3420 Geary Blvd (Stanyan), 668-8778, 7am-5pm, Sat to 2pm, closed Sun. With fries & coleslaw--deep-fried fish $3.75, deep-fried prawns $4.35. Tempura (deep-fried) prawns, fish, vegetable, with rice & tea $4.50. Simple, clean, counter & booth service. ****(13)

VERY GOOD***

TINA'S, 83 Eddy St. (Mason), 982-3451, 6am-6pm, Sat to 7pm, fish & chips $4.85. ***(9)

LE CAFE' DU COIN, 696 Geary (Leavenworth), 441-6770, 11:30am-10pm. With soup or salad, fish & fries $5.75. ***(1)

SUTTER STREET BAR & GRILL, 1085 Sutter (Larkin), 474-2077, 11:30am-11pm. Fish & chips $2.75. ***(1)

VALLEY CAFE', 1089 Sutter (Larkin), 885-4412, 8am-7pm, fish & chips $2.75

SUN'S SUPERIOR, 312 8th Avenue (Clement), 221-9165, 7am-3pm. With salad, fish & chips $4.25. ***(22)

MIZ BROWN'S, 731 Clement (8th Av), 752-5017. See phone book for 3 more locations. With soup or salad & vegetables $6.15. ***(22)

Fast Foods

America's favorite, and cheapest, eat-out food--especially among children--is in the fast-food restaurants. First place goes to hamburgers, second place to chicken. One good development healthwise are the salad bars at Burger King, Carl's Jr and Wendy's.
BURGER KING
CARL'S JR
DONUTS & THINGS
INTERNATIONAL HOUSE OF PANCAKES
JACK-IN-THE-BOX
KENTUCKY FRIED CHICKEN
McDONALD'S
PIONEER (FRIED CHICKEN)
POPEYE'S CHICKEN
ROUND TABLE PIZZA
VIKING'S GIANT SUBMARINES
WENDY'S OLD FASHIONED HAMBURGERS
WINCHELL'S DONUTHOUSE

4. Intermediate Restaurants $5-$10 Per Person

Since there are so many restaurants in this category, I am listing them in ethnic groups, beginning with *Chinese* restaurants and ending with *Continental & American*. (The *Italian & Basque restaurants* are included separately right after this section).

Note: An asterisk (*) in front of a name denotes "especially recommended". I am putting those at the top of the listing in order to facilitate a choice.

For menu terms of Asian & Mexican restaurants, see Glossary at end of book.

A tip on wines. Bottled wines are sometimes marked up as much as 300-400%, although some restaurants in this category serve bottled wines reasonably, in the $7-10 range. In most cases, the "house wine" is good and costs about $5-/ a liter. Do not hesitate to ask for it. It is often the same as one of the bottled wines.

Chinese

BEST BUY****

*TSING TAO, 3107 Clement (32nd Ave), 387-2344, 11:30am-9:30pm daily. Szechuan cuisine, some dishes very spicy-hot. For 3 or 4 persons choose among the following: hot and sour soup $3.25-4.95, mushu pork (highly recommended) $5.75, pepper prawns $6.75, sizzling beef $5.95, hot braised chicken $5.25, Szechuan eggplant $4.95, shredded pork with garlic. $4.95, crispy fried fish $6.95, spicy chicken salad (cold) $4.95, 1/2 tea-smoked duck $8.50. Family dinners are very attractive: for 2 persons, 6 courses, including dessert $16.95; for 3, 7 courses, $23.95; for 4, 8 courses $33.95; for 5, 9 courses, $40.95; for 6 persons, 10 (sic, ten) courses $49.95. An all-time favorite.

****(23)

*YUET LEE, 1300 Stockton (Broadway), 982-6020, & 3601 26th St. (Guerrero), 550-8998, 11am-3am, closed Tues. One of the very best Chinese restaurants in the Bay Area, especially for seafood. The special fish dishes can be overly expensive. Therefore, you may want to stick to the dishes on the printed menu. Hot & sour soup $4.75, sizzling spareribs (clay pot) $5, beef with cashews $5, cashew chicken $5.50, sweet-sour pork $4.50, mixed vegetables $5, prawns chow mein $4.75, rice soup, with pork, beef, chicken, or fish $3-5.50. ****(2)

*NARAI (Chinese/Thai), 2229 Clement (23 Av) 751-6363. 11am-10pm Tues-Sun. Chow-chow (South China) cuisine, also Thai dishes. Thai egg rolls $3.25, Thai spicy & sour soup with chicken & Thai spices $4.75, garlic eggplant $4.95, Thai BBQ chicken with light curry or sweet-sour sauce $5.50, simmered duck in garlic sauce $5.25, Thai-style pork or beef curry $5.25, prawns with garlic $7.75, deep-fried squid with sweet hot sauce $5.25, Thai-style seafood hot pot $10.50, jumbo prawns & silver noodles hot pot $7.75. Extensive lunch menu of soups, rice and noodle dishes $3.25-3.95. One of the best. ****(23)

*SUN HUNG HEUNG, 744 Washington (Grant/Kearny), 982-2319. 11:30am-midnight, closed Tues. Egg flower soup $2.50, almond chicken $4.50, mandarin duck $5, prawns with cashew nuts $6.75, beef with snow peas $5.75, sweet-sour pork $5, mongolian lamb $7, crabmeat egg foo young $4. One of China-town's oldest and best. ****(2)

*TAI CHI, 2031 Polk (Pacific/Broadway), 441-6758, 11:30am-10pm Mon-Sat, 4-10pm Sun. Hunan-Mandarin cuisine. Hot-sour soup $3.25, curry beef $5.75, mu shu pork(with 4 crepes) $5.95, sizzling shrimp $6.75, bean-sauce chicken $5.50, vegetables deluxe $4.75. Also, a number (15) of strictly vegetarian dishes $3.95-5.75. A favorite. ****(10)

*HOUSE OF NANKING, 919 Kearny St (Pacific/Broadway), 421-1429, 11am-10pm. Inspired homestyle Shanghai cooking in a simple barebones location. Soup: hot & sour $1.75, Nanking fish soup $2.50 (both soups enough for 2). Appetizers: egg rolls $2.50, potstickers $3, Shanghai buns (specialty) $3.20. Entrees: Nanking beef $5.25, Nanking chicken $5.25, Nanking pork $4.95, prawns with Tsing Tao beer sauce (specialty) $6.95, mu shu dishes with 4 pancakes $5-6.95 (shrimp), fried rice or chow mein noodles with beef, pork, chicken or shrimp $3.30-3.95. Tsing Tao beer $1.75. Large portions. A favorite. ****(2)

*OCEAN, 726 Clement (8th Ave), 221-3351, 11:30am-9:30pm. Cantonese cuisine. Westlake beef soup (thick with beef, coriander, egg white) $4.75; chicken with onions in clay pot $5.25; satay beef (sauteed beef slices with hot chili and 5-spice) $5; chicken with plum sauce $5. Popular with young Chinese. 7-course Family Dinner for 4, $7.95 per person. ****(22)

POT STICKER, 150 Waverly Place (Grant/Stockton), 397-9985. 11:30am-9:45pm. 4 Potstickers $1.85, 8 potstickers $3.15, 2 spring rolls $1.85, 4 spring rolls $3.15. Hot-sour soup $4.15, mandarin or twice-cooked pork $5.25, green onion or broccoli beef $5.95, lemon beef $5.95, 1/2 hunan crispy chicken $6.25, garlic chicken $5.55, mu shu pork (4 crepes) $5.25, assorted vegetables $4.50, Szechuan prawns $7.25. ****(2)

KING TIN, 826 Washington (Grant/Stockton), 982-7855, 8am-midnight, Sat to 3am. Roast duck $4.50, BBQ pork $4.50, spicy shrimp $7, beef with vegetables $5.50, orange-juice spareribs $4.50, clay pots $4-5.50. Simple, busy place for Chinese clientele. ****(2)

PACIFIC COURT CAFE', 728 Pacific Ave (Grant/Stockton, in Miriwa Center, ground floor), 781-8312, 8am-9pm. Lunch entrees served with soup or green salad, jello or ice cream--1/2 fried chicken $5.15, pan-fried salmon steak $5.75, snapper almondine $6.15, deep-fried prawns $6.45, roast prime rib of beef $7.45. Dinner about $2 higher. ****(2)

BRANDY HO'S HUNAN, 450 Broadway, 362-6268 & 217 Columbus (Pacific Av), 788-7527, 11:30am-midnight, to 11pm at Columbus Sun-Thurs. Onion cakes with peanut sauce $1.75, steamed dumplings with sweet-sour sauce $3.50, cold eggplant salad $4.25. Smoked chicken with onions & carrots (they smoke their own meats) $6.25, sauteed pork with black beans & red pepper $5.95, fried rice with beef, chicken & shrimp $6.25. They advertise "absolutely no MSG". ****(2)

OCEAN KING SEAFOOD, 684 Broadway (Stockton), 989-8821, 11am-3am. 6-course Family Dinner for 6 persons, 6 dishes, mostly seafood (includes seafood soup, hot & spicy prawns, clams with black bean sauce, whole steamed rock cod), $39.95; 8-course Seafood Dinner for 8 persons, with whole crab and whole fish, $58; 10-dish deluxe Family Dinner for 10 persons, mostly seafood, $108. Also non-fish dinners for 2 $12.75 and 3 or 4 $23.50. In season, this restaurant offers live lobsters and live crab for under $10, made the Chinese way. ****(2)

WOK SHOP CAFE', 1307 Sutter (Franklin/Van Ness), 771-2142, 11am-10pm. Validation parking. For complete dinner add $1.50 to the price of the entree and you also get egg roll, soup, rice and dessert. Appetizerts: egg roll (2) $1.75, pan-fried dumplingh (3) $1.95, BBQW spareribs $2.50. Entrees: Hot &

spicy or lemon chicken $5.50, orange beef $6.75, beef with snow peas $5.05, ginger shrimp $6.95, mixed vegetables$5.25. ****(10)

SAN WANG, 1682 Post (Buchanan), 921-1453 and 2239 Clement, 221-1870. 11:30am-10pm daily. Hot and sour soup $3.95, beef with shredded ginger $5.95; steamed, whole fish in wine sauce with ginger $10.95; baby shrimp in hot pepper sauce $7.50, twice cooked pork $5.50, mushu pork $6.50, vegetables deluxe $3.95, eggplant with garlic sauce $4.50. Very popular, very crowded, large portions. ****(12)(23)

HAPPY VALLEY SEAFOOD, 2346 Lombard (Pierce/Scott), 922-9179. Hot & sour or westlake soup $3.75, potstickers (6) or egg rolls (4) $3.75. BBQ pork ribs (8 ozs.) $4.50. Dinners--the following dishes can be had with samosa, rice & dessert for $1.50 extra, making a full single dinner--chicken with almonds or cashews, or hot braised chicken $5.50, lemon spareribs $5.95, beef with broccoli or mushrooms $5.95, orange beef $6.75, prawns with tender greens or cashew nuts $6.95, mixed vegetables $4.75. Seafood dinner $8.95 per person--5 courses for 3 persons, 6-courses for 4, 7 courses for 5 (the 7-course dinner includes a whole fish). ****(6)

TAIWAN, 445 Clement (6 Av), 387-1789, North Chinese & Taiwan cuisine. Hot & sour soup $3.95, mushu pork or beef (with 4 crepes) $5.25, sizzling chicken platter $5.50, curry chicken $4.50, 1/2 crispy chicken $6, snow peas beef $5.50, sweet & sour spareribs $5.50, spicy prawns $6.95, lemon fish filets $5.50, vegetables deluxe $3.95. ****(22)

MIKE'S, 5145 Geary Blvd (15/16 Avs), 752-0120, 4:30-10pm, closed Tues. Combination plate for 2 (spareribs, prawns, fried won ton, shrimp chips) $5.50, egg flower soup $3.75, hot & sour soup $4.25. boned chicken with cashews $5.95, 1/2 crispy chicken $7, pressed duck $4.75, beef with sugar peas $5.75, sweet & sour pork deluxe (specialty) $5.95, mixed vegetables $4, shrimp chow mein $4.95, shrimp fried rice $3.75, pan-fried prawns in shells (Cantonese style) $6.25, toss-fried clams $4.75. Said to be one of the best Cantonese restaurants in the Bay Area. ****(13)

ALICE'S, 420- Judah (9 Av), 566-1646, 11:30am-9pm, 3:30-9:30 Sat-Sun, closed Mon. Hot & sour soup $3.50, spring rolls (2) $2.50, chicken spring rolls (6) $3.50, chicken with snow peas $5.25, lychee sweet & sour pork $4.25, beef with ginger $5.25, prawns with mushrooms $5.95, scallops with snow peas $6.25. Family Vegetable Dinner $6.50, 5 courses for 2, 6 courses for 3 & 7 courses for 4 persons. 8-course family dinner for 4 $6.75-

7.95 per person. ***(19)

YIN HAY, 1936 Irving (20/21 Avs), 665-3404, 11am-10pm. Hakka cuisine, e.g., they cook with wine. Crispy egg rolls (2) $2.50, pot stickers (6) $2.95, 1/2 crispy fried chicken $6.50, 1/2 crispy fried duck with lemon $7, chicken with snow peas $5, spareribs in orange jam sauce $5, BBQ pork with snow peas $4.75, beef with ginger & pineapple $5, onion chicken clay pot $4.25, assorted meat clay pot $4.75, spiced prawns (hot) $6.25, wine-flavored squid with pickled greens $5.25, mixed vegetables deluxe $4.25. Hakka specialties–1/2 salted baked chicken $6, wine-flavored meat-stuffed bean curd with pickled greens $4.50. Also, 7-course family dinners for 4, $7.25 & $8.95.

VERY GOOD***

JOY, 3258 Scott St (Chestnut/Lombard), 922-0270. Hot-sour soup $3.95, orange-peel beef (specialty) $5.95, mu shu chicken or pork (with 4 pancakes) $5.95, prawn dishes $6.50-6.95. 12 vegetarian dishes $4.75-5.50. For $2.50 extra charge on any main entree in menu, a dinners is served for one person with egg roll, won ton soup, and oat bran rice. ***(6)

CHAN'S, 336 Clement (5 Av), 387-8370, 11am-10pm. Hot & sour soup $3.95, spring roll $2.75. Chicken with pineapple $4.50, 4-season vegetable lamb $5.50, beef with black mushroom $4.95, beef with cashew nuts $4.50, prawns with greens $5.95, sweet & sour rock cod $4.75, 4-season vegetables $3.75, noodle dishes $3.50-3.95, Chinese porridges $3.25-3.75, country-style clay pots $3.95 (stuffed bean cake in soup)-4.95 (beef stew with bean cake). ***(22)

YET WAH RESTAURANT, 1829 and 2140 Clement (19 and 22 Avs), 387-8056 and 387-8040. Latter is a lovely garden-like setting. This is a small chain of Mandarin-cuisine restaurants of high quality. Hot and sour soup $3.75, Szechuan spiced beef $6.75, hot and sour pork with bamboo shoots, onions, peppers $5.50, ginger fried prawns $7.50, cashew chicken $6.25, noodles with pork and scallions $4.25, vegetables deluxe $4.50. Also, excellent 6-course Family Dinners for $7.95, $8.95 & $9.75 per person. ***(23)

HUNAN RED PEPPERS, 450 Balboa (5/6 Avs), 387-1680, 11:30am-9:30pm. Hunan (hot) specialities, no MSG. Dumplings (with or without hot sauce) $2.75, egg rolls (2) $2.50, pot stickers (6) or fried wonton (12) $2.50. Mu shu soup (with eggs, pork, bamboo shoots, & spinach) $2.95 & $3.95, eggplant salad $3.50. Curry chicken with hot sauce $5.25, Hunan chicken (with bell peppers, garlic onions, & hot & sour sauce) $$4.95, curry beef $5.25, Hunan prawns $6.95, prawns with snow peas

$6.95. Also, a 7-course Family Dinner for 4, $8.25 per person. ***(19)

SILVER BOWL, 1501 Noriega Street (22nd Av), 664-7766, 10:30am-10:30pm. Chao chow cuisine. 6 potstickers $2.95, 3 egg rolls $2.95, prawns $3.95, assorterd appetizers (for 2) $5.50. Hot & sour soup $2.95, seafood soup $3.50. Mu shu pork $4.25, Peking spareribs $4.50, tender greens with beef $4.25, beef with ginger & pineapple $4.25, lemon chicken $4.25, spiced prawns in garlic sauce (hot) $5.95, mixed seafood $6.50, mixed vegetables $3.50, roast duck over rice $3.55. Very modest prices. ***(20)

Vietnamese

*AUX DELICES, 1002 Potrero Ave (22nd St, opposite S.F. General Hospital), 285-3196, and 2327 Polk Street (Green), 928-4977, 11am-2:30pm & 5-10pm Tues-Sun, 5-10pm 7 days. Onion soup $1.95 cup, salad $1.75, imperial rolls (2) $4.25, pork-noodle soup with shrimp $3.95 (enough for 4 as starter), crab-asparagus soup $4.95. Pork with mushrooms, bamboo shoots, & vegetables $5.50' shrimp curry with vegetables $5.95; 1/2 chicken stuffed with rice, ground pork, chicken, mushrooms, onions $5.50; beef with bean-curd $6.95; pan-fried marinated catfish $6.50; pork curry with vegetables $6.50. Fried banana $1.50; mango, jackfruit or lychee ice cream $1.50. *French specialities*, with French onion soup or salad–8-oz steak with garlic & butter $9.50, 1/2 duck in orange sauce $9.50. One of the best Vietnamese restaurants in the City. ****(17)(10)

*ROSE, 791 O'Farrell (Larkin), 441-5635, 10:30am-10pm. Beef 7-Ways (7 different beef dishes, including beef fondue, beef salad, la lot, etc.), $16 for 2 persons. Seafood & beef fondue, $16 for 2 persons. Also, $22, 6-course Family Dinner (on Chinese or Vietnamese menu only) for 4-5 persons, which includes shrimp soup, catfish clay pot, iron platter beef etc. Popular with Vietnamese crowd. Specialty: live crab, seasonal price, ****(9)

*AN HONG PHU-NHUAN, 808 Geary Street (Hyde), 885-5180, 3-10pm Mon-Thurs, 11am-10:30pm Fri-Sun. Appetizer combination of fried wonton, egg roll, crab's claw, shrimp on sugar cane $4.95; asparagus soup with crabmeat $2.25 (for 1-2), seafood soup $2.25. Special combination served with rice, salad & soup and grilled at the table–beef, shrimp, pork, chicken & squid $7.95 per person. Seven Courses of Beef, $10.95 per person. ****(1)

KIM SON, 3614 Balboa (36/37 Avs), 221-3811, 10am-9pm. Imperial rolls $2.95, chicken salad $3.95. Crab & asparagus soup $3.50. Chicken, pork & beef dishes $3.95-4.50, seafood dishes $4.50-6.50 (prawns). 7 Flavors Beef (7 beef courses) for 2 $14.99. Seafood dinner for 4, 7 courses, including whole catfish, $8.95 per person. ***(13)

MAI'S, 316 Clement (4th Ave), 221-3046, & 1838 Union (Laguna), 921-2861, 11am-10pm Mon-Sat, 4-9:30pm Sun. Imperial rolls with crab & shrimp $5.25, Saigon-style soup $4.25. Rice plates: lemon grass BBQ ribs $5.25, lemon grass chicken $5.50, Lalot beef $5.95, coconut chicken $5.50, fried prawns, sweet-sour $6.95. ***(22)(5)

KIM'S (Vietnamese, Continental), 508 Presidio Ave (California), 923-1500. Vietnamese--chicken breast sauteed in lemon grass & coconut sauce, with peanuts $4.50; sauteed coconut beef $4.75, sweet-sour prawns & sizzling rice $6.50, catfish in clay pot $4.95. ***(11)

Japanese

*SANPPO, 1702 Post (Buchanan), 346-3486, 11:45am-10pm, Sun 3-10pm, closed Mon. Dinner, with soup, rice, pickled cabbage, tea--tempura combination (prawns, chicken, fish, vegetables) $7 95, salmon teriyaki $7.95, seafood nabe (bouillabaisse) $7.95, shabu shabu (beef & vegetable fondue in broth, with dipping sauce) $7,95, beef cooked in butter with orange & lemon-flavored soy sauce--$8.25. Donburi (meal in a bowl, over rice) average $6.50. One of the best Japanese for the price. ****(12)

*HANA, 408 Irving (5th/6th Ave.), 665-3952. Lunch 11:30am-2pm Mon-Fri, dinner 5-9:30pm Mon-Sat. Extremely popular for lunch, so it's best to be early. Dinner--including soup, salad, pickled cabbage, rice tea--beef & vegetables $6.20, shashimi $6.70, yosenabe (Japanese fish stew with shrimp, oysters, fish, chicken) $6.95, salmon teriyaki $8.20, sashimi and tempura $7.95, shabu shabu (fondue) $6.95, and much, much more. ****(19)

*MOSHI MOSHI, 2092 Third St (18 St), 861-8285, 11:30am-3pm Mon-Fri & 5-9:30pm Mon-Thurs, to 10pm Fri-Sat. Combination dinners with choice of sushi or gyoza (potstickers), soup, cucumber salad, steamed rice & ice cream or sherbet for dessert--tempura shrimp & beef teriyaki $10.95, shrimp tempura & chicken karaage $10.45. A la carte--beef teriyaki $8.95, royal eel, smoked & grilled, over rice $9.95. A bit out of the way, but worth the trouble. ****(17)

*AZUMA (Japanese/Korean), 3520 20th Street (Mission/Valencia), 282-1952, 11am-2:30pm & 5-10pm, closed Sun. *Japanese menu*: with appetizer (vegetables), rice, salad, tea--beef or fish teriyaki $6.50, tempura $6.95, sashimi (tuna) $7.25, Yosenabe (seafood, chicken, vegetable soup) $6.75, assorted sashimi $8.50; combinations $9.95--sushi & teriyaki, tempura & teriyaki etc. *Korean menu*: with vegetable appetizer, soup, rice, salad, tea--short ribs $7.95 (recommended), pan-fried beef & noodles $5.95, spicy seafood soup with bean-cake & vegetables $6.95 (recommended), special vegetable dish with garlic & ginger $6.75. ****(16)

OZUMA, 1331 Polk (Sacramento), 474-0882. With soup, rice, salad, and choice of vegetable tempura, prawns tempura, deep-fried breaded prawns, broiled salmon, grilled beef teriyaki $6.75. Combination dinners $7.50, e.g., tempura & salmon teriyaki. Sushi special, with soup, $6.50, sashimi & sushi special, with soup, $9. ****(10)

MIYABI, 253 Church (Market/18 Sts), 861-0447, noon-3pm Mon-Fri & 5-10:30pm 7 days. Sushi dinners with miso soup $7.95-12.95. Sashimi dinners with miso soup, salad, & rice, with 2 kinds of fish $7.95, with 5 kinds of fish $12.95. With vegetables & tofu--chicken sukiyaki $7.50, beef teriyaki $8.50. 5-course special dinners $11.95, e.g., sashimi, salmon teriyaki, tempura, gyoza, & sukemoni. New, popular. ****(15)

DORAEMON, 2512 Clement (26/27 Aves), 387-4999, 11:30am-2:30pm & 5-10pm, no lunch Sat-Sun. With salad, soup, sunomo & pickles--shrimp tempura with rice $7.60, salmon teriyaki $6.90, deep-fried breaded pork $6.70, sashimi (raw tuna) $7.70, beef teriyaki $7.90. Combination of 3 items--e.g., sashimi, tempura & teriyaki--$8.90. ****(23)

SANRAKU, 704 Sutter (Taylor), 771-0803, 11am-10pm, Sat 4-10pm, closed Sun. Dinners, with soup, salad, pickles, green tea--chicken teriyaki $5.95, pork teriyaki $6.95, salmon teriyaki $7.95; shrimp tempura $7.95; yosenabe (Japanese bouillabaisse, served with pickles, rice & green tea) $7.95. Dinners, with soup, salad, pickles, rice, green tea and green tea ice cream $9.95 & $10.25 (salmon). Sushi with soup, salad, green tea $7.95-13. ***(1)

KABUKI HIBACHI, Japan Center, 931-1548, 11am-midnight. Food is cooked on table-top grills. Dinners include soup, salad, rice, tea & dessert, $8.50-10.50--beef, pork, chicken; short ribs, shrimp plate; combination seafood plate. ***(12)

COUNTRY STATION SUSHI, 2140 Mission (17/18 Sts), 861-0972. Sushi Special with soup & tea $4.95-6.95. Dinner, with soup, salad, rice--teriyaki chicken $5.50, salmon $5.80, ginger beef $5.95, tempura (vegetables & shrimp) $6.95. ***(16)

TAKEYA, 5850 Geary Blvd (22/23 Avs), 386-2777, 11:30-9:30pm Mon-Fri, 5-9:30pm Sat, closed Sun. With soup, salad, pickle, rice, tea--tuna or chicken teriyaki $6.99, beef $7.50; deep-fried breaded fish $7.75, shrimp $7.75; seafood nabe (soup) $8.25. Chocolate mousse $2. Sake $1.75 glass. ***(13)

HOUSE OF TERIYAKI, 2191 Irving (23 Av), 566-5540, 5-9pm, closed Mon. Dinners include soup, salad, steamed rice, green tea & dessert--tempura (jumbo prawns & vegetables) $8.95, deep-fried marinated chicken $8.45, pan fried salmon steak $8.45, broiled mixed seafood $9.55, ***(20)

Thai

*NARAI (Thai-Chinese), 2229 Clement (23 Av) 751-6363. 11am-10pm Tues-Sun. See under Chinese above. ****(20)

*MARNEE THAI, 2225 Irving (23/24 Avs), 665-9500. 11am-9:30pm, closed Tues. Imperial rolls (with prawns) $3.95, chicken soup in coconut milk & lemon grass $5.50, chicken salad with mint leaves $5.25, BBQ chicken $5.50, red beef curry $5.50, BBQ chicken $5.75, garlic pork $5.75, vegetables deluxe $5.50, prawns with hot pepper $7.95. Elegant, one of best Thai restaurants in the City. ****(20)

*PLOY, 2232 Geary Blvd (Divisadero), 563-8602, 11am-3pm & 5-10pm. Egg rolls with shrimp, chicken etc. $4.25, silver-noodle salad with shrimp, chicken, chili & lime juice $5.25, chicken soup with coconut milk & lemon grass $5.25. Curries $4.95 & $5.25, pork & beef dishes $5.75-6.25, BBQ chicken (no one does it better than the Thais) with Thai herbs in sweet & sour sauce $6.25, deep-fried whole pompano fish $7.25, garlic & pepper prawns $8.50. Tropical fruit ice cream $1.75, with fried banana $2.75. A favorite. ****(13)

*ROYAL THAI, 951 Clement (11 Av), 386-1795, 11am-3pm & 5-10:30pm, no break Sat-Sun. Appetizers--prawns with lime juice, lemon grass, mint & chili $4.95, Thai crepe stuffed with shrimp. pork, shredded coconut, bean cake, ground peanuts, & bean sprouts, served with cucumber sauce $5.75. Chicken coconut milk soup $4.95, green salad with bean cake, tomatoes, cucumber, bean sprouts & dressing $4.50. Roast duck with red curry, coconut milk, tomatoes & bell pepper $5.25, 7-ingredients beef with zuchini $5.50, BBQ chicken with sweet &

sour sauce $5.25, sauteed prawns with snow peas, baby corn, & mushrooms $6.95, marinated grilled trout with chili red sauce $7.95, deep-fried whole pompano topped with spicy sauce & bell pepper $7.95. There is also a large lunch menu with noodle, rice & BBQ plates $3.95-4.95 per dish. Considered to be one of the best Thai restaurants in the Bay Area. ****(19)

MANORA'S, 3226 Mission, 550-0856, 5-10pm. See phone book for other 2 branches. Appetizers--imperial rolls filled with shrimp, pork, shredded vegetables & glass noodles $3.95, prawns marinated in lemon grass & mint leaves $5.25, chicken soup in coconut milk $4.95. Entrees--BBQ chicken, marinated in herbs, with sweet garlic sauce $5.75, yellow chicken curry with coconut milk served, with cucumber sauce $5.25, duck curry in coconut milk with pineapple & red chili sauce $5.25, pork marinated in garlic & black pepper $5.25, fish curry $5.75, sauteed Japanese eggplant with shrimp, chicken & pork in basil spicy garlic sauce (also available as vegetarian dish) $6.50, deep-fried marinated crab, shrimp, pork in crab shells with sweet plum sauce $6.75, assorted seafood in garlic spicy sauce served on hot plate $9.95, jumbo prawns served with 2 sauces $8.95. Oriental fruit ice cream with Thai fruit dressing $1.75. One of the oldest & best Thai restaurants in the Area. ****(16)

SAMUI THAI, 2414 Lombard (Scott), 563-4405, 11:30-2:30pm & 5-10pm, closed Sun. Appetizer--Thai crepes stuffed with shrimp, pork, shredded coconut, peanuts, mint leaves, spicy lime sauce (2 can share) $5.95. Chicken coconut soup with lemon grass $6.95. Beef curry with basil & coconut milk $5.75, roasted duck with orange-curry, spinach, tomatoes & coconut milk $5.95, prawn curry with Thai eggplant, bamboo shoots $5.75. Marinated pork with Thai spices $5.75, marinated beef with Thai herbs & lemon sauce $6.75, BBQ marinated chicken with Thai herbs $5.75, prawns marinated with garlic $7.50, deep-fried whole pompano fish with ginger & garlic $7.95. Fried banana with ice cream $2.25. According to a restaurant critic, some of the best appetizers & curries in the local Asian scene. ****(6)

RAMA THAI, 3242 Scott (Lombard/Chestnut), 322-1599, Sun-Thurs 11:30am-2pm, 5-9pm Sun-Thurs, 5-10pm Sat-Sun. Dinner with soup or salad, rice, & dessert--$7.95, choice of pork & chicken dishes,. e.g., pork spareribs, bean cake & vegetables, or charbroiled chicken with papaya salad; $8.95, beef dishes, e.g., beef & eggplant with chili sauce; $9.95, dishes, choice of fish or prawn dishes, e.g., whole fish with sauce, or fish stew with prawns, crab, red snapper, in chili sauce; $6.95, choice of 10 vegetarian dishes. Bananas with coconut ice cream $1.50, lychees with coconut ice cream $1.50. ****(6)

THAI HOUSE, 151 Noe (Henry), 863-0374, 5-10pm. Chicken coconut soup (can be sensational) $3.95, shrimp noodle salad with lemon & chili $4.50. Spicy beef with mint leaves or ginger beef $4.95, pork & garlic pepper $4.10, spicy chicken $5.75, prawns with silver noodles $7.95. Pleasant neighborhood restaurant. ****(15)

SIAM LOTUS, 2732 24th Street (Potrero), 824-6059, 11:30am-2:30pm & 5-10pm. Thai crepes with shrimp, pork, coconut etc. $3.50; lime-prawn soup with lemon grass & mushrooms $5.50. Spicy beef or pork $4.95, crispy duck with sweet sauce $4.95, sauteed prawns with red curry $5.95, pan-fried whole pompano fish with chili sauce $6.50. Lotus ice cream $1.25. ****(15)

SIAMESE GARDEN, 3751 Geary (2nd Av), 668-8763. 5:30-10pm, Tues-Sun. Special dinner $9.95, consists of choice of 2 appetizers and entree, e.g., beef with curry, peanuts, coconut milk; beef with zucchini, hot chili sauce; pork with sweet-sour sauce, onion, pepper. Other dishes--marinated pork sauteed with garlic and pepper $4.95, ginger chicken $4.95, whole deep-fried fish with chili sauce $6.95, beef or pork dishes $4.25-4.95, chicken and seafood dishes $4.95-7.95. ****(13)

LITTLE THAI, 2348 Polk (Green), 771-5544, 11am-3pm Mon-Sat, & 5-10pm Mon-Sun. Thai egg rolls with shrimp $3.95, noodle salad with shrimp $4.25, hot & sour prawn soup $4.75, spicy chicken soup with coconut & lemon grass $4.75, spicy seafood soup with lemon grass $5.95. Spicy sweet & sour pork $4.95, silver noodles with pork & shrimp & vegetables $5.25; beef, chicken or pork curry in hot, sweet sauce $5.50; roast duck with red curry, tomatoes, pineapple & basil $5.95; broiled marinated chicken with sweet & sour sauce $5.50; chili beef with bamboo shoots $5.25; jumbo shrimp & pork in spicy sauce $6.75. ****(10)

NEECHA, 2100 Sutter (Steiner), 922-9419, & 500 Haight (Fillmore), 861-2550, 11am-3pm & 5-10pm. Thai & vegetarian food. Chicken soup with coconut milk, lemon grass, mushrooms, galanga, lime $4.95; roast duck in red curry, basic, tomatoes & spinach $5.25, beef with red curry & basil $5.25, sauteed prawns with garlic & pepper $7.95. Fried banana $1.50, with ice cream $2.50. See also under Vegetarian. ***(11)(14)

THEP PHANOM. 400 Waller (Fillmore), 431-2526, 11am-2:30pm & 5-10pm. Papaya salad $4.95, egg rolls stuffed with shrimp, with plum sauce $4.95, spicy soup with coconut milk & lemon grass $5.95. Sliced sirloin of beef in peanut sauce $6.95, marinated duck on hot plate $6.95, deep-fried whole fish with curry sauce $8.95. Curry dishes $5.95-6.95, prawns in chili paste $6.50, combination seafood in hot chili sauce & lemon leaves $6.95, noodles with shrimp & beancake $5.95. Pleasant atmosphere. ***(14) (13)

SONGKHLA, 3815 Geary Blvd (3rd Av), 386-0203, 11am-9:30pm. Small, intimate, reasonably-priced. Egg rolls $3.75, beef salad with cabbage & onion $3.65, chicken soup with coconut juice, lemon grass, tomatoes, mushroom, garlic & chili $3.95. Silver noodles with pork, egg, shrimp, & vegetables $4.50; stir-fried beef with tender green beans & fungus $4.50, yellow curry chicken with coconut juice, bamboo shoot, onion & green pepper $4.50; roast duck with spinach & sauce $4.75; shrimp with mushrooms & oyster sauce $5.45; deep-fried fish with curry sauce $6.25. Noodles with brocolli & shrimp $3.60, fried rice with pineapple, shrimp, & Chinese sausage $3.75. ***(13)

Mexican

*EL TAZUMAL (Salvadoran, Mexican), 3522 20th St. (Valencia/Mission), 550-0935. 10am-10pm daily. Paella Valenciana $20 for 2, with dinner. All dinners include salad, salsa & chips, most dishes with beans and/or rice. Salvadoran specialities--Spanish sausage with eggs $4.50, pork in green chile sauce $6.95, beef tongue in red-wine sauce $6.25, marinated pork loin with fried plantains & fried cheese $8.50; prawns with vegetables & rice $8.95; pan-fried whole red snapper $8.95, bouillabaisse (clams, crab, fish, squid, prawns), with rice $8.50; chicken in mole (chocolate) sauce $6.95, charbroiled chicken with rice & salad $6.25. Sometimes available is birria (goat stew) $6.95. Also, large selection of Mexican dishes--flautas, enchiladas, chile relleno etc. $5.95-6.50. They have a good taqueria next door. ****(16)

*LA VICTORIA, 2937 24th St. (Alabama), 550-9292. 10:30am-10pm daily. Two tacos, rice and beans $5.95; 2 tostados, rice and beans $6.35; Machaca (meat, onion, chili, eggs, sausage) $6.45; steak ranchero, rice and beans $6.45; combination (chili rellenos, tamales, taco, rice and beans) $6.55; birria (goat stew) $6.45. This is a family-run restaurant and bakery. ****(16)

NEW CENTRAL (Mexican,Peruvian), 301 S. Van Ness (14 St), 431-8587. With chips, rice & beans--chicken mole $7, pork sauteed in a red sauce $6.50, steak ranchero. spicy with hot peppers $6.50, prawns sauteed with tomatoes & onions $7.25, birria (Sat-Sun only) lamb stewed in red chili $5, combination (e.g., flautas & chile relleno) $6. ****(16)

LOS JARRITOS (Mexican, Peruvian), 901 S. Van Ness (20 St), 648-8383. Same mgt, same menu as New Central above. ****(16)

LAS PALMERAS (Salvadoran/Mexican), 2721 Mission (23 ST), 282-7796, 8am-10pm. See under Salvadoran below. ****(16)

MOM'S PLACE (Mexican/Salvadoran). 1192 Geneva Ave (Naples), 586-7000, 10am-11pm. Huge menu. Soups (very large portions, a meal for 1 or an appetizer for 4-5), e.g., chicken soup in mole sauce, chilies & sesame seed--$5.25; or pozole, a beef broth with chunks of meat, raw onion, radishes and lettuce, $4.25 Some appetizers--quesadillas (tortilla with melted cheese) $1.50, boquitas (tortilla chips with beans, guacamole, sour cream and choice of meat), $2.50 & $3.95; pupusas (fried thick corn tortillas with cheese & meat) $1.50; pasteles (fried corn tortillas filled with potatoes, cheese & meat) $1.95. Entrees, served with beans & rice, include: hot & spicy shrimp $7.25, roast pork $7.25, chicken mole (with chocolate sauce, chilis, sesame seed) $5.25. As dessert, fried bananas with sour cream $2. A bottle of acceptable California wine is $4.25. Very low prices, and inspired Mexican cooking by Mom. ****(16)

ENSENADA (Salvadoran/Mexican), 2976 Mission (25/26 Sts), 826-4160, 9am-9pm, closed Mon & Tues. See under Salvadoran below. ***(16)

BRISAS D0 ACAPULCO (Mexican, Salvadoran), 3137 Mission, 826-1496. Specialty: seafood. With rice, salad, tortillas--grilled or breaded shrimp $8.95, crab with green sauce $10.95, whole fried fish $9.95, breaded fish filet $6.95, seafood combination in red wine sauce $10.95. Seafood soup, with tortillas--fish & vegetable $5.95, shrimp & vegetable $6.95, shrimp, fish & vegetable $7.95, seafood combination $12.95. Paella Valenciana with seafood, meat & saffron rice, $17.95 for 2 persons. Menudo (tripe soup) $3.50. With rice & beans--l cheese enchilada $2.95, 1 taco $3.10, 1 super-burrito (with meat, sour cream, avocado, cheese) $3.75; 2 flautas (beef or chicken) $4.25, 2 chile rellenos (stuffed peppers) $5.25, 1 super tostado $3.75. With rice, beans, salad, tortillas--grilled steak $6.50, beef in red sauce $4.95, pork in green sauce $4.95, beef tongue in sauce $5.75, chicken Mexicana in sauce $4.95, Salvadoran steak (with grilled onions, tomatoes, & peppers) $6.50. ****(10)

Indian

*GITA'S, 1048 Market (6/7 Sts), 864-4306, 11:30am-8pm, Fri to

9 pm, Sat-Sun 5:30-9pm (no lunch). Thali dinners served with vegetable, basmati spiced rice, lentil soup, mango chutney, raita, chapati, papadum (lentil wafer), & dessert (honey balls)–lamb curry $8.95, spiced chicken with spinach $9.25, vegetable dish $8.25, chicken in yoghurt sauce $9.25. Lunch prices for the same are $3 cheaper. Other Indian dinners range from $7.95 (vegetarian) to $12.50 (lamb with spinach cooked with herbs). ****(7)

DARBAR, 448 5th Street (Market/Mission), 957-0140. Dal (lentil soup) $2.50, "hot" if requested; samosas (patties stuffed with vegetables) $2.50. Tandoori chicken (half) $8.95, tandoori lamb $9.95, tandoori rack of lamb $13.95. Curries $8.50 & $8.95, prawn $9.95, vegetarian dishes $6.95-7.95. Complete dinners, including lentil soup, eggplant, rice, yogourt & cucumber, dessert, coffee or tea–vegetarian $10.95, chicken $12.95, lamb $12.95. ****(7)

MAHARANI, 1129 Post (Polk), 775-1988, 11:30am-2pm Tues-Fri, & 5-10pm Tues-Sun. Buffet lunch $5.95. Vegetable biryani (rice with mixed vegetables, nuts & herbs) $5.25, vegetarian Thali dinner $7.50, chicken biryani $6.95, chicken Thali dinner $9.75, lamb biryani $8.25, lamb Thali dinner $10.75. Curries $6.25-8.75, tandooris (Indian BBQ over charcoal in a special clay oven) $7.25-16.75. 9 vegetarian dishes $4.75-5.75, vegetarian soup $2. Spinach curry with white cheese $5.75, Tandoori chicken with vegetables $7.95, chicken Vindaloo curry (very hot) $7.75, lamb with yogourt sauce $8.25, Goas fish curry (very hot) $9.75, prawn curry $10.75, lamb kebab $11.75. Big Splurge dinners with samosa & papua, salad, pulao, chicken curry, lamb, dessert $15.50 & $18.50. ****(10)

PASAND MADRAS CUISINE, 1876 Union (Laguna), 922-4498. 11:30am-10pm. Thick lentil-vegetable soup $1.25, Indian breads $1-1.50. Complete Thali dinner, $8.50-11 (price is determined by the entree) includes choice of entree (vegetable curry, curry lamb, chicken cooked with yogurt, or curry shrimp etc.), lentil curry, thick lentil vegetable soup, mango chutney, lentil wafer, deep-fried Indian bread, rice pilaf & dessert. Entrees alone are $5-8. Madras crepes (specialty), with lentil soup & hot & mild sauces are $3-4.50. Pasand has a full bar and live music nightly, no cover charge, minimum 1 beverage per set. ***(5)

Burmese

*BURMA'S HOUSE, 720 Post (Jones), 775-1156, 11am-10pm. Black pepper soup with vegetables & fish $3.75, Burmese fish chowder $3.95. Rangoon beef $5.75, Rangoon chicken $5.25; Rangoon smoked pork with bamboo shoots, green pepper, mushrooms & cabbage $5.25, pepper sauteed prawns or prawns with garlic sauce $6.75. Burmese dessert made with cream of wheat, coconut milk, eggs, sprinkled with poppy seeds $2; "paluda ice cream" (tapioca, coconut juice and paluda syrup, topped with chopped peanuts and ice cream) $2.50. ****(1)

MANDALAY, 4348 California (at 6th Ave), 386-3895. 11:30am-3pm and 5-10pm, closed Mon. Black pepper soup $4.50, Mandalay chicken $6.75, Mandalay beef with garlic $6.75, large prawns cooked in sauce $7.50. An interesting dessert is a coconut pudding-cake topped with poppyseeds. $2.75. First Burmese restaurant in the City, still very good but getting pricey. ****(22)

BURMA, 309 Clement (4 Av), 751-4091, 11am-9:30pm, closed Sun. Pepper soup $3.50 & $4.75, catfish soup with noodles & cilantro $3.95, Burmese vegetarian rolls (4) $3.25, fresh ginger salad $4.95, Burmese potstickers filled with curried potatoes & green peas (served with hot dipping sauce) $3.75. Iron platter beef $6.95, curried chicken with cashew nuts, raisins $5.95, deep-fried pompano with spicy sauce $6.95, curry-squid $6.50, Burmese curry vegetables $5.25. Burmese sundae with roasted peanut ice cream, tapioca, grass jelly & red bean $2.95. ****(19)

ON LOK YUEN, 3721 Geary Blvd (Arguello/2 Av), 386-6208, 11:30-3 & 5-9:30pm, Fri-Sat to 10:30pm. Mango salad $4.85, black pepper soup $4.65, fish chowder $3.65. Burmese pineapple chicken $5.45, Burmese Kung Pao chicken $5.45, Burmese-style beef (stir-fried with onion, chili, tomatoes & special sauces) $5.85, pan-fried pompano with curry $7.95, Burmese eggplant $5.45. Rangoon meal for 3 (5 dishes & rice) $23.95, Burmese meal for 5 (7 dishes & rice) $39.95. ***(13)

Salvadoran

*EL TAZUMAL (Salvadoran, Mexican), 3522 20th Street (Mission/Valencia), 550-0935. See under Mexican above. ****(16)

ENSENADA (Salvadoran/Mexican), 2976 Mission (25/26 Sts), 826-4160, 9am-9pm, closed Mon & Tues. Salvadoran menu: Tripe & vegetable soup, or beef & vegetables $3.50 & $4.50. Lunch & dinner with rice, beans & salad--grilled NY steak with salad $6.75, beef stew Salvadoran style $6.25, stuffed green pepper with pork & vegetables $6, whole fried fish $8.75.

Mexican menu: with rice, beans & salad–combinations $6.50-7.50, beef simmered in sauce $6.50, flautas with steak, meat, guacamole & sour cream $6.75. Tacos $1.45, enchiladas $2.15, tostados $2.15, burritos $2.15-3.50. ***(16)

LAS PALMERAS (Salvadoran/Mexican), 2721 Mission (24 St), 285-7796, 8am-10pm. Salvadoran menu: fish soup $3.75, prawn soup $4.50 & $6.50 (large), mixed seafood (shrimp, clams, crab, fish, calamari $8.50. With beans & salad–rice with chicken, Salvadoran-style $3.50, whole fish with tomatoes, onions & vegetables $6.75, fried breaded prawns $7.75, shrimp ranch-style $7.95, rib-eye steak with fries only $6.50, Salvadoran steak with tomatoes & peppers $6.75, beef tongue with sauce $5.25. Chicken, with fries, 2 pieces $2, 3 pieces $2.80, 4 pieces $3.60. Simple, clean, large portions. ***(16)

Greek

*SALONIKA, 2237 Polk (Green), 771-2077. 5:30-10pm, closed Mon. Former location of Xenios, similar menu. Egg-lemon soup $2.25, tarama (creamy white caviar) $3, hot spinach-cheese pie $3.50, mixed cold plate for 2 (tarama, grape leaves & eggplant salad) $5 (enough for 2 as appetizer) & $8.50. Moussaka (eggplant casserole with meat & cheese) $8.50, chicken in red-wine sauce $8.75, mixed grill (4 meats) $11.50, rabbit in red-wine sauce $11.75, chunks of lamb & cheese-wrapped in dough $11.25, rack of marinated lamb $16.75. ****(10)

STOYANOF'S, 1240 9th Ave (Irving/Lincoln), 664-3664. 10am-9pm, closed Mon. This restaurant is open for lunch, cafeteria style. Appetizers–tarama (fish-egg paste) $3, dolma (stuffed grape leaves) $2.95, lemon and rice soup cup $2, bowl $3, Greek salad $4.25. Entrees, with rice pilaf and vegetables–lamb shish-kebab $10.95; moussaka (casserole of eggplant baked in layers with lean ground beef and tomato sauce, with bechamel sauce & cheese) $8.95; spanakopita (chopped spinach and feta cheese baked between layers of filo dough) $8.95; roast leg of lamb $10.95, baked 1/2 chicken with tomato, green pepper, & spices $7.95. ****(19)

ATHENS, 39 Mason (Market), 775-1929, 11am-11pm. Mon-Sat. Simple, counter, small tables, no-nonsense food atmosphere, wholesome, tasty Greek food. Lamb dishes with vegetables and potatoes $6.25-6.95, lamb stew $6.50, mousaka $5.75, calamari $7, stuffed cabbage (with beef) $4.95. Lemon soup with meal 85 cents. ***(9)

Czech

*GOLDEN DUCK GRILL, 2953 Baker (Greenwich/Lombard), 922-7144, noon-2:30pm & 5-10pm. With soup *and* salad--paprika goulash with dumplings $9.25, paprika chicken $8.95, 1/2 duck with winekraut & dumplings $10.95, veal wienerschnitzel with potato salad $11.95, Marinated herring $3.50, palatschinken (thin crepes Czech-style) $2.95. Small, intimate, picturesque. There's an interesting political story attached to the name--ask. ****(6)

VLASTA'S, 2420 Lombard (Scott), 931-7533, 5-11pm, closed Sun. With soup *and* salad--stuffed cabbage $9.50, goulasch $11.50, veal wienershcnitzel $11.95, sauerbraten $11.95, 1/2 duck with cabbage & dumplings $11.95. Strudel $1.50, cheese cake $2.50. ****(6)

HEART OF EUROPE, 685 Sutter (Taylor), 441-5678. With real German rye bread & butter, vegetable & parslied potatoes--Polish kielbasa with red cabbage $7,95, Swiss bratwurst with red cabbage $4.95, Hungarian beef goulasch $8.95, Bohemian goulasch $9.95, wienerschnitzel $9.95, Dessert--palatcinkas (crepes) topped with strawberry jam & whipped cream $3.75. Pickled herring $3.75, potato pancakes $3.25, bowl soup $2.75. Spaten beer on tap 1/2 liter $3.75, Czech Pilsner Urquell in bottle $3. ***(1)

Persian

*MAYKADEH, 470 Green Street (Grant Av), 362-8286. 12 noon-11pm Tues.-Sun. Yoghurt with cucumbers (served with hot pita bread), $2.90, is a good appetizer for 2, as are stuffed grape leaves $5; barley & vegetable soup $3. Entrees, served with saffron rice--skewered mixture of ground lamb & beef $7.25, skewered slices of marinated filet mignon $10.50, baby lamb chops with garlic & mint $11.75, chicken marinated in yoghurt & saffron $9.25, lamb shank cooked in onions, scallions, leeks, beans etc. $9. Rose-petal flavored ice cream $3. Restaurant is elegant (cloth tablecloth & napkins, fresh flowers). ****(4)

HAFEZ, 2001 Union (Buchanan, end of lobby), 563-7456. Similar to Maykadeh in decor (elegant) and menu, but with complimentary opening appetizer with feta cheese, scallions, mint & basil leaves, pita bread. Persian soup $1.50, yoghourt with shallots $1.95. Skewered lamb & beef mixture, with onion, saffron rice $5.95, skewered filet mignon with rice $8.95, lamb shank special (Thurs) $7.50, eggplant with lamb pieces, rice $7.50, fish with basmati rice, greens $9.50. Persian ice cream with rose-water & nuts $1.95. ****(5)

KASRA, 349 Clement (3/4 Avs), 752-1101, noon-10pm, Fri 1-11pm. Broiled tomatoes 75 cents, eggplant with carrots & cauliflower $1.25. All meat is marinated and served with rice--mixed ground lamb & beef, broiled $5.95, marinated filet mignon $7.95, lamb shashlik $10.95, chicken kabob $7.50. Persian desserts $0.60-2.50. ***(22)

French

*BAYON (French Cambodian), 2081 Lombard (Webster), 922-1400, 5:30-10:30pm, Tues-Sat. 3-course French dinner with Cambodian touch, $9.90--soup or salad, entree (choice of duck confit, grilled pork chops, beef skirt steak with mushroom sauce, or catfish meuniere), and dessert (ice cream, or creme caramel). Superb cuisine. See also under Splurge Restaurants further on for a la carte menu. ****(6)

CHEZ MOLLET, 527 Bryant (3/4 Sts), 495-4527, 11am-3pm & 5:30-10:30pm. Soup or salad $1.50. Specialties: NY steak teriyaki with rice & vegetables $8.50, English-cut prime rib of beef, choice of soup or salad, and mashed potatoes & vegetables $10.50 (Sun, Mon & Tues only), seafood platter (deep-fried) with fries $7.50, soup & large dinner salad $5.50. ****(7)

Peruvian

*DON QUIJOTE, 2351 Mission (20 St), 550-8325, 11am-9pm Wed-Sun, closed Mon-Tues. Elegant setting. Seafood combination, with salad $9; fried fish, rice & beans $6.95; steamed fish with tomatoes, onions & wine $6.95; grilled steak with rice, beans, lettuce & tomatoes $7.25; seafood combo soup $8.25; prawn soup with rice, milk & vegetables $5.95; beef soup with onions, tomatoes & milk $3.75. ****(16)

FINA ESTAMPA (Peruvian/Spanish), 2374 Mission (19/20 Sts), 824-4437. Attractive. Paella marinera $9.95, sarzuella de mares $9.75, prawns & steak $9.50, seafood platter with onions & tomato $8.95, deep-fried fish combination $7.95. ****(16)

German

*SCHROEDER'S, 240 Front (Embarcadero), 421-4778. Split pea soup $2.25, marinated herring $4.25, German meat balls & sauerkraut $6.75, Swiss sausage (veal) & red cabbage $7.75, German sausage platter $7.75, goulasch & noodles $9, sauerbraten & pancakes $10.25, wienerschnitzel $12. Coleslaw or potato salad 75 cents, imported beer $1.75. Oldest German restarant in town. ****(8)

*GERMAN COOK, 612 O'Farrell (Jones), 776-9022, 4:30-9:30pm Tues-Sat. Menu changes daily, all items a la carte. With potatoes and red cabbage or vegetable--bratwurst or knockwurst $5.95, calve's liver $6.95, sauerbraten $7.95, wienerschnitzel $8.95, 1/2 roast duck $8.95, cheese omewlette $4.95. Applestrudel $1.35, with whipped cream $1.85. Intimate German atmosphere, small but adequate menu, and very reasonable prices. ****(9)

GERMAN OAK, 2257 Market (Sanchez/Noe), 861-9669, 5-10pm, closed Mon. With soup or salad--bratwurst with sauerkraut & potatoes $7.75, filet of herring marinated in sour cream, potatoes $7.95, Kasseler (smoked pork chops), sauerkraut, & potatoes $9.65, roast pork in dark beer, red cabbage, potato pancakes & applesauce $10.45, paprika schnitzel, vegetables, spaetzle $10.95, sauerbraten, red cabbage, spaetzle $11.25, pan-fried trout German-style, vegetables, potato $9.95, salads with herring in sour cream $7.20. ***(15)

Mid-Eastern

*LA MEDITERRANEE', 2210 Fillmore (Sacramento/Pine), 921-2956 & 288 Noe (Market), 431-7210, 11am-10pm. Soup $1.75 cup, $2.50 bowl. Soup de jour & salad $5.25. Mediterranean meza, for 2 or more, consisting of dolmas, humous, tabuleh & other specialties $9.25 per person. With cup of soup & Armenian potato salad--Middle Eastern Plate (also as vegetarian plate) $6.50, ground lamb with spices over pilaf rice $6.50. Quiche of the day $5.95. Fillo dough specialty, with soup & salad $6.25. ****(11)(15)

*LA FORCHETTA, 536 Broadway (Kearny), 433-4636. Open lunch & dinner. Dinner is served with complimentary appetizer, sometimes with complimentary soup (if so, choose the lentil) & salad--lamb with honey, nutmeg, prunes, apricots & almonds $9.95, brochette of prawns $10.95, mixed grill of lamb, chicken & prawns $11.75. Couscous (specialty, very filling), lamb $9.95, chicken $8.95, seafood $10.95. You can make a good meal of their merguez (homemade Tunisian sausage) $4.25, and the tomato-lentil soup $2.95. Complete dinner (if they no longer give complimentary appetizer or soup) $14.95 includes soup, salad, any entree, dessert & coffee. Excellent for a very hungry person who likes good Mid-Eastern food. At site of Enrico's. ****(3)

SUNRISE DELI, 2115 Irving (22 Av), 664-8210. Besides sandwiches & mid-eastern plates, now serving dinner as well, with salad, rice & pita bread–1/2 broiled chicken $5.49, lamb or chicken shish-kebab $7.99, kafta kebab (ground sirloin) $7.99, vegetarian plate $4.49. Spinach pie $1.95, feta-spinach pie $2.09. Generous servings, excellent food. ****(20)

Korean

NEW VILLAGE, 4828 Geary Blvd (Park Presidio), 668-3678. Dinner served with appetizer (12 small dishes), soup, salad, rice, rice tea & dessert (rice pudding or jello)--cooked at table for 2 or more--marinated beef short ribs with sauce $11.95, marinated chicken $9.95, seafood & vegetables $11.95. Hot pots--with vegetables etc.--$6.95-9.95. Broiled fish $8.95 & $9.95. ***(13)

MUN'S, 401 Balboa (5 Av), 668-6007, 9:30am-9:30pm. Same short BBQ menu lunch & dinner. Dinner ribs $7.95, beef or pork $6.95, chicken $5.95. Lunch, all dishes $4.95. ***(13)

Cambodian

*BAYON (French Cambodian), 2081 Lombard (Webster), 922-1400, 5:30-10:30pm, Tues-Sat. 3-course French dinner, with Cambodian touch, $9.90. See under French above for details. ****(6)

*ANGKOR-BOREI (Cambodian), 3471 Mission (30 St), 550-8417, 11am-10pm. An elegant & worthy replacement for Angkor Wat which has closed. Appetizers (good starters for 2)--Chicken salad with mints, cabbage, red onions, cucumbers, bell pepper, bean sprouts, ground peanuts & a lemon-garlic dressing $3.95, with shrimp $4.95; crispy crepe stuffed with shrimp, ground pork, tofu, shredded coconut & bean sprouts, served with ground peanuts in a lemon-garlic sauce, & a vegetable salad $4.75; Cambodian crispy spring rolls with ground pork & vegetables $3.95. Entrees--Green curry with fish chunks, eggplant & mushrooms, in a coconut milk broth $5.95, with shrimp $6.95; shrimp & pineapple curry in yellow coconut sauce $5.95; charbroiled beef balls with water chestnuts & a vegetable salad $6.25; sauteed shrimp in coconut milk & red curry, on a bed of spinach $7.25; sauteed seafood combination with vegetables $7.95. ****(16)

ANGKOR PALACE, 1769 Lombard (Laguna), 931-2830. Dinner can be expensive (dishes run as high as $20) but doesn't have to be. We started with a wonderful crepe stuffed with shrimp & bean sprouts, and a dipping sauce ($5), which was big enough to split, then 1 entree each, sauteed pork with mushrooms & cashews ($6), and a whole fish in spices ($8) which was great. The two other members of our party splurged and had the 8-course dinner --$20 per person, and worth it. There are many entrees for $6-$8, e.g., prawn curry ($8), breast of chicken & shrimp over eggplant (($6), sweet & sour pork ($7). Desserts are overpriced at $4, wine is reasonable (we had a bottle of French Bordeaux for $10). Worth a visit. ****(6)

PHNOM PENH, 631 Larkin (Eddy/Ellis), 775-5979, 11am-3pm & 5-9:30pm, Fri-Sat to 10pm. Cambodian classical entertainment Fri & Sat at 8:30pm. Charbroiled marinated chicken in ginger & spices $6.75, spareribs with Japanese eggplant, carrots simmered in red curry sauce $6.95, pan-fried whole fish simmered in Cambodian sauce $7.95, sauteed prawns with bamboo shoots in coconut milk & hot sauce $7.95, baked eggplant in lemon sauce $5.75, charbroiled lamb with lemon grass $8.50, 2 smoked quail with pepper lemon sauce $7.95. Quality is high. Be sure to reserve. ****(9)

Cuban

EL CUBANE (Mexican/Cuban), 1432 Valencia (25/26 Sts), 824-6655, 12noon-10pm Tues-Sun, closed Mon. Corn tamales with beef $2.50, deep-fried green plantains $2.25, garbanza soup with pork & ham $2.20 & $3.60, Sopa de mariscos (Mexican bouillabaisse, with clams, crab, shrimp. fish, squid) $8. Entrees, served with green salad, beans, rice, bread and butter--16-oz broiled porterhouse steak $12, ox-tail stew (no beans) $9.25, beef tongue in tomato sauce $9, goat stew $9.50, roast pork with yucca $9.50, paella valenciana $14, prawns sauteed in tomato sauce & white wine $9, whole deep-fried fish (no beans) $9. ***(16)

Russian

*CINDERELLA BAKERY, 436 Balboa (5 Av), 751-9690. 9am-6:00pm, closed Sun-Mon. Soups (borsht, barley, spinach, or kidney) $2.40 bowl, cheese omelette or ham & eggs $2.85. Beef stroganoff, leg lamb with kasha, or cutlet a la Kiev $6.60; beef, chicken or fish cutlet $4.40; Cabbage rolls or stuffed peppers $4.80; vareniki with cheese $4.40; pirogi $1.70-1.80. Hearty Russian cooking. Most customers speak the language. ****(19)

ACROPOLIS BAKERY (Russian-Greek), 5217 Geary (16th Ave), 751-9661. 8:30am-9pm. Borscht $2.80, Beef Stroganoff $6.95, stuffed cabbage with sour cream $5.85, calves liver with onions $5.50, vareniki (ravioli with sour cream) $4.95, dolmades (stuffed vine leaves) $2.80, blintzes $3.80, soups--barley, spinach, vegetables & meatballs, or borsht, $2.80. New ownership but old, longtime cooking staff. ****(13)

Ethiopian/East African

*NYALA (Ethiopian/Italian), 39A Grove Street (Civic Center), 861-0788, 11am-2am. Ethiopian dishes served with vegetables & Ethiopian bread (which is used in lieu of knife & fork to scoop up the food)--chicken in spices & specially prepared butter $7.50, beef cubes sauteed in onions & peppers & garlic butter $7.50, lamb curry $7.75, Ethiopian steak tartar $8.50, pan-fried fish with spicy lentils, peas, with fresh salad $8.50. Same entrees at lunch are $2 cheaper. Italian dinners are served with salad & bread & butter--spaghetti $7.50, lasagna $8.50, sauteed prawns with fresh tomatoes, garlic butter & white wine, tossed with pasta & parmesan cheese $9.50. Same dishes at lunch $2-3 cheaper. Italian food is surprisingly good. They now also have a vegetarian buffet at lunch, Mon-Fri, $3.95, and dinner, 7 days, $6.95. ****(9)

*MASSAWA, 1538 Haight (Ashbury/Clayton), 621-4129, 11am-11pm, dinner 5-11pm. All dinners served with injera (flat-round bread), lentil stew, and salad--chicken stew with berbere (red pepper & spice mixture) $6.95, beef stew with berbere $6.95, lean beef with spices & served with home-made cottage cheese $8.50, lamb cubes with vegetables, prepared with herbs & spices $6.95, fish & spinach stew, with tuna & sardines (specialty) $6.95, combination of 2 kinds of lentil, spinach & chicken sauce, with yoghourt $8. Five vegetarian dishes $6.50-8. Also, a small Italian menu, served with salad & bread & butter, e g.--lasagna (with tomatoes, cheese & ground beef)

$7.50, spaghetti, macaroni or ravioli with meat sauce $6.50. A good addition to S.F.'s ethnic culinary culture. ****(14)

Brazilian

*EUNICE'S, 3392 24th Street (Valencia), 821-4600, 5-10pm, closed Sun-Mon. With salad, rice & vegetables--feijoada (national dish consisting of spareribs & sausage smothered in black beans, with rice & collard greens) $7.95, cajun jambalaya (shrimp & ham cubes) $8.95, creole gumbo (with crab, shrimp, chicken, sausage. okra, over rice) $11.95, Spanish paella $11.95, . ****(16)

BAHIA, 41 Franklin (Market), 626-3306, 11:30am-2:30pm Mon-Fri, Mon-Sat 5-10pm, closed Sun. Beef or chicken croquettes $2.95, black bean soup cup $1.50, bowl $2.25. Feijoada $10.95, roast leg of pork stuffed with vegetables, bacon & black olives, served with refried beans & collard greens $9.95; fish of day marinated in lime juice & simmered with fresh tomatoes, bell peppers & coconut sauce $11.95. ****(15)

Irish

*MAD HATTER, 3848 Geary (3rd Av), 752-3148. 11:30am-9pm Mon-Sat. Bar & restaurant with good food and reasonable prices. Pub Grub Menu, from 4pm--BBQ pork ribs with fries $5.95, 2/3-lb burger on French roll $6, fries $1.50, Texas-style chili with onions & cheddar $3.95, grilled Thai chicken wings with dipping sauce $3.50, all-beef old-fashioned hot dog with mustard & relish $2.25. Some typical dinner entrees--southern-style chunks of monkfish with black beans, Mexican rice, & cilantro pesto $8.95; Catalonian seafood stew (ahi tuna, seabass, mussels, clams, shrimp) in tomato broth with ground almonds, pine-nuts, garlic-parsley pesto, with garlic bread $8.95. ****(13)

IRELAND'S, 3920 Geary Blvd (3 Av), 386-6173. Lunch, Sat-Sun only--1/2-lb burger with fries $4.25, Irish stew $4.50, shepherd's pie $5.50, 10-oz sirloin steak & fries $7.95, fish & chips $5.25. Sandwiches, with choice of fries, potato salad or soup--ham & Italian salami with melted Swiss cheese on French bread $4, corned beef or Reuben $4. Irish stew & shepherd's pie served during bar hours, 10am-2am. ****(14)

English

PENNY FARTHING PUB, 679 Sutter (Taylor), 771-5155, dinner 4:30-11pm. Bangers & mashed potatoes $6.95, steak & kidney pie with vegetables $7.50, shepherd's pie with mashed potatoes & vegetables $7.50, roast cross rib of beef $8.50. Bread pudding with bourbon sauce, or sherry trifle $2.50. ****(1)

LIVERPOOL LIL'S, 2942 Lyon (off Lombard), 921-6664, 11am-4pm & 5-midnight, Sat-Sun 10am-4pm Decorative pub atmosphere. Dinner--smoked salmon, pate', or shrimp cocktail $4.95, French onion soup with 2 cheeses $3.95. Special burger with sauteed onions & cheese, & fries, $6.95, a meal in itself. Dinner entrees with soup or dinner salad & fresh vegetables--English fish & chips $8.95, chicken breast with white wine, cream & Dijon mustard $8.95, steak & kidney pie $8.95, BBQ ribs English style (with chutney) $8.95, tournedos (beef filets with mushrooms & bernaise sauce) $11.95, 12-oz N.Y. steak with seasoned butter $12.95. Sat/Sun brunch with orange juice or champagne $7.95. Lunch entrees are about $2 less than for dinner. Excellent pub fare English-style at reasonable prices. ****(6)

Danish

*EINER'S DANISH, 1901 Clement (20th Ave), 386 9860. 5-10pm daily, to 11pm Fri-Sat, closed Sun. Dinner begins with a complimentary salad of raw carrots, celery, melon & a dip. With "real" mashed potatoes & vegetables--8oz top sirloin with mushrooms $9.95, 12oz $11.95, veal stew $7.95 (come early, they run out), bratwurst $7.95, cheese fondue (specialty. made with harvarti & Swiss cheeses & wine) $12.95 for 2 persons, $5.50 extra for each person over 2, with homemade bread. ****(23)

Singaporan/Malaysian

SINGAPORE-MALAYSIAN, 836 Clement (9/10 Avs), 750-9518. Malaysian salad with prawn paste sauce $3.95, satay (beef, pork, chicken marinated in coconut sauce) with spicy peanut sauce $6.95. Soup--rice noodles, cucumber, mint leaves, onion, in fish broth $4.50 (for 2), $5.50 (for 3-4). Entrees--Fried chicken with curry $5.95, fried rice with shrimp, egg, salt fish, peas $4.95, curry beef with coconut red sauce $7.25, sauteed prawns with lemon grass, onion tumeric, coconut $8.50, whole pompano with curry, tumeric, onion $8.50, fried prawns with tamarind & soy sauce $8.50, mixed vegetables Malaysian $4.95. Malaysian desserts $1.75. ***(22)

Jamaican

PRINCE NEVILLE'S, 1279 Fulton Street (Divisadero), 567-1294, 11:45am-10pm. Dinner 4-10pm. Moved from Haight Street. With soup (5-bean) or salad, rice & peas, mixed vegetables-- stewed or curried chicken $7.95, Jamaican jerk chicken $10.95, mixed curried vegetables $6.95, curried shrimp $9.95, stewed oxtails $9.95, curried prawns $10.95, curried goat $11.95, red snapper Jamaican style $11.95, ackee fruit (national dish) $13.95. Rum cake $2, Guiness stout or Jamaican beer $2, Jamaican coffee $1. Very small, interesting decor. ****(14)

Laotian

MALAI LAO, 3189 16 St (Valencia/Guererro), 626-8528, 5-10:30pm. Paper rolls stuffed with pork, crabmeat, cucumber, tofu & mushrooms $4.95. Chicken soup with coconut milk, mushrooms, lemon grass, & galanga $4.95, combination seafood soup $5.55. Vegetable curry with coconut milk $4.45, BBQ marinated chicken in herbs, with spicy sauce $5.75, curry roast duck cooked with coconut milk, red chilis, pineapple, tomato & spinach $5.55; BBQ beef marinated in herbs, with spicy sauce $5.75, steamed catfish in banana leaves, with chili, lemon grass & coconut milk $6.75; shrimp sauteed with bamboo shoots & bell peppers in garlic sauce (spicy) $6.95, deep-fried whole pompano topped with chili-garlic sauce & bell peppers $7.95. Fried banana with honey $1.25, with ice cream $2.25. ****(16)

Dutch

DE WINDMOLEN, 120 9th Ave (Irving/Lincoln), 753-0557. 8am-2:30pm, breakfast & lunch. 5-9pm. Soup of day $1.50, house salad $1.50, tuna salad $3.95, crab salad $4.95, split pea soup with sausage & bread $3.90, meat balls with potatoes & salad $6, croquettes (specialty) with potatoes & salad $7. Windmolen burger, with sauteed onion, mushroom, cheese & egg, served with hot potatoes $4.95. ***(19)

PHILIPPINE

PHILIPPINE, 3619 Balboa (37 Av), 752-8657, noon-10pm Wed-Sat, 3-9pm Sun. Combination Plate dinners $5.99-7.99. Including beef lumpia, soup & tea--Adobo (pork or chicken) $5.99, chicken curry $6.99, estofado (beef) $7.99, halibut steak $7.99. ****(13)

Jewish

DAVID'S DELI, 474 Geary (Taylor/Mason), 771-1600, 7am-1am, Sat from 8am. Appetizers (enough for 2)--Gefillte fish with horseradish $4.95, kishka $5.95, matjes herring $6.95, chopped chicken liver $6.95, Scottish lox $7.95. Entrees, with potatoes, vegetables & pickle--beef meat loaf $7.95, roast chicken $8.95, stuffed cabbage $9.75, boiled brisket of beef $9.75, Hungarian goulasch $9.75, sauerbraten $9.75. Also, kosher frankfurters with beans or salad $6.95; crisp potato pancakes with apple sauce or sour cream $6.95. ***(1)

SHENSON'S DELI, 5120 Geary Blvd (15/16 Avs), 751-4699. 8am-5:45pm Tues-Sun. Lunch plates $4.50--3 potato pancakes & sour cream, gefillte fish with horse-radish & potatoes, frankfurter & potato salad, chopped liver & potato salad, knockwurst & sauerkraut. 1/2 sandwich with soup or salad $3.50. Sandwich platters with roast kishke (stuffed intestine) or potato pancake, coleslaw--corned beef, pastrami $5.50. ***(13)

Swiss

SWISS ALPS, 605 Post (Taylor), 885-0947, 5-10pm Tues-Sat, closed Sun-Mon. With soup *and* salad--bratwurst $7.75, sweetbreads with mushrooms in brandy cream sauce $9.95, sauerbraten with German noodles $10.45. Specialties--cheese fondue for 2 $16, beef fondue with sauces, for 2 $26. ***(1)

Afghan

THE HELMAND, 430 Broadway (Kearny/Montgomery), 362-0641, 11:30am-3pm & 6-10pm. Ravioli filled with leeks on yoghourt-mint $2.95, pan-fried eggplant with tomatoes & spices in yoghourt & garlic sauce $2.95, a soup made with beef, mung beans, chick peas, black-eyed peas & yoghourt $1.95. Entrees served with Afghan bread--spinach sauteed with chunks of beef and Afghan seasonings & challow (rice with cumin & other spices) $7.95; beef meatballs sauteed with sundried tomatoes, hot peppers & green peas in tomato sauce, with challow $6.95; tenderloin of lamb with raisins & glazed carrots, with pallow (Afghan-style rice) $9.95. Afghan desserts $1.95. Wines tend to be high; stick to the house wine which is good. A worthy addition to the ethnic cuisines of San Francisco. ****(3)

Nouvelle Pacific

L'ORIENT, 1666 Market (Gough), 863-3103, 1-4pm & 7-10pm. A new category of cuisine which derives its products from the Pacific Basin. New Zealand green mussels with mint & chilis $3.75, Thai bouillabaisse with toasted shallots $4.75. Entrees served with green salad, rice & vegetables--grilled seafood with tumeric rice & East Indies herbs $8.75, blackened catfish a la Singapore $9.75, BBQ Thai pork $8.75, New Zealand lamb chops $10.75, stuffed prawns Thai-style $9.95. Jackfruit ice cream with mango sauce $3.25, mango coconut cheesecake with grand marnier sauce $3.25. Lunch has same dishes but considerably cheaper. They also serve a Midnight Express for $5.50, from 12:30am-4am, i.e., a late-night breakfast, with garlic fried rice, 2 fried eggs, pickled papaya, and choice of the following--2 Phillipine sausages, marinated sweet pork, marinated beef, deboned marinated milkfish, or Filipino noodles. Interesting cuisine. ****(15)

East-West cuisine

*TEMASEK, 1555 Clement Street (17 Av), 387-6556, 5-10pm. This is a major find. This cuisine is based in Southeast Asia (Temasek is the ancient name for Singapore), prepared by a cook who also trained in first-class French restaurants in Europe. The menu is small, & each complicated dish is prepared with devotion. Appetizer--small tarts filled with sauteed mushrooms, East-Indan herbs, & fresh oysters $3.75. Shrimp bisque with thyme & basil, with lemon grass, galanggal, & bay shrimp $4.75. Entrees are all $9.75 or $9.95, except vegetarian entrees, prepared Southeast-Asian style, which are $7.75 or $7.95. All are served with a house salad & special sauce, e.g., salmon a la Singapore: marinated in lime juice, cayenne, oyster sauce, shallots, & then blackened, served with jasmine rice & vegetables; medley of seafood sauteed with jicama, squashes, chestnuts, sun-dried mushrooms, basil & chopped pecans, with jasmine rice; & 2 or 3 entrees not on the menu, but which are special. Desserts are $3.25, and unique--lime & coconut cheesecake with Grand Marnier, almond torte, or chocolate triple truffle with cardamon sauce (sinful). Inspired cooking, served in a small area (8 tables), starkly decorated. Expect the prices to go up soon. I consider this to be a major find, not yet discovered by the critics (but, possibly will be by the time this Edition goes to press). ****(22)

Continental & American

BEST BUY****

*PACIFIC COURT CAFE, 728 Pacific Avenue (Stockton/Grant, on ground floor of Miriwa Center), 781-8312. With soup, green salad, dessert (jello or ice cream), garlic bread--hamburger steak & onions $5.95, 1/2 garlic fried chicken $5.95, filet of sole $7.55, calamari steak $7.95, Pacific snapper almondine $7.95, roast prime rib of beef au jus $8.95 (extra large cut $10.95), T-bone steak or steak forestiere $10.55. Lunch is up to $1 cheaper, with one less course, soup *or* salad, and a few more entrees (e.g., pan fried salmon steak or rainbow trout $5.75, filet of sole $5.45). Very simple decor, no tablecloths, clean, pleasant service. There's a good chef at work. See, also, Splurge Restaurants for higher-priced entrees. ****(2)

LEHR'S GREENHOUSE PATIO CAFE', 740 Sutter (Taylor), 474-5047, 6am-10pm. Lunch or dinner entrees with salad bar (some 50 items) $3 extra, with soup & salad bar $4--hot turkey or roast beef plate, with mashed potatoes & vegetables $5.50, chicken & mushroom crepes with rice & vegetables $6.50, beer-batter fish & chips with French or sweet-potato fries in a basket $6.50, grilled liver & onions with mashed potatoes & vegetables $6.25. Sandwiches are served with sweet-potato fries or French fries, & their "fireworks" cole slaw, on choice of bread, including sour-dough. e.g., roast beef $5.25, turkey & avocado $5.25, ham & cheese $4.75. Ice cream $1.50, hot fudge sundae $3.25, banana split $3.50. ****(1)

HYDE STREET BISTRO, 1521 Hyde (Jackson/Pacific), 441-7778, 5:30-10:30pm. They use organically-grown vegetables. Also, a Viennese cook is at work here. Appetizers--two can share--warm vegetable strudel with herb sauce $4.25, grilled country sausage with polenta $5.25. Pastas & entrees--Viennese spinach gnocchi with gorgonzola & pancetta sauce $6.75, pasta with pesto & chicken $7.80, ravioli with wild mushroom sauce $8.25, spaetzle with smoked ham, gruyere, mozzarella & parmesan cheeses $8.95, grilled red snapper on bed of spinach with tagliarini $9.50, veal fricasse with wild mushroom sauce & spaetzle $10.75. ****(9b)

THE DELI, 1980 Union (Buchanan), 563-7274, 11am-2am. A meeting place on Union Street. Large deli servings. Chicken liver $5.50, cold borscht & sour cream $2.75. Cold plates-- corned beef or pastrami $9. Entrees-- blintzes with sour cream $8.25, knockwurst & sauerkraut with baked beans $8.75. Sandwiches--hot corned beef, pastrami or tongue $6.50, chopped liver $6.50, smoked salmon $9.50, reuben $7.95. ****(5)

MARINA CAFE', 2417 Lombard (Scott), 929-7241, 5-10:30pm Tues-Sat, 4-10pm Sun, closed Mon. 10th Anniverary Dinner, $10, valid for all of 1990. With soup or salad, vegetables, rice or potatoes, and choice of entree--N.Y. steak, jumbo prawns saute', fresh Eastern scallops, fresh fish of the day, breast of chicken, or cioppino. Validated parking. ****(6)

LUPANN'S CAFE', 4072 18th St. (Castro), 552-6655. 6-10:30pm Tues-Sun, closed Mon. Calves liver with mushrooms & bacon $10.50, pot roast with red potatoes $9.95, calamari with French fries & vegetables $8.95, roast loin of pork with sauteed pippin apples $11.50, 2 6-0z lamb chops broiled over wood, with red-wine aioli & mashed potatoes $16.95. Special desserts $3.50. One of the best restaurants in the Castro area. ****(15)

LE CAFE' DU COIN, 696 Geary (Leavenworth), 441-6770, 7am-10pm. With soup or salad, vegetables & sourdough bread--fried chicken (with fries) $5.75, broiled halibut steak (with rice & tartar sauce) $5.95, fish & chips (with fries) $5.75, vegetable lasagna $4.50, spaghetti with meat sauce $4.50, T-bone or rib steak (with fries) $7.95, sauteed prawns (with mushrooms & broccoli) $5.95. ****(1)

NOB HILL NOSHERY, 1400 Pacific (Hyde), 928-6674, 7am-10pm, from 8am weekends. With rice or potato (except pasta), bread & butter--1/2 BBQ chicken $4.95, whole $6.95, crab & seafood broccoli $5.95, spinach & cheese lasagna $6.95, old-fashioned meat loaf $6.95, quiche of the day $3.95, with salad $5.95, pasta with meatballs & sausage $6.95, pasta with red sauce $4.95. Baked brie with French bread $3.95, dry salami & cheese $3.95, pate' & cheese platter $4.95. ****(9a)

THE CURBSIDE CAFE', 2417 California (Fillmore), 929-9030, 9am-10pm. Intimate, small. Mixed green salad $2.50, baked brie with seasonal fruit $3.50. Entrees--fettucine alfredo $6.95, eggplant sorrento $6.95, Greek-style prawns $8.95, sauteed spicy chicken with peppers & mushrooms $8.95, grilled sirloin steak with herb butter $9.95. ****(11)

CLOUD NINE, 1428 Haight (Masonic), 864-8484, 8am-9:30pm. With soup or tossed salad, fresh vegetables & rice, pasta or baked potato–chicken Canadienne (chicken breast charbroiled with Canadian bacon, cheese & mushrooms) $8.95; chicken in lemon juice with white wine, topped with capers $7.29; veal with mushrooms, apples in brandied cream sauce $8.29; 10-oz rib-eye steak, or au poivre with mushrooms, peppers & onions in a sherry sauce $10.95. Also, creole jambalaya entrees, with tossed salad & rice–$7.75-8.95. Pastas, with garlic bread, $4.95-6.25. ****(14)

CRESCENT CITY, 1418 Haight (Masonic), 863-1374, 10am-10pm Wed-Thurs-Fri, Tues 5-10pm, 8am-10pm Sat, 8am-3pm Sun. Specialty: New Orleans' dishes. With soup or salad & corn bread, pasta–creole gumbo (chicken, sausage, crabmeat) $6.95, shrimp creole $7.95, crab cakes plate $6.95, grilled pork chop with red beans & rice $5.95. With soup or salad & corn bread–catfish platter $8.95, Louisiana crawfish, tomatoes, cream sauce $11.95. Creole gumbo, cup $2.95, bowl $5.50. All seafood comes from Gulf of Mexico.

****(14)

ALL YOU KNEAD, 1466 Haight (Masonic/Ashbury), 552-4550, 8am-11pm, to 8pm Sun, dinners 5-10pm. With soup or salad, French bread & butter–eggplant parmigiana $5.50, cheese ravioli with mushrooms $5.25. With salad–pastas $5.95-6.75. French bread pizza with salad $3.50. ****(14)

VERY GOOD***

TINA'S, 83 Eddy Street (Mason), 982-3451, 6am-6pm, Sat 7am-7pm. With soup or salad, potatoes or rice, bread & butter, coffee or tea–calves liver $6.70, roast pork $6.25, lamb $6.75, baked meat loaf $5.50, 12-oz N.Y. steak $9.95. ***(7)

PACIFIC BAY DINER, 522 Jones (O'Farrell), 775-5414, 10am-10pm. Pastas–spaghetti with mushrooms or meat sauce $3.95, with baby clams $4.50, fettucine Alfredo $3.95, linguini with baby clams $4.50. Roast chicken stuffed with chicken livers, onions, spinach, & bread crumbs $5.95. Dinner, with soup, salad, baked potato or rice, rolls & butter–grilled halibut steak with tartar sauce $5.50, salmon with lemon & butter $5.50, roast prime rib of beef (Sat-Sun only) $8.75, grilled pork chops $5.35, T-bone steak $6.75, NY steak $6.75 (with shrimp $8.75). Banana split with 2 bananas $2.95, mug of ice cream $1.95, pie $1. On ground floor of completely rebuilt Pacific Bay Hotel. Surprisingly good for the low price. ***(9)

SUTTER STREET BAR & GRILL, 1085 Sutter (Larkin), 474-2077,

11am-11pm. With soup or salad, mashed potatoes, vegetables, muffin--turkey $7.95, chicken fried steak $6.95, 2/3-lb hamburger steak $6.95, 6-oz NY steak $9.95. ***(1)

PING YUEN, 650 Jackson (Grant/Kearny), 986-6830, 7am-9pm. This Chinese-American restaurant, which has been serving very good meals at knock-down prices ($4-6.50) for years, has now added a gourmet menu (one of the owners is a top chef at one of San Francisco's most prestigious deluxe hotels). Dinners include soup, salad, fresh vegetable, potato or rice, dessert (sherbet or ice cream), coffee or tea--cajun-style chicken steak $6.25, linguini with sauteed seafood in cream sauce $6.50, filet of sole almandine $6.85, grilled salmon steak $7.85, NY steak & prawns $9.85. Simple decor, service tends to be brusque, and the quality of the food is often uneven. ***(2)

HARRINGTON'S BAR & GRILL, 245 Front Street (Embarcadero), 392-7595, 11:30am-3:30pm Mon-Fri, Sat 11:30am-7:30pm. Dinner entrees served with soup or salad, vegetable, french fries & French bread--baby beef liver with grilled onions $7.75, fried filet of sole $8, halibut $9.25, N.Y. steak $9.95. 1/2-lb superburger with fries $5.75, club sandwich (turkey, ham, cheese, tomatoes, pickles, lettuce) with fries $6, bowl of chili or soup $2.25. ****(8)

SUGAR PLUM, 3490 California (Laurel), 922-3111, open 24 hours. With soup or salad, potatoes or rice, vegetables, bread & butter--spaghetti & meat sauce $5.95, fish & chips (white cod of Nova Scotia) $7.95, veal parmigiana with spaghetti (no potatoes or vegetable) $7.75, 8-oz NY steak $10.95, 14-oz NY steak $15.50, cross rib of beef (Sat-Sun only) $8.95. Dinner Special daily--with soup or salad & beverage $7.95. ***(11)

CHURCH STREET STATION, 2100 Market (Church), 861-1266, *open 24 hours*. With soup or salad, potatoes, vegetables, bread & butter--pan-fried liver with onions & bacon $5.65, charbroiled rib-eye steak $7.95, fish & chips $4.95, dinner salad $1.15. ***(15)

CAFE' FLORE, 2298 Market (Sanchez/Noe), 621-8579, 8am-11pm, 8am-8pm Sun. Crowded gay hangout, garden tables. Breakfast & lunch menu is limited but the cafe' has been renovated and new items, e.g., pizzas, are being added. Focus is on organizally-grown fruit & vegetables. Prices have gone up since last reporting. A few items on the menu: bowl of soup, with bread & butter, $3.75; prosciutto plate with artichokes & marinated vcegetables $6.50; shrimp salad with spinach & marinated vegetables $6.50; fruit salad with yoghourt $3.75. ***(15)

DUO, 4094 18th St (Castro), 552-8388. 5:30-10pm. With soup or salad, rice & vegetables--moussaka $9.75, Swiss veal with cheese & avocado $9.50, chicken cordon bleu (with Canadian bacon & Swiss cheese) $9.50, veal or eggplant parmigiana $8.95, ricotta-stuffed meatloaf $8.95. Specialities: Brazilian feijoada (black bean cassoulet with sausages, ham, & pork) $10.50, jambalaya (ham, chicken, sauasage, & bay shrimp in a spicy creole sauce) $10.50. Spanish gazpacho soup (cold) $2.75. Various crepes $7.95-9.50. Turn-of-century decor. ***(16)

WELCOME HOME, 464 Castro (Market/18 Sts), 626-3600. With soup or salad--meat loaf $6.25, grilled liver with bacon & onions $6.25, deep-fried prawns $8.25, broiled 10-oz N.Y. steak with salad & cottage cheese $9.75, charbroiled 1/2-lb burger with fries, potato salad, or coleslaw $4.95. ***(15)

WITHOUT RESERVATION, 460 Castro (Market/18 Sts), 861-9510, 7:30am-2:30am. With soup or salad, vegetables, potatoes, bread & butter--grilled chicken breast on bed of spinach $6.60, 8-oz ground-round hamburger steak $6.60, grilled liver & onions $8.25, 8-oz N.Y. steak $9.55. ***(15)

MEL'S DRIVE-IN, 2165 Lombard (Steiner), 921-3039 & 3355 Geary Blvd (Beaumont), 387-2244, 6am-1am Sun-Thurs, Fri-Sat to 3am. American chow. Grandma's chicken soup $2.50 bowl, clam chowder (Fridays only) $2.25 & $3, homemade chili, with onions & grated cheese, cup $2.25, bowl $3.50. Chicken pot pie, with salad & roll, $5.95, All-American meat-loaf with lumpy mashed potatoes, mushroom gravy, vegetables, roll & butter $6.95; fish & chips, coleslaw, tartar sauce & roll $5.95. Thick milk shake $2.75, banana split $3.95, hot apple pie with cinnamon sauce $2.50. ***(6)(13)

TOM'S PLACE, 5716 Geary Blvd (21 Av), 221-9890. With soup or salad, vegetables & choice of pasta, rice or potato--stuffed sole (with shrimp, scallops) $7.95, seafood crepe $6.50, escallope of veal with marsala $8.50, N.Y. steak $10.95. Onion soup $1.95, fettucine Alfredo $6.50. ***(13)

CAFE' RAIN TREE, 654 Irving Street (8th Ave, 665-3633, 4-10pm. $6.50-7.95. With soup *and* salad, vegetables or rice--moussaka $6.50, beef teriyaki with mushrooms, tomato, garlic $6.50, 10-oz N.Y. steak $7.95, filet mignon shish kebab $7.95. ***(19)

KIESER'S, 1833 Irving (19/20 Avs), 681-6100, 7am-8pm. With soup or salad--8oz NY steak $7.95, 8oz NY steak & fried prawns $8.95, veal cutlet $6.95. ***(20)

NEW YORK DELIGHT, 2222 Irving (23/24 Avs), 753-1112. 4-

9pm Mon-Sat. With soup or salad, potatoes--broiled sea bass $8.45, N.Y. steak $7.95, roast beef or turkey plate $4.95. ***(20)

TENNESSEE GRILL, 1128 Taraval (21/22 Avs), 664-7834, 6am-9pm. Dinners--with soup or salad, potatoes, vegetables, French bread & butter--8-oz club steak $7, 14-16-oz rib steak $7.75, roast beef au jus $6.05, spaghetti & meat sauce $5.35, grilled pork chops & applesauce $6.35, breaded veal cutlets $5.45, grilled calves liver & bacon $5.45, 16-oz sizzling rib steak $7.75. Large, simple, counter & tables. ***(20)

GRANADA CAFE', 4753 Mission (Ocean Av), 586-1515. Dinners are colossal, simple, hearty meals consisting of soup or salad, antipasto, pasta and choice of many entrees, e.g., roast chicken $6.50, pot roast $6.50, chicken cacciatore $6.75, roast beef au jus $7, veal cutlet $7.50, veral parmigiana or scallopini $8.50, Italian steak $9.50, salmon or halibut $10, N.Y. steak $11, rib-eye steak $12. A la carte--spaghetti & meat sauce $3.25, with meat balls $4.50, ravioli with meat sauce $4, with meat balls $4.75, salad $1,25 small, $2 large. Child's plate $4.50. Great value. ***(16)

Italian & Basque Dinners

These are all BEST BUYS and among the best values of all restaurants in San Francisco. The Italian family dinners are 5-6 course affairs, the lunches serve 1 course less (soup *or* salad). The Basque dinners include *two* entrees (on Friday, meat *and* fish) as well as soup, salad, dessert, and coffee (one includes wine in the price). They are fixed-menu meals, some with a few choices.

Italian Family Lunches & Dinners

Note: An asterisk(*) in front of a name denotes "especially recommended". For the sake of convenience, and to facilitate choice, those so noted are put at the top of the list.

*CAPP'S CORNER, 1600 Powell (Green), 989-2589, 11:30am-2:30pm & 4-9:30pm. This is a well-frequented bar-restaurant. Lunch is $7.50 and consists of soup or salad, pasta, entree with vegetables, spumoni ice cream--baked chicken, fish of the day, pasta, roast beef sandwich or rib-eye steak sandwich; with rib eye steak $9.50. Dinner starts at $9.50, and includes ministrone soup, green salad, pasta of the day, entree with vegetables, & spumoni ice cream--meat ravioli, linguini with steamed clams & mussels, fettucine with shrimp. Dinner for $11.50, same as above, with roast beef, roast veal, veal t-bone chop, fish of the day. Finally, the $13.50 dinner has a 12-oz rib-eye steak, chicken breast piccata, roast duck (Sat only) or rack of lamb (Sat only), marinated in pomegranate juice, as the entree. ****(3)

*NEW PISA, 550 Green (Columbus/Grant), 362-4726. 2:30-11pm, closed Wed. 5-course lunch is $8, 6-course dinner is $12, N.Y. steak dinner is $14.

Entrees include roast beef, roast veal, breast of lamb, veal saute, chicken cacciatore. ****(3)

*GREEN VALLEY, 510 Green (Columbus/Grant), 788-9384. 11am-2:30pm, 4:30-10pm Tues-Fri 2-10pm, Sat-Sun. 5-course lunch $6.95, 6-course dinner $11.75. ****(3)

*GOLD SPIKE, 527 Columbus (Union/Green), 421-4591. 5-10pm Tues-Sun. With antipasto, minestrone soup, salad, pasta, spumoni and coffee $11.95--roast beef, chicken cacciatore, veal saute. A big Special every Friday is their crab cioppino, with dinner $14.95. ****(3)

BUSHATI'S, 2526 Lombard (Scott), 346-5156, 4-11pm, closed Mon. With antipasto, salad, soup, pasta, entree, & coffee--chicken Toscana with mushrooms & wine sauce $10.50, veal scallopini or parmigiana (with red-wine sauce) $12.95, veal stuffed with prosciutto & cheese, & mushroom sauce $13.50, sauteed calamari $9.75, prawns in butter & wine $14.95, N.Y. steak $15.50. ****(6)

GOLD MIRROR, 800 Taraval (18 Av), 564-0401. See Big Splurge Restaurants. ****(20)

Other Italian Dinners

Most of the following, with few exceptions, are a la carte, i.e., they do not include soup or salad in the price of the entree. But most make up for it by charging very moderately for soup or salad, some only $1-1.50. They also have reasonably-priced wines, including the house wine.

*U.S. RESTAURANT, 431 Columbus Ave (Stockton), 362-6251, 6am-9pm Tues-Sat, closed Sun-Mon. With pasta or vegetable--veal parmigiana $8, pot roast $7. Pastas--spaghetti $5, with meatballs $6.50, al pesto $6. Spumoni $1.25. Bottle Louis Martini $6.50-7.50. Hearty food at reasonable prices. ****(3)

*MILANO, 1448 Pacific (Larkin/ Hyde), 673-2961. 5:30-10:30pm Tues-Sat, closed Sun & Mon. Gnocchi in gorgonzola cream sauce $8.95, fettucine with sausage & cream sauce $8.95, spaghetti with fish $8.50, chicken with peppery sauce $8.25, veal with gorgonzola sauce $11.75, chicken breast with prociutto & cheese $10.50. Appetizers, soups & desserts are somewhat high, pasta and chicken reasonable, as is veal, for the quality served. ****(10)

*PADRINO'S, 900 Stanyan (Frederick), 665-5333, 4:30-10:30pm. Dinner is a la carte but soup with meal is only $1.50. Appetizers--baby shrimp in basil sauce $3.25, crepes filled with spinach & mushrooms $3. Pastas (excellent)--fettucine with 4 cheeses $6.50, with shrimp $7; pasta al pesto $7, linguini with baby clams $7, lasagna with 3 cheeses & meat $6.75; veal scallopini $8, veal parmigiana $8, prawns sauteed in brandy $9. ****(14)

LITTLE JOE'S, 521 Broadway (Columbus), 433-4343 & 1919 Van Ness Ave (Jackson), 776-4600, 11:30-10pm. Ministrone with meal $1 (without meal $3.95), calamari appetizer $3.95. Entrees served with spaghetti or vegetables or beans--10-oz N.Y. steak $10.95, boiled chicken $6.95, beef tongue or pork chops $7.95, pot roast or roast pork $8.95, veal cutlet $8.95, veal scaloppini $11.95. Vegetable plate $5.95. Daily specials $7.95-$11.95. Spumoni $1.95, cheese cake $2.95. Same menu at lunch $1-2 cheaper. ****(3)(10)

BASTA PASTA 1268 Grant Ave (Vallejo), 434-2248, 6am-2am. Mixed green salad $2.75, fisherman's soup $2.25, garlic bread $2.25 (2 can share as appetizer). Pastas--fettucine al pesto, spaghettini bolognese, or gnocchi Piemontese, $7.95; tortellini in butter sauce $8.95, linguini with baby clams, or lasagna $9.75, veal cannelloni $9.25, seafood cannelloni $10.75. Entrees--eggplant parmigiana $7.95, calamari with lemon & butter sauce $8.25, filet of sole in lemon & butter sauce $8.75, whole broiled fish $9.50, veal marsala $10.50, veal parmigiana $9.75, broiled salmon or halibut $11.75. A North Beach standby. ****(3)

NORTH BEACH PIZZA, 1499 Grant Ave (Union) & 1310 Grant Ave (Green), 433-2444, 11am-1am Sun-Thurs, to 3am Fri-Sat. Pasta dinners with soup or salad--fettucine Alfredo, or gnocchi with cream or meat sauce $7.05, spaghetti with meat balls $7.40, cannelloni or baked lasagna $7.70, veal scallopini $8.95, chicken cacciatore $7.85, BBQ spareribs 1/2-lb $7.50, 1-lb $11.50. Garlic bread $1.50, ministrone soup $1.85, sauteed vegetables $1.85. ****(3)

FETTUCCINE BROS, 2100 Larkin (Vallejo), 441-2281, 11:30am-2:30pm Mon-Sat & 6:30-9:30pm Wed-Sun. They make and sell pastas & sauces in their deli which is open daily from 12noon-7pm, Sun from noon. The restaurant serves pastas only. Dinner--fettucine alfredo $7.95, tortellini Alfredo or pesto $8.95, tagliarini (thin spaghetti) with walnuts & herbs on spinach pasta $7.95, al pesto $8.50, with marinara sauce $7.75. Lunches are $2-3 lower. Strong coffee $1. House wine $3.50 1/2 liter, $6.75 liter. Italian bottled wines $7.50--11.75. ****(10)

BUCA GIOVANNI, 800 Greenwich (Columbus), 776-7766. 5:30-11pm Mon-Sat. Minestrone $2.75, fettucine Alfredo $7.50, fettucine with Italian ham $7.95, fettucine with rabbit & chicken sauce $7.95, pasta stuffed with venison $9.95. Large portions. Veal dishes are $14.95-18.95, chicken dishes $12.55-14.50, both on the high side. The pastas are a great value. ****(3)

CAFE RIGGIO, 4112 Geary Blvd (5/6 Avs), 221-2114. 5-11pm Mon-Sat. Minestrone cup $1.75, bowl $2.50, antipasto $4.95, house salad $2.25. Fettucine Alfredo $7.25, spaghetti al pesto $7.25, stuffed tortellini $7.95, veal piccata $11.95, saltimbocca (veal with ham & cheese) $11.95. Peach melba $2.95. Very busy. ****(13)

MESCOLANZA, 2221 Clement (23 Av), 668-2221, 5-10pm. Specializes in pastas & pizzetas. Antipasta (2 can share) $4.25, ministrone $2.50. Fettucine Alfredo, with parmigiana $7.75, green tortellini with prociutto, peas, parmigiana $8.25, linguini with garlic sauce $7.50, gnocchi with meat sauce $7.75, linguini with clams, tomatoes, garlic $8.25, pizzetas, 109 varieties, $7.25-7.75. ****(23)

PACIFIC BAY DINER, 622 Jones (O'Farrell), 775-5414, 8am-10pm. Pastas--spaghetti with mushrooms or meat sauce $3.95, with baby clams $4.50; fettucine Alfredo $3.95; linguine & baby clams $4.50. See Intermediate Dinners above for non-Italian menu. ***(9)

PASTA DE PESCE, 418 Larkin (Golden Gate Av), 885-5710, 6am-5:30pm, Sat 8am-4pm. Pastas served with fish & garlic bread--calamari $4.25, al pesto $4.25, seafood platter with linguini $5.25. Pasta & soup $4.25, pasta & meat sandwich $4.25, pasta & meat balls $4.25. Clean, interesting lunch operation. ***(9)

DE PAULA'S 2114 Fillmore (California), 346-9888, 5-11:30pm, Fri-Sat to 1am. Fettucine alfredo $6.50, fettucine de Paula's $6.85, special eggplant, with rice $8.65. mixed salad $2.55. ***(11)

JACKSON FILLMORE, 2506 Fillmore (Jackson), 346-5288, 5:30-

9:30pm. Prices have gone up considerably since the last listing, but it is still very popular with the local crowd. Cold antipasto (for 1 or 2) $6.75, linguini marinara or pesto $6.25, ravioli $7, tortellini $7.25, linguini with prawns $9, prawns a la Jack $12, fried calamari $8.75, eggplant parmigiana $6.50, veal dishes $12.75. ***(11)

PASTA II, 381 S. Van Ness Ave. (15 St), 864-4116. Minestrone $2.50. Pastas--garlic & oil $5.75, Polonaise (with mushrooms, cheese, eggs, parsley) $5.75, pesto $6.75, vongole $8.75. Lunch--pastas are about $1-2 cheaper. House wine liter $7.75. ***(16)

SPARKY'S (Italian), 242 Church (Market), 621-6001. Pasta dinners with vegetables, bread & butter--fettucine or spaghetti $5.95, ravioli $7.95. Dinners with soup or salad, vegetables, potato--2 pork chops $8.95, 8-oz chicken breast $8.95, 12-oz N.Y. steak $10.95. 9-oz hamburger with fries or salad $6.95. ****(15)

PSGHETTI, 2304 Market (16 St), 621-0503, 10am-10pm. All pasta dishes--angel hair, fettucine, linguini, rotelle, spaghetti, spinach--with choice of sauce--alfredo, marinera, pesto, red meat, tomato basil, clam--are served with tossed green salad, choice of sauce, parmesan cheese and bread. $3.99 regular, $5.99 grande, $7.49 all-you-can-eat. Meat or cheese ravioli $4.49, meat balls $1.49. Salads $1.75, e.g., seafood, tuna, chicken, garden, egg. Sandwiches $2.50 & $3.25. Cheese cake $1.65, chocolate chip cookie 35 cents each. Counter service. ***(15)

ERNESTO'S, 2311 Clement (24 Av), 386-1446, 4-11pm. Soup $1.50, mixed salad $1.95. Pastas--linguine a la marinara $5.95, with meat sauce $6.25, with Italian sausage or meat balls $6.25, with calamari $6.95, fettucine alfredo $6.25, ravioli with meat balls $6.25; lasagna or cannelloni $6.95, tortellini stuffed with beef ,veal & Italian ham $6.25. Veal marsala or piccata $8.95, chicken cacciatore $7.95. Elegant setting. ***(23)

Basque Dinners

*OBRERO HOTEL, 1208 Stockton (Pacific, 989-3960. A 7-course dinner, $13 including tax and tip, starts at 6:30pm sharp, and includes soup, salad, *two* entrees, dessert, wine, and coffee. Examples are (Monday) oxtail stew and roast beef; (Wednesday) clams with pasta and roast pork; (Friday) rex sole and lamb. Convivial family atmosphere. ****(2)

*DES ALPES, 732 Broadway (Stockton/Powell), 788-9900. 5:30-10pm $10.50 (10-12-oz NY steak every day $12.50). This restaurant is no longer true Basque: they no longer serve 2 entrees with the dinner. Instead, a 2nd salad has been added. It now calls itself a French restaurant. Menu is different each day and posted for the week. Phone for daily details. ****(3)

*THE BASQUE HOTEL, 15 Romolo Place (near Broadway/Columbus), 788-9404. 5:30-9:30pm Tues-Sun. Dinner includes *two* entrees, soup, salad, french fries, ice cream, coffee--$10.50, steak $13.50 (as substitute of the meat dish). Menu changes daily, e.g., Tues Basque chicken or red snapper *and* N.Y. steak or chicken leg, Fri trout *and* steak, or sweetbreads *and* roast lamb. Owner is French-Basque. ****(3)

Early Dinners

A number of restaurants offer "Early Dinners" or "Twilight Dinners" at $6.95 and $7.95, some a bit higher, between 4 and 7pm. Most are for weekdays only, but a few are for weekends, too. These dinners include soup or salad, entree and, some, even drink or dessert. Since some of these restaurants may discontinue the specials, especially for the tourist season, be sure to check first.

An asterisk (*) before a name denotes "especially recommended". I am putting those at the top of list in order to facilitate making a choice.

BEST BUY****

*FISHERMAN'S COTTAGE, 1040 Columbus Avenue (Taylor), 885-4910. $7.95, 44-5:30pm, choice of steak kabob or fish of the day, unlimited soup & salad bar, and choice of beer, wine, or soda. ****(4)

*CAESAR'S (Italian), Bay & Powell Streets, 989-6000. 4:30-6pm Tues-Sun, closed Mon, $8.50 ($6.95 for Seniors). Soup, salad, vegetables, potatoes, coffee and choice of filet of sole, Italian pot roast, baked Virginia ham, roast chicken, or ground sirloin. Also, Senior lunches $6.95, 11:am-2pm, Tues-Fri--soup, salad, potato, vegetable, coffee, choice of 5 entrees (for all ages, same meal $8.50). Validated parking. ****(4)

*SOUTH PACIFIC (Polynesian), 2500 Noriega (32nd Av) 564-3363. 5-6pm daily, Sun 4-6pm. With clam chowder or salad, coconut ice cream and choice of entree, e.g., shrimp louie, snapper, sole, trout. Seniors also receive 10% discount on lunch 11:30am-2pm (closed Mon); Sunday brunch, 11am-2:30pm, $6.95, includes salad, potatoes, choice of 4 entrees, coffee or tea. ****(23)

*FISHERMAN'S CAFE, 7001 Geary (34 Av), 751-0191. 4-6:30pm. $7.95. With soup or salad, coffee or tea, ice cream, & a glass of wine--entree, e.g., red snapper, English sole, N.Y. steak. ****(13)

*ORIGINAL JOE'S, 144 Taylor (Market), 775-4877. A Super Special for Seniors, $6.25, 7 days a week, 2-5pm. Choice of 4 entrees (pot roast, boiled beef, roast pork, or filet of sole), sourdough bread, fresh vegetable, pasta or potato, coffee or tea. ****(9)

*NORTH INDIA, 3131 Webster (Lombard), 931-1556, 5-6:30pm Sun-Thurs, $9.95. Early Bird Dinner consists of soup, entree, rice, vegetable, bread, condiments & dessert (e.g., mango ice cream). A good deal in a very good restaurant. ****(6)

HOULIHAN'S, 2800 Leavenworth (Fisherman's Wharf), 775-7523, 4-6pm Mon-Fri. $8.95. With French onion soup, Boston clam chowder or Caesar salad, entree & dessert (ice cream or hot apple strudel pie--8-oz rib-eye steak with mushrooms and natural-cut fries, chicken parmigiana with garlic toast & pasta, London broil with garlic toast & pasta, half-pound teriyaki steak with fries, herb grilled chicken with rice pilaff and vegetable etc. ****(4)

MERMAID, 524 Irving (7th Ave), 759-9644, 5-7pm Sun-Thurs. $7.95. With soup *and* salad, glass of wine, and choice of blackboard specials. ****(19)

LUCKY FRENCH PIERRE BISTRO, 200 23rd Ave (California), 386-3571, 5-9:30pm. With salad and a choice of meat & fish dishes, $6.95.****(23)

VERY GOOD***

MAYE'S, 1233 Polk (Sutter/Bush) 474-7674. 3-6pm Mon-Fri. $8.25. With soup, salad, choice of 4 entrees. Same dinner for Seniors is $7.25. ***(10)

CARLENE'S OF MAUI, 1237 Polk Street (Sutter/Bush), 441-8200. 4-7pm, Early Dinner $6.95, entree (e.g., pork chops, meatloaf, Hungarian goulasch, linguine with red clam sauce) with soup or salad, ice cream & coffee. Nightly piano music. ***(10)

CASABLANCA, 2323 Polk (Green), 441-2244. Before 6:30pm-- with soup, "Rick" salad, sorbet, at price of the a la carte entree, e.g., cannelloni $9.50, breast of chicken with lemon sauce $11.50, roast pork tenderloin with mustard sauce $12, prawns sauteed in white wine $13.50, 1/2 roast duck $14.50, peppered N.Y./ steak with brandy cream sauce $15.50, rack of lamb with port sauce $16.50. ***(10)

DISH, corner Masonic & Haight, 431-3534. 6-7:30pm Mon-Fri, 4-6pm Sat-Sun. $4.95-5.95. With soup or salad and choice of entree--prawn fettucine, grilled pork chops, teriyaki chicken, grilled mahimahi. ***(14)

DI GRANDE'S (Italian), 1439 Taraval (25 Ave), 665-0325, 4-10:30pm, closed Mon. $8.95, with soup or salad, pasta, vegetables--chicken cacciatore, veal parmesan, filet of sole, spaghetti & meatballs. ***(20)

Seafood Restaurants & Oyster Bars

San Francisco is famous for its seafood. In this section, I've concentrated on those that give value as well as high quality. I've also included Oyster Bars because they serve some of the best seafood in San Francisco, and are very reasonable in price.

Some of the fish dinners described below are more than $10 and really should be in the Splurge section ($10-$15), or even Big Splurge ($15+). However, I have put them in this section because I think this is where you would look for them if you wanted a fish dinner.

An asterisk (*) before a name denotes "especially recommended". I am putting these at the head of this list in order to make a choice easier.

Seafood Restaurants

BEST BUY****

*TU LAN (Vietnamese), 8 Sixth Street (Market/Mission), 626-0927. Simple-looking restaurant with good food. 4-course seafood dinner for 2, $8.95 per person--asparagus soup with crab, shrimp salad, fried fish with ginger sauce, sauteed prawns with bamboo shoots & mushrooms. For 4 persons add fried prawns with sweet & sour sauce, for 6 persons add also marinated fish. ****(7)

*YUET LEE (Chinese), see under Intermediate Restaurants. (2)(16)

*LOBSTER TUB, 7379 Mission Street, Daly City, 755-9993. 5-10pm Tues-Sat, 2-9 Sun. This is just outside of S.F. city limits but worth the trip. Be prepared for a very simple setting resembling a Boston lobster house with bare common tables.

They get the lobsters from New England and pick them up regularly at the S.F. Airport. $11.99 one-pound lobster dinner with salad or clam chowder, baked potato or corn on cob, bread & butter. Phone first to be sure this special is still available and, if not, what is. They also have 2-lb & 3-lb lobsters ($23.50 & $34.50), bouillabaisse ($8.99), cioppino etc. at very modest prices. A major feature is their wine list: Fetzer at $7.95 bottle, a very modest markup over the retail price. ****

MON KIANG (Chinese), 683 Broadway (Stockton), 421-2015, 11am-10:30pm Sun-Thurs, Fri-Sat to midnight. Seafood dinner for 5-6 persons $45--7 courses plus rice & tea, including whole baked crab & whole steamed fish. Also, Hakka-style dinner with wine-flavored beef (specialty), with whole fish $10 per person. ****(3)

R & G LOUNGE, 631B Kearny (Sacramento/Clay), 982-7877. $60 for 6-8 persons--soup, deep-fried squid, 2 kinds seafood, clams with hot bean sauce (hot), sizzling prawns in garlic sauce, live whole crab with ginger, whole steamed fish. ****(8)

TON KIANG (Chinese), 3148 Geary Blvd (Spruce), 752-4440 & 5827 Geary (22/23rd Avs), 387-8273. 11am-10pm. 7-Course family fish dinner for 5-6 persons $50. Includes a whole fish. Very good feast meal. A Hakka dinner for 5-6 with chicken, beef, spareribs, whole fish $50. Also, a 9-course fish dinner for 10 persons, with whole crab & whole fish, $90. Recommended for "big occasions". ****(3)(13)

ADRIATIC, 1755 Polk (Clay), 771-4035. 11:30-2:30pm, 5:30-10pm. Seafood platter $9.50, filet of sea bass (recommended) $10.95, fish stew $9.50, frog legs $9.95, green salad $2, soup $2. Also beef, lamb, veal, poultry dishes 9at comparable prices ****(10)

GARDEN (Chinese), 716 Kearny (Washington), 956-2480, 7am-9pm. Seafood dinner for 4 $8.95 per person--steamed clams with ginger onion sauce, crab meat wintermelon soup, prawns in black bean sauce & with black beans, green peppers & onions, sauteed scallops with broccoli, sweet & sour filet of rock cod, whole Maine lobster or dungeness crab in ginger onion sauce, steamed rice, & tea. ****(2)

SEA CHANTEY'S, 1233 Van Ness Ave (Sutter/Post), 673-0558, 11am-2:30pm & 5-11pm. They get fish from Boston & Florida. With soup or salad, vegetables & potatoes--Idaho mountain trout, fried in butter & wine $8.95, English sole with shittake mushrooms $10.95, sand dabs $9.25, grilled monk fish $10.75, clams or mussles with white wine & garlic $10.50, bouillabaisse with saffron & pernod $11.25, swordfish $11.25. ****(10)

PACIFIC GREEN, 2424 Van Ness Ave (Green), 771-3388, 5-9:30pm. With clam chowder, soup de jour, or house salad, & vegetables & potatoes--Pacific snapper with red peppers, tomatoes & capers $9.95, sauteed calamari provencale $9.95, linguini de mare with clams & shrimp $8.95, calamari & baby prawns $9.95, grilled salmon $14.95, grilled 1-lb lobster $19.95, but it is often on Special, so ask first by phone,, & make a reservation. Seniors get 10% off on all meals, except Specials. 2-hour validated parking. ***(10)

BRANDI'S, 2775 Van Ness (Lombard, in Quality Hotel), 928-5000, 5-9pm. Seafood & salad bar $7.95--clams, scallops, shrimp, squid, pasta, clam chowder etc. ****(6)

BENIHANA (Japanese), 1737 Post (Japantown), 563-4844. With onion soup a la Japanese, Benihana salad, shrimp appetizer, rice, green tea, & apple pie--hibachi (cooked at the table) shrimp $16.50, swordfish $16.25, hibachi $16.50, seafood combination (including lobster tail, scallops, jumbo shrimp) $24.95. Last-named is a Big Splurge seafood dinner for a special occasion. ****(12)

RED CRANE (Chinese), 115 Clement, (12th Av), 751-7226, 11:30am-10pm. This is a Chinese seafood and vegetable restaurant. Soups: crabmeat & corn $4.50, vegetarian hot-sour $3.75. prawns with cashews $5.50, ginger garlic squid $4.75, sliced fish with black bean sauce $5, sweet-sour walnuts $5.25, black mushrooms with greens $5, scallops Hunan $6.25, steamed whole fish $10, vegetable chow mein $4.25, chow mein with 5 kinds of mushrooms $3.75, kung pao vegetable "duck" $5, vegetable "chicken" with cashews $5. ****(22)

SILVER MOON (Chinese), 2301 Clement (24 Av), 386-7852. 11:30am-10pm. Seafood & vegetarian, opened by former cook of Red Crane, above. Crab meat soup $5, vegetarian hot-sour soup $4, sizzling prawns $6.95, vegetarian "duck" or "chicken" $5, sliced fish with black bean sauce $5.50, Szechuan eggplant $5, abalone with black mushrooms $6.25, sweet & sour walnuts $5.25, snow peas with imitation shrimp $5.25, mandarin scallops $6.25. ****(23)

TAIWAN, 307 Church (15 St), 863-7121, 11:30-2pm Mon-Sat & 5-10pm 7 days. Seafood & vegetarian. Seafood--Fishball spinach soup $4.75, seafood potstickers (6) $3.95, scallops a la Hunan $7.25, clams with ginger garlic sauce $6.95, prawns with snow peas $6.95, sliced fish with black bean sauce $5.75, seafood fried rice $4.75, shrimp chow mein $4.75. Vegetarian--Garlic eggplant $2.50, vegetarian spring rolls (2), $2.95, vegetarian hot & sour soup $3.75, vegeterian duck or chicken $4.75, sweet & sour walnuts $4.75, vegetarian almond shrimp $4.95, vegetables fried rice $4.25. ****(15)

SILVER CLOUD, 1994 Lombard (Webster), 922-1977. Steak & lobster Special, with soup or salad, baked potato & vegetable--$9.95. Also, Sat & Sun brunch with eggs benedict, fresh fruit & glass of champagne for $3.95. ****(6)

THE BEACH HOUSE, 4621 Lincoln (49th Av), 681-9333, 5-10pm. With green salad, vegetables, rice, French bread--broiled halibut $13.50, broiled English sole $11.50, broiled swordfish or salmon $13.95, bouillabaisse $15.95, steamed crab $11.95, fried oysters $12.95. Elegant dining. ****(20).

VERY GOOD***

MAYE'S OYSTER HOUSE, 1233 Polk (Sutter/Bush), 474-7674. Over 100 years old. Recently under new management with an aggressive program, including Early Dinner, Senior Specials, etc. Snapper $7.95, sand dabs $7.95, sea bass $8.95, swordfish $9.90. For $6 more you can have a colossal dinner including soup, shrimp cocktail, pasta, ice cream or cheese, tea or coffee. The complete dinner is a good deal if you're hungry. ***(10)

WING LEE, 1810 Polk St (Washington), 775-3210, 11am-9pm, closed Tues. Seafood Dinner for 4-5 persons $40--seafood soup, shrimp with Chinese broccoli, squid in shrimp sauce, deep-fried oysters, clams in black bean sauce, crab in black bean sauce, steamed rock cod fish, including tea & rice. ***(10)

SEA GULL, 535 Irving Street (6/7 Avs), 681-4373, 11am-10pm. Special Seafood Dinner for 2-6 persons $8.20 per person--subgum seafood soup, fried shrimp, Kung Pao shrimp (hot), squid with oyster sauce, dessert, for 3 add abalone with oyster sauce, for 4 add combination seafood hot pot, for 5-6 add sweet & sour whole fish. Includes rice & tea, of course. ***(19)

HEUNG HEUNG (Chinese), 3608 Balboa (37 Av), 221-9188, 11:30am-9:30pm. Seafood dinner for 4, $7.50 per person, 6 courses plus rice & tea,--including prawn cutlet, sweet & sour fish, oyster & roast pork clay pot, squid saute, mixed seafood basket. ***(13)

ERNIE'S NEPTUNE FISH GROTTO, 1816 Irving (19th Ave), 566-3344, 11am-3pm and 5-10pm Tues-Sat. Lunch, with clam chowder or salad, and fries $5, e.g., rex sole, sand dabs. Dinner entrees served with mixed green salad, clam chowder, ice cream and coffee, e.g., brook trout $9.50, halibut $10.50, red snapper $10.20, rex sole (specialty) $10.20, swordfish $11.25, bouillabaisse $11.99, N.Y. steak (8ozs) $12. This a no-nonsense, old seafood restaurant. ***(20)

Oyster bars

*SWAN OYSTER DEPOT, 1517 Polk (California/Sacramento), 673-2757. Counter-only. Cocktails--shrimp $3.95, prawns $4.50, crab $5.50. Salads--shrimp $8.95, prawns $9.75, crab $9.95, lobster $11.95. Always crowded. ****(10)

*THE HYDE STREET SEAFOOD HOUSE & RAW BAR, 1509 Hyde (Jackson/Pacific), 928-9148, 5-10:30pm. Caesar salad $3.50, prawn cocktail $5.95, oysters (6) $5.95, steamed clams or mussels $6.95, New England clam chowder cup $2.50, bowl $3.95. With vegetables & baked herbed garlic bread--rainbow trout $9.95, steamed clams or mussels $9.95, cioppino $9.95, red snapper en papillote (sealed in parchment paper and baked), salmon or mahi mahi en papillote $11.95. ***(1)

ANCHOR OYSTER, 579 Castro (19 St), 431-3990. Cocktails--Shrimp $4.50, crab or prawn or combination $5.50. Oysters (6) $5.50 (3 oysters $2,95), clams $3.95. 1/2 cracked crab, salad, bread & butter $9.95. Boston clam chowder cup $1.95, bowl $2.95. 12 oysters, 8 clams, 4 prawns, bread & butter $18.95, 1/2 order $9.95. ****(15)

LA ROCCA'S OYSTER BAR, 3519 (California (Laurel), 387-4100, 8am-8:30pm. Cocktails--shrimp $3.95, prawns $4.95, crab $5.25, combination $5.95. Salads--shrimp $10.95, prawns $11.95, crab $10.95, combination $12.95. Salads are on high side but they are very large & quality is impeccable. ****(11)

P.J.'S OYSTER BED, 737 Irving (9 Av), 566-7775, 11:30am-10pm Mon-Fri. Cocktails--shrimp $4.75, prawn $6.95. Salads--shrimp louie $9.95, crab louie $11.95. Also, housemade pastas & seafood sandwiches (crab, shrimp, oyster, calamari, red snapper) at reasonable prices. Retail fish market on the premises. ****(19)

Steak

There are few steak-only or steak-and-rib-only restaurants in San Francisco, and, with one or two exceptions, they are expensive. They start above $15 for a 12-oz steak, perhaps even charging a few dollars extra for potatoes or a vegetable. I am, therefore, including "normal" restaurants which offer good-quality steaks, 8-16-oz in size, at much lower prices than the exclusively-steak restaurants.

Some of the steaks shown below are more than $10 and should

really be in the Splurge section ($10-$15), or even Big Splurge ($15+). However, I thought it better to list them under *Steaks* since that is probably where you would look for them.

Note: An asterisk (*) in front of a name denotes "especially recommended". I am putting those at the top of the list in order to make the choice easier.

BEST BUY****

*ORIGINAL JOE'S (Italian), 144 Taylor (Market), 775-4877. 10:30am-1.30am. In Splurge range. Top sirloin 18-oz $15.95, N.Y. cut (18-oz) $15.75, filet mignon (14-oz) $15.45, 18-oz $17.95. All come with choice of ravioli, spaghetti, vegetables or French fries. Also, a wide range of Italian foods. ****(9)

*POLO'S (Italian), 34 Mason (Market), 362-7719, 11am-11pm Mon-Sat. One of the oldest Italian restaurants in the city. Their charbroiled steaks--after 5pm--are a specialty and are served with spaghetti, ravioli or vegetables, e.g., N.Y. cut 12-14oz, $10.90; rib 16-oz, $10.50; top sirloin, l6-oz, $9.90. Also, large choice of Italian dishes. ****(9)

*WHITE HORSE TAVERNE, 637 Sutter (Mason/Taylor), 673-9900, 5:30-10pm Tues-Sat. 16-oz+ Porterhouse steak, with vegetables & baked potato, $13.95, 12-oz filet mignon $11.95. Elegant dining. ****(1)

*DES ALPES, 732 Broadway (Powell/Stockton), 788-9900, 5:30-10pm. With soup, salad, dessert, coffee--10-12-oz NY steak $13.50. ****(3)

* THE BASQUE HOTEL, 15 Romolo Place (Broadway/Columbus), 788-9404, 5:30-9:30pm Tues-Sun, closed Mon. With soup, salad, dessert, coffee, *and 1 more entree*--12-oz NY steak $9.50 Tues & Fri, $12.50 on other days of week. ****(3)

*UNITED STATES RESTAURANT (Italian), 431 Columbus Ave (Stockton), 362-6251, 6am-9pm, closed Sun & Mon. With vegetables or pasta--16-oz NY steak $10, 16oz+ rib steak $10. ****(3)

*JAY' N BEE'S CLUB, 2736 20th St (York), 648-0518, 11am-2:30pm, Mon-Fri, closed Sat & Sun. A very busy bar-restaurant serving very good lunches at very low prices. With soup & salad, small bottle of wine--14-oz NY steak $8.50. ****(17)

HARD ROCK CAFE', 1699 Van Ness Avenue (Sacramento), 885-1699, 11:30am-midnight, Fri-Sat to 1am. Smoke House Steak, 12-oz aged N.Y. steak with fresh garlic butter, with baked potato and a green salad $11.95. Soup & 1/2-sandwich (Mon-Fri only), with green salad $4.95. Banana split $2.95. "Hard Rock Cafe' uses no preservatives or additives". ****(10)

OPPENHEIMER, 2050 Divisadero (Sacramento), 563-0444, 5:30-9:30pm, Fri-Sat to 10:330pm. Mesquite grilled steaks, with fried potatoes--13-oz NY strip with fresh peppercorns $13.50, Danish baby back ginger pork ribs $10.90. Other entrees from $8.50 (chicken pub pie) to $13.50 (spicy prawns). Hazelnut cheesecake $3.75. Elegant restaurant, haute cuisine. ****(11)

BULLSHEAD, 840 Ulloa (West Portal) 665-4350. Noon-10pm. All steaks come with soup or salad bar (repeats), potatoes or rice, vegetables and French bread--T-bone 16-oz $13.95; N.Y. steak 10-oz $11.95, 12-oz filet mignon $14.95. ****(13)(21)

LIVERPOOL LIL'S, 2942 Lyon (off Lombard), 921-6664, 11am-4pm & 5pm-midnight. Dinner, with soup or salad, 12-oz N.Y. steak $12.95. ****(6)

EL CUBANE (Mexican/Cuban), 1432 Valencia (25/26 Sts), 824-6555. 16-oz porterhouse steak with green salad, beans rice, bread & butter--$12. ***(16)

TENNESSEE GRILL, 1128 Taraval (20/21 Avs), 664-7834, 6am-9pm. Large, simple, clean restaurant, also counter. Dinners--with soup or salad , potatoes, vegetable, French bread & butter--sizzling 14-16-oz rib steak $7.75. Pork chops $6.35, lamb chops $7.30. Seniors (60 or over) receive 10% discount. Children's Plate (12 or under)--roast sirloin of beef au jus, ice cream, soft drink or milk $3, spaghetti or hamburger $2.70. ****(20)

CLOUD NINE, 1428 Haight (Masonic), 864-8484, 8am-9pm. With soup or tossed salad, sauteed vegetables, rice, pasta, or baked potato--12-oz rib-eye steak $9.95, 10-oz NY strip $9.95. ****(14)

CUBA (Mexican-Cuban), 2886 16th Street (S. Van Ness Av), 864-9871, 12 noon-10pm. 16-oz+ porterhouse steak, with fries, yucca & salad $12.50. ****(16)

VERY GOOD***

TAD'S, 120 Powell (Ellis), 982-1718, with potatoes, French roll, salad--steak $4.99, 1/2-lb hamburger steak $4.20, 1/2 grilled chicken $4.99. ***(9)

VILLA NONNA, 869 Geary (Larkin/Hyde), 441-1228, 7am-10pm. With soup or salad, rice or steak fries--12-oz N.Y. steak with garlic, or 12-oz rib-eye steak $8.95; prime rib (Fri-Sat) $8.95. ***(9)

GEARY STEAK HOUSE (cafeteria), 901 Geary (Larkin), 776-6300. 11am-11pm. With soup or green salad, baked potato, garlic roll--12-oz N.Y. steak $7.45, 12-oz club $6.45, 10-oz filet mignon $9.95, 1-lb T-bone $8.95, prime rib $9.95. ***(9)

LITTLE JOE'S, 523 Broadway (Columbus Av), 433-4343 & 1919 Van Ness Ave (Jackson), 776-4000, 11am-10:30pm Mon-Sat, Sun noon-10pm. With choice of vegetables, spaghetti, rigatoni or beans--12-oz NY steak $10.25, lamb chops $7.75, pork chops $8.25. ***(10)(3)

DENNY'S, 1700 Post (Japantown), 563-1400, *open 24 hours*. Dinner, with bowl soup or garden salad--8-oz NY steak $6.95, 5-oz steak & shrimp $7.95, pork chops $5.95. Chain restaurant, good food. ***(12)

SUGAR PLUM, 3490 California (Laurel), 922-3111, *open 24 hours*. With soup or salad, potatoes or rice, vegetables, bread & butter--8-oz NY steak $10.95, 14-oz NY steak $15.50. A very clean chain restaurant with good food & low prices. ***(13)

PALACE STEAK HOUSE, 3047 Mission (Army), 647-2011. 11am-11pm Mon-Sat, 1-10pm Sun. Cafeteria. One hour courtesy parking. With green salad, vegetables, baked potato & bread--charbroiled 12-oz N.Y. cut $6.29, 14-oz club $7.29, broiled chicken $6.95, chuck hamburger with green salad & fries $4.75. ***(16)

Ribs

There is a great dearth of ribs-only restaurants in San Francisco. Recently, a few Thai BBQ houses have opened, which enhances the scene a lot. I have included in this section some restaurants that *also* serve ribs.

Note: An asterisk (*) denotes "especially recommended". I have put those so marked at the top of the list in order to facilitate a choice.

BEST BUY****

*SAN FRANCISCO BBQ (Thai), 1328 18th St. (Missouri/Texas), 431-8956. 11am-2pm and 4:30-9:30pm Tues-Sun, closed Mon. With carrot salad, rice, bread & butter--BBQ pork ribs (with spices, garlic) $5.95, 1/2 chicken $4.75, lamb $6.75, frog legs $6.95, BBQ salmon steak $7.95. BBQ & noodle dishes $4.50, BBQ chicken or beef salad $4.50. Beef soup cup $1, bowl $2.50, bowl beef noodle soup $4, practically a beef stew. ****(20)

THAI BBQ, 730 Van Ness Ave (Turk/Eddy), 441-1640, 11am-2:30pm & 4:30-10pm, Mon-Fri, noon-9pm Sat-Sun. With carrot salad, sweet rice, bread & butter--pork ribs $5.95, BBQ lamb or veal $6.75, BBQ frog legs $6.95. Noodles with pork, duck, or chicken and peanuts $4.50. ****(10)

SIAM BBQ, 500 Fell (Laguna), 863-5140. BBQ dishes, With rice--pork spareribs $5.95, beef $5.95, chicken $5.95, calamari $6.50, prawns $6.95. ****

HARD ROCK CAFE', 1699 Van Ness Avenue (Sacramento), 885-1699, 11:30am-midnight, Sat-Sun to 9pm. With green salad & fries--baby ribs $9.95. Favorite very loud spot for the young, expect a long wait. ****(10)

BOBBY RUBINO'S, 245 Jefferson (Fisherman's Wharf), 673-2266, 11:30am-11pm, Fri-Sat to midnight. With baked potato, coleslaw & biscuit--baby back ribs (14-16 count) $12.95, 24-count $14.95. ****(4)

BROTHER-IN-LAW'S BAR-B-QUE, 705 Divisadero (Grove), 931-7427, 11am-midnight, Fri-Sat to 2am, closed Mon. Takeout only. With coleslaw, spaghetti or potato salad and bread--1/2 order pork spareribs $4.95, full order $8.75 (7-8 ribs, more than enough for 2), 1/2 order short end $6.75. A slab--13-14 ribs is $15. Beef brisket 1/2 order $5.50, full order $9.85; chicken $4.50 and $7; beef links $4.15 & $8.50. Combos also available. Sweet potato pie or deep-dish peach cobbler $1.50. Great hot sauce, and large portions ****(14)

EVERETT & JONES, 5130 3rd Street (Shafter), 822-7728. Including potato salad & bread--pork rib lunch $5.55, dinner (with more meat, salad, & bread) $6.75; sliced beef lunch $4.95, dinner $5.95; chicken lunch $3.50, dinner $4.50. 2-way combination (for 2 persons) $9.50, 3-way combination (for 3) $12.50, 4-way combination (for 4) $15. Pork rib slab for 4 (with 4 salads & 8 slices of bread) $15. Sweet potato pie $1.35. They also have highly-regarded BBQ restaurants in Berkeley, Oakland & Hayward. ****

COLLIER'S BBQ, 1516 Ocean (Miramar), 585-6568. 4:30-12pm Mon-Thur, Fri & Sat 11am-2:30pm, Sun 12-9pm. Spareribs with 1 side dish, 1/2 order $6.45, full order (with 2 side-dishes) $8.50, combinations (with 2 side dishes) $10.75, slab of ribs for 3-4 persons $17. Peach cobbler $1.70, sweet potato pie $2. ****(20)

VERY GOOD***

LEON'S BARBEQUE, 1911 Fillmore (Pine), 922-2436 and 2800 Sloat Blvd. (46th Av), 681-3071. 11am-10pm. Lunch or dinner plates include corn muffin and choice of baked beans, potato salad, spaghetti or coleslaw. Lunch--pork or beef ribs $5.95, 1/2 chicken or hot links $5.50. 1/2-lb BBQ hamburger with potato salad $4.95. Dinner--pork or beef ribs $9.95, 1/2 chicken $5.95, hot links $7.95. Sampler for 1 $10.95, for 2 $19.95. ***(11)(23)

BOBBY RAY'S BBQ, 4063 18th Street (Castro), 863-0484. 4-10:30pm, noon-10:30pm Sat-Sun. With coleslaw, baked beans or corn on cob, & corn muffin--4 pork ribs $6.95, BBQ beef plate $6.50, 3 beef ribs $6.95. Combinations $8.75--3 pork ribs & 1/2 chicken, or 4 pork ribs & 3 beef ribs. Pig Out, $11.95, served with 2 accompaniments & 1 corn muffin,--2 pork ribs, BBQ beef, and 1/2 chicken. Chili, with onions, cheese, cilantro $2.95, sour cream 50 cents extra. ***(15)

BIG HEART VIDEO CAFE', 5700 Geary Blvd (21 Av), 668-2919, *open 24 hours*. With green salad or cup soup, French fries or mushrooms, rice, bread & butter--BBQ pork spareribs marinated with honey sauce $6.45. ***(13)

LIVERPOOL LIL'S, 2942 Lyon (off Lombard), 921-6664, 11am-4pm & 5pm-midnight. BBQ ribs, English-style with chutney, with soup or salad, $8.95. ***(16)

Prime Rib

Prime Rib of Beef is a specialty known to most Americans, but not to foreigners. Hence, a word of explanation: prime rib consists of meat only, not the bone. It is the choice cut of beef next to the 7 ribs immediately before the loin. It is often served rare and always au jus, with the natural juice left from the roast. In specialty (expensive) restaurants, it is served with Yorkshire pudding, since prime rib is also a British specialty.

BEST BUY****

*PACIFIC COURT, 728 Pacific Avenue (Grant/Stockton), 781-8312, 5-course prime-rib dinner $8.95, $10.95 for "extra-large cut". Restaurant is simple, no tablecloth, mostly Chinese clientele, pleasant service. ****(2)

*RUBINO'S, 245 Jefferson (Fisherman's Wharf), 673-2266. 12-oz cut $10.95, 18-oz $13.95. Served with cole-slaw, baked potato or French fries, and fresh horseradish sauce. ****(4)

HENRY VIII, 673 Geary (Leavenworth/Jones), 775-5258, 5:30-10:30pm, closed Sun. $17.75-21.25. See Big Splurge section for details. ****(1)

PING YUEN, 650 Jackson (Grant/Kearny), 986-6830, 7am-9pm. 4-course prime- rib dinner $7.95. See Intermediate Restaurants above for more details. ****(2)

HOUSE OF PRIME RIB, 1906 Van Ness Avenue (Jackson), 885-4605. $19.95 & $21.95. You can pig out with seconds on the prime rib, the excellent creamed spinach, and the mashed potatoes. Excellent but getting pricey. See Big Splurge section for details. ****(10)

HARRIS', 2100 Van Ness Ave (Pacific), 673-1888. With fresh vegetables, Texas red potatoes, and homemade horseradish--Harris Cut $19.50, Executive Cut $21.50. Comparable in quality with House of Prime Rib above. Steaks, chops, tartar etc. are excellent but pricey, too. Their window display is worth seeing. ****(10)

CHART HOUSE, 2801 Leavenworth (The Cannery), 474-3476, noon-10pm. Regular Cut $17.95, Callahan Cut $22, with fresh horseradish, sourdough bread, and extensive all-you-can-eat salad bar (salad bar only, $8.95). Good Big Splurge value, considering the salad bar. ****(4)

CHARLEY BROWN'S, 2801 Leavenworth (The Cannery), 776-3838. $10.95 for 4-course dinner. Prime rib is a specialty of theirs. See Early Dinners for more details. ****(4)

CHEZ MOLLET (French), 527 Bryant (3/4 Sts), 495-4527, 5:30-10:30pm. Sun, Mon, Tues only, $10.95, with soup or salad. ****(7)

THE GALLEON, 718 14th St (Market), 431-0253, 6-11pm, Piano bar. With soup or salad, horseradish, & red potatoes $13.50. ****(15)

VERY GOOD***

JOE JUNG'S, 1098 Sutter (Larkin), 673-1818, 11am-9pm. $9.95, with soup or clam chowder, spaghetti salad, dessert, coffee or tea. ***(1)

FISHERMAN'S COTTAGE, 1040 Columbus Ave (Taylor), 885-4910. $12.95--10-oz prime rib dinner includes potatoes & rice, unlimited soup & salad bar, & drink. ****(4)

SILVER CLOUD, 1994 Lombard (Webster), 922-1977, 5-10pm. With soup or salad, $9.95. *** (6)

SUGAR PLUM, 3490 California (Laurel), 922-3111, open 24 hours. Prime rib Sat-Sun only, $7.95, with soup or salad, potatoes or rice, vegetable, bread & butter. ***(11)

JAY N'BEE'S CLUB, 2736 20 Street (York), 648-0518, 5:30-9pm Fri night only, $8.50. See under Hamburgers for more details.

***(117)

Vegetarian

San Francisco has a large number of vegetarian restaurants. A tip: If you live in the Area, or if you are here for a longer stay and frequent vegetarian restaurants, join the S.F. Vegetarian Society, 1450 Broadway, San Francisco, CA 94109 (phone 775-6874 or 776-3960). This group has a comprehensive list of restaurants and salad bars that gives its members a discount. Membership $12/year.

Note: An asterisk (*) in front of a name denotes "especially recommended". I have put those at the top of the list in order to facilitate a choice.

BEST BUY****

*LOTUS GARDEN (Chinese), 532 Grant Ave (California), 397-0707., 11:30am-9pm, closed Mon. Hot-sour soup $3.25, spring roll $2.75, deluxe mixed vegetables with noodle soup $3.95, straw mushrooms with vegetables $4.35, 2 kinds mushrooms with broccoli $5.25, stuffed eggplant $5.50, combination vegetarian $4.95, hot walnut pudding $1.50. Family Dinner for 2, $7.95 per person, changes from time to time, e.g., pot stickers, soup of the day, deluxe vegetables, sweet & sour "pork", snow peas & sweet corn, fried rice, fortune cookie, tea. Elegant. ****(2)

*GANGES (Indian), 775 Frederick (Arguello), 661-7290, 5-9:30pm Mon-Sat, closed Sun. Former location of Higher Taste. The chef, Malvi Dosi, has written a cookbook and teaches cooking classes. There are 2 prix fixe dinners, $9.95 & $10.95. Both are very extensive and include lentil pancakes, yoghourt dip, breads, curries, fried bananas, nutty rice etc. All a la carte dishes are under $3.50 (curries). Food is prepared salt-free and dairy-free on request. ****(14)

*SHANGRI-LA (Chinese), 2026 Irving St (22 Av), 731-2548, 11:30am-9:30pm. Family Dinner $6.95 per person (minimum 2)--wonton soup, spring rolls, combination vegetables, rice, fried banana, tea; for 3 add mu shu with pancakes, for 4 add mu shu and eggplant with hot sauce. Large selection-- 6 soups $1.25-1.40, 5 appetizers $1.60-3.25, 7 chow mein & noodle soups

$3.50-4.20, & 16 vegetarian dishes $4.25-5.20. ****(19)

*RED CRANE (Chinese), 1115 Clement (12 Av), 751-7226. See

under Fish Restaurants. ****(22)

*SILVER MOON (Chinese), 2301 Clement (21 Av), 386-7852. See under Fish Restaurants. ****(23)

*VEGI-FOOD (Chinese), 1820 Clement (19th Av), 387-8111. 11:30am-3pm and 5-9pm Tues-Fri, no break on Sat-Sun. Hot and sour soup $3.65, walnuts sweet & sour $4.95, vegetable deluxe (with 4 kinds of mushrooms, 2 kinds of fungus, tofu, gluten), $6.50, braised bean curd with black mushrooms and greens $4.95. One of the best. ****(23)

LUCKY CREATION (Chinese), 854 Washington St (Stockton/Grant), 989-0818, 11am-10pm, closed Wed. Appetizers $3, e.g., fried won ton, spring egg rolls, or pot stickers. Soups $3.50, e.g., hot & sour, seaweed & beancake, or won ton. Entrees, e.g., braised beancake with mushrooms $3.75, vegetarian sweet & sour "pork" $3.95, sauteed straw mushrooms & bean cake $3.75, deep-fried crispy taro rolls & bean curd $4.25, fried honeyed walnuts & taro cake with sweet-sour sauce $5.25. Also, large selection of clay-pot dishes, pan-fried noodle dishes, rice plates $3.50-3.95. ****(2)

KOWLOON (Chinese), 909 Grant (Washington/Jackson), 362-9888, 9am-10pm. Newest vegetarian-only restaurant addition to Chinatown, with an unusually large menu. 16 soups, e.g., sweet corn & white fungus $3.80. Almost 100 vegetarian dishes, e.g., mixed vegetables $4.50, deep-fried white mushrooms $5, black mushrooms with thread fungus $5, vegetables with taro rolls $5. 24 dim sum specialities at 40 cents each, & 4 hot puddings, e.g., walnut or almond, at $1.50 each or $4.50 for 4 persons. ****(2)

AMAZING GRACE, 216 Church (17 St), 626-6411. Cafeteria. 11am-10pm Mon-Sat. Entree with vegetables & brown rice $5.55, with cup of soup $6.10. Sandwich with cup soup $4.50. Salad bar $3.39/lb (expensive). ****(15)

GOVINDA'S (Indian, formerly 7-Mothers), 86 Carl (Cole), 753-9703, 11:30am-9pm, Closed Sun. All-you-can-eat buffet, including salad bar and lasagna, $9. All-you-can-eat organic salad bar alone $5, soup & salad bar $6.50. ****(14)

TAIWAN (Chinese), 307 Church (15 St), 863-7121, 11:30am-2pm Mon-Sat & 3-10pm 7 days. See under Fish Restaurants above. ****(15)

POT & PAN, (Chinese) 1243 9th Avenue (Irving/Lincoln), 665-2833, 11:30am-9:30pm. Large vegetarian menu--e.g., 3 appetizers, 5 soups, 10 sautees, 4 sweet-and-sour dishes, and 8 vegetarian dishes. Range $2.45-7.85. Simple, very busy place. ****(19)

VERY GOOD***

BURMA'S HOUSE (Burmese), 720 Post (Jones), 775-1156, 11:30am-10pm. 11 vegetarian dishes, most at $4.75, including mu shu vegetables with 4 pancakes, Rangoon eggplant, sauteed broccoli, Burmese fried string, hot sauce bean curd; egg noodles with vegetables Burmese style $3.95, paluda ice cream dessert $2.50 (tapioca, coconut juice, paluda syrup, chopped peanuts, & ice cream). ***(1)

HUNAN VILLAGE (Chinese), 839 Kearny (Columbus), 956-7868. Vegetarian Lunch Special $4.50--spring roll, hot & sour soup, steamed rice, choice of 12 entrees. ***(2)

DARBAR (Indian), 48 - 5th Street (Market/Mission), 957-0140, 9am-9pm. 15 different Indian curries $6-6.95, 6-course vegetarian dinner $9.99, vegetarian Thali dinner (13 items) $14.95. ***(7)

MAHARANI (Indian), 1115 Polk (Post), 775-1988. 10-12 vegetarian dishes, including vegetarian Thali dinner $7.50, or deluxe vegetarian Thali $10, spinach cooked with herbs & served with cheese cubes $5.75, garbanzas with tamarind sauce $4.75, green peas & mushrooms sauteed with onions & spices $5.75, eggplant with spices $5.75, an okra specialty $5.75. All can be ordered mild, medium or hot. ***(10)

TAI CHI (Chinese), 2031 Polk (Pacific/Broadway), 441-6758. This is one of our favorite Chinese restaurants, and is listed under Chinese Lunches Under $5, also under Intermediate Restaurants. They list 16 vegetarian dishes, in addition to noodles & rice, e.g., bamboo shoot, fried gluten bean curd, straw mushroom, fungus, baby young corn, lotus root, fried bean curd with tender green $4.95; black mushroom with tender green $5.25, mixed vegetable deluxe $4.75, hot spicy eggplant $4.95, Szechuan bean curd $4.95. ***(10)

TAIWAN (Chinese), 289 Columbus Avenue (Stockton), 989-6789, 10am-3am. 16 vegetarian dishes on the menu, plus rice & noodles, e.g., red-cooked eggplant $4.50, snow peas with mushrooms & water chestnuts $4.95, hot & sour soup $4.25, bean sauce noodles $3.50. Be sure to specify: no fish or meat, or fish or meat sauces. ***(2)

PASAND MADRAS CUISINE (Indian), 1876 Union (Laguna), 922-4498. See under Intermediate Restaurants (Indian). ***(5)

GREAT CITY DELI (Mid-Eastern), 1801 Divisadero Street

(Bush), 931-5455. Falafel burger with home fries $4.95, mid-east vegetarian plate with falafel, humous, tabuli, tahini, dolma, & pita bread $4.99. ****(11)

REAL GOOD KARMA (Indian), 501 Dolores (18th St), 621-4112. 11:30am-2:30pm, and 5-10pm Mon-Fri, 5-10pm Sat-Sun. Daily lunch special with soup and salad $3.95, e.g., tempura with 5 vegetables and tofu, with soup and salad $6.75; mushroom fried rice and vegetables $4.35. Ice cream (made with honey) $1.35. ***(15)

NEECHA (Thai), 2100 Sutter (Steiner), 922-9419 & 500 Haight (Fillmore), 861-2550, 11am-3pm & 5-10pm. Has 7 vegetarian appetizers, 3 soups, 3 vegetarian curries in coconut milk, 10 vegetable, tofu & noodle dishes. Thai-style corn cake with cucumber sauce $4.25, spicy & sour soup with mushroom, lemon grass & tofu $4.25. ***(11)(14)

JOY (Chinese), 3258 Scott Street (Chestnut/Lombard), 922-0270. 12 vegetarian entrees $4.75-5.50, e.g., mu shu vegetables with 4 pancakes $5.50, eggplant in hot & sour sauce $4.75, sauteed spinach with garlic root $4.75. ***(6)

INDIAN OVEN, 237 Fillmore (Haight), 626-1628, 5:30-10pm, closed Tues. See under Splurge Restaurants above for the vegetarian Thali dinners at $7.95. ***(14)

BURMA (Burmese), 309 Clement (3 Av), 751-4091, 11am-9:30pm, closed Sun. 12 vegetarian dishes on menu, plus rice & noodles--vegetable rice or chow mein $3.50, braised tofu with tomatoes, onions & rice $4.95, tofu a la Burma $5.25, tofu with vegetables in red pepper sauce $5.25, Burmese curry vegetables $5.25, eggplant in spicy garlic sauce $5.25, black mushroom tofu $5.25, stir-fried vegetables $5.25, steamed Burmese whole yellow bean stir-fried with garlic & onion $4.95. ***(22)

SEA GULL (Chinese), 535 Irving (6/7 Avs), 681-4373, 11am-10pm. Choice of 14 bean curd & vegetarian dishes plus rice & noodle dishes, e.g., bean curd Szechuan-style (hot) $4.25, eggplant Szechuan-style $4.25, mixed vegetables $4.25, sauteed tender greens $4.25, black mushrooms with pea pods $4.75, vegetables chow mein $3.50. ***(19)

CANTON WINTER GARDEN (Chinese) 1125 Clement (11/12 Avs), 668-8368, 5:30-10:30pm. Half the menu is vegetarian. Westlake vegetarian soup $3.25, spinach & bean-curd soup $3.50. Mu shu vegetables with pancakes $4.25, sweet & sour walnuts $5.95, tofu dishes $4.95 & $5.95, vegetarian "chicken" $4.95-6.95, vegetarian "pork" $4.75-5.95. ***(22)

5. Splurge Restaurants, $10-$17 Per Person

To make the choice easier, I am listing these restaurants by ethnic groups.

Note: An asterisk (*) before a name means "especially recommended". I am putting those at the top of each ethnic group. Actually, every one of the restaurants listed in this section could qualify for the asterisk.

A tip on wines--bottled wines are often marked up 300-400%, particularly in deluxe restaurants (of which there are a number in this section). Some, surprisingly, remain at a decent $10-$15 level. However, almost all have a good "house wine" in the $6-$9 per liter category (slightly more than half for a half-liter). On a few occasions, I have found the same wine in a bottle at a much higher price. Don't hesitate to ask for it.

French

*LE DOMINO, 2747 17th St (Bryant/Harrison), 626-3095. 5-10pm. Appetizers--duck pate with pistachios $4.75, snails in chablis $6.25, onion soup $4. With green salad--sweetbreads in vermouth $14.75, rack of lamb $16.95, medallions of veal in cream sauce $15.75, rabbit in Dijon-mustard sauce $13.95. jumbo scallopps in champagne sauce $14.75. French desserts $3.75-5. Food is presented artistically; sometimes, it looks too good to eat. ****(16)

*LA BERGERIE, 4221 Geary (6th/7th Av), 387-3573, 5-10pm Tues-Sat. With soup, salad, ice cream, coffee--duck with orange $13.75, veal sweetbreads $12.50, rabbit braised in red wine, herbs, tomatoes $13.50, coq au vin $11.75, rack of lamb $13.50, Australian lobster tail $18.50. Unusually low prices for a 5-course meal of excellent quality. ****(13)

*LE CYRANO, 4134 Geary Blvd. (6th Av), 387-1090, 5-10:30pm, except Sun. With soup (French onion soup or du jour), salad and choice of 7 desserts (e.g., cheese, chocolate mousse, ice cream, sorbet). Cheese or mushroom omelette (excellent) $9, rack of lamb $17.50, frog legs in garlic butter $14.75, deep fried rex sole $13.25, chicken in wine $12, beef in burgundy wine $13. Quality French country-cuisine. Very reasonable prices for a 4-course dinner. ****(13)

*BAYON, 2018 Lombard (Webster), 922-1400, 5:30-10:30 Tues-Sat, 4:30-9:30 Sun, closed Mon. Appetizers,some of a spectacular nature, e.g., snails in a sauce that has a touch of lemon grass, 6 for $5.25, or an unusual chicken salad made with basil and roasted peanuts, shaped like a bird's nest $5.50, or tiny, greasless spring egg rolls (12) $5.50. Main dishes--duck with orange (with a touch of lemon grass) $13.50, prawns with lemon grass, Dijon mustard, coconut milk & herbs $12.95, and rack of lamb $14.95. While high and a la carte, these prices are cheaper than those of well-known French restaurants serving similar dishes. They also serve a 3-course French meal, with Cambodian overtones and herbs, for $9.95--soup or salad, entree with fresh vegetables, dessert (ice cream or creme caramel). ****(6)

LUZERN (Swiss-French), 1427 Noriega, 664-2353. 5-10pm Wed-Sat, 4-9pm Sunday. With soup, salad. dessert (creme caramel, ice cream or sherbet)--poached salmon with shrimp sauce $15, veal with artichoke & mushrooms $14.75, duck with orange sauce $16, cordon bleu $14.75, sweetbreads in brandy & with mushrooms $14, rack of lamb $18.25. Fondue is served with soup or salad--beef fondue $16, cheese fondue $9 per person, minimum order for 2. Intimate small, neighborhood restaurant. Reasonable price, considering the full menu. ***(20)

Japanese

*OSOME, 1923 Fillmore (Bush/Pine), 346-2311, 5:30-11pm. With appetizer, soup, sunomono, dessert--sashimi & tempura $13.95, sashimi & beef teriyaki $14.20, tempura & chicken teriyaki $13.95, tempura& beef teriyaki (flavored with garlic & sesame seed, on request) $14.20. With appetizer & soup--sushi, tempura & chicken teriyaki $13.75. Yosenabe (Japanese bouillabaisse, with chicken & vegetables) $12.95. With appetizer & soup--Sashimi, tempura, & teriyaki $12.95. Osome was once called the best Japanese restaurant in the Bay Area in a poll of experts. ****(11)

*KICHIHEI, 2084 Chestnut (Steiner), 929-1670, 5-10pm. With soup, salad, rice, dessert--sashimi & tempura $11.65, sashimi & beef teriyaki $11.75, tempura & chicken teriyaki $11.95, yosenabe (Japanese fish soup) $11.75, tempura & salmon teriyaki $13.25, pot cookery, e.g., shabu-shabu (fondue, cooked in broth at table) $11.75. Good value on Chestnut Street. ****(6)

*MA TANTE SUMI (Californian cuisine with Japanese touches), 4243 18th Street (Diamond), 552-6663, 5:30-10pm. Small but interesting menu. Steamed clams or mussels, with sake $4.95, three-mushroom salad with endive and greenleaf lettuce in a soy sesame dressing $4.50, sashimi with Wasabi vinaigrette $5.95. Entrees include miso soup & vegetables, rice or potatoes--"Vegetarian Medley" cooked oriental style $7, chicken breast with mushrooms $9.25; prawns with mushrooms, tomato, basil & cream $13; grilled marinated rack of lamb with mustard-chive sauce $15; grilled marinated ahi tuna $14; 1/2 duck glazed with Japanese plum-wine sauce $13.50. Homemade cheese cake $3, with berries $4. One of the best restaurants in Castro area. ****(15)

*TEMPURA HOUSE, 529 Powell (Bush/Sutter), 392-3269, 5:30-10pm. Family Dinner for 4, $14.50 per person, includes soup, salad, dessert, rice, green tea, tempura, chicken teriyaki, tonkatsu (deep-fried pork), yakitori, beef teriyaki, lobster, & sashimi, dessert. Same dinner without lobster, beef teriyuaki, & dessert $10.50 per person. ****(1)

ALL SEASON HIBACHI (Japanese), 737 Washington (Grant), 421-1188, 11:30am-12am. All meals cooked at table, on hibachi ovens. Special combinations with house soup, chef's salad, steamed rice, tea & dessert--steak, pork chop, chicken & prawns, or seafood combination (prawns, octopus, oysters, scallops, squid) $13.95. Also, hot pots a la carte--lamb $7.95, steak $5.95, pork chop $4.95. Vegetable or rice noodles $1.95 extra. A fun meal, good quality. ***(2)

Thai

*KHAN TOKE THAI HOUSE, 5937 Geary Blvd (23/24 Avs), 668-6654, 5-11pm. The Thai Royal Style Dinner, $14.95--fried fish cakes cucumber sauce, spicy sour shrimp soup (served mild, medium or hot), choice of beef or egg salad, sliced beef, choice of 2 entrees, dessert, Thai coffee or tea. Entrees include interesting beef, prawns or fish dishes. An elegant dinner, especially on Sunday evening when there is Thai dancing, begins 8:30pm. ****(13)

Vietnamese

*GOLDEN DEER, 908 Clement (10 Av), 751-8089, 10am-2am. 10-course banquet dinner, $12.95 per person, includes pan-fried whole crab, sizzling shrimp, dessert. 7-beef dinner for 4, $12.95 per person. This is a Vietnamese restaurant that gets most of its trade from its own nationals, a good sign. The a la carte menu provides traditional Vietnamese dishes at reasonable prices, with a culinary flair, e.g., shrimp rolls $3.95, stuffed chicken wings $4.95, 5-spice chicken rubbed with herbs $4.95, lemon-grass pork $6.95. ****(22)

German

SPECKMANN'S, 1550 Church (27/28 Sts), 282-6850, 11am-9pm. With lentil or goulasch or potato soup, or salad--Kasseler (smoked pork chop) with sauerkraut & mashed potatoes $11.95, sauerbraten with red cabbage & potato pancakes $11.95, eisbein (pickled & boiled pig's joint) $12.95. German Gasthaus ambience. Is becoming a bit pricey, has now moved to Splurge category. ****(15)

Indian

INDIAN OVEN, 237 Fillmore (Haight), 626-1628, 5:30-10pm, closed Tues. Curries are varied and interesting, from all parts of India, e.g.--lamb with ginger sauce, lamb & spinach curry, each $10.95. Chicken curries are $8.95-$12.95, prawns & fish curries $12.95. Also, multi-course thali dinners--which include dal lentil) soup, chutneys, raita (yoghourt dish with onions, tomatoes, spices), nan bread, dessert (rice pudding with saffron)--at cost of the entree plus $2. Some entrees--choice of several vegetarian specialties $7.95, chicken with apricots $9.95, roasted quail biryani (seasoned rice) $12.95, tandoori salmon biryani $12,95, tiger prawns tandoori $13.95, rack of lamb tandoori $14.95. ****(14)

Moroccan

*EL MANSOUR (Moroccan), 3123 Clement (31/32 Avs), 751-2312, 5-10pm. Two fixed meals nightly $14.75 & $16.75. The $14.75 meal includes spicy lentil bean soup, salad, bastela (pastry filled with chicken, almond & spices), entree (choice of a couscous & lamb dish, chicken with almonds or honey & prunes, or a lamb dish, e.g., with honey & almonds or with prunes, or rabbit), dessert (banana fritter or pastry), mint tea. Entree choices include couscous, chicken with prunes, lamb with honey & almonds. The $16.75 dinner includes all of the above plus couscous, banana fritter, & a Moroccan pastry. Live belly-dancer nightly. ****(23)

Polynesian

RAFFLES, 1390 Market St (Hayes), 621-8601, 11am-4pm, & 4-9pm, closed Sun. Dinners with soup or green salad (with shrimp), pupus (hors d'oeuvres), & coconut ice cream--cashew chicken with black mushrooms $10.95, Polynesian Plate (spareribs, prawns, cashew chicken, chow mein) $10.95, petrale sole or sea bass $12, scallops & prawns $12, lamb chops $13, 8-oz N.Y. steak or filet mignon $14.50. ***(7)

Lebanese

GRAPELEAF (Lebanese), 4031 Balboa, 668-1515, 6-10pm, Sun from 5pm. Dinner includes a Lebanese salad, pilaff with Lebanese vegetables, Turkish or Infidel coffee--baked lamb $14.25 breast of chicken $12.75, N.Y. steak $18.75, baked fish filets in casserole $12.75. ****(23)

Jewish

David's Deli, 480 Geary (Taylor/Mason), 771-1600, 7am-1am. Complete Dinner, $14.95--appetizer (e.g., lox, chopped herring, kishka, gefilte fish), entree (e.g., baked brisket of beef, stuffed cabbage, Hungarian goulasch), dessert (choice of pastries), coffee of tea. ***(1)

Continental & American

*JACKSON PAVILLION, 640 Jackson (Grant/Kearny), 982-2409, 7:30am-10pm. A new addition to continental cuisine in Chinatown, next door to the successful Ping Yuen (see next listing). Dinner includes soup or salad, dessert, coffee or tea--T-bone steak $9.95, sauteed scallops with filet of sole $10.95, grilled salmon $11.75, filet mignon with pepper sauce $11.95, N.Y. steak with giant prawns $13.95. They also have a continental lunch menu, at which time they are jammed with

Chinese who want non-Chinese food. ****(2)

PACIFIC COURT CAFE', 728 Pacific Ave (Grant/Stockton, on ground floor of the Miriwa Center), 781-8312, 8am-9pm. This is the third gourmet continental restaurant in Chinatown. Entrees are served with garlic bread, vegetables, potatoes or rice, coffee or tea--hamburger steak with onions $5.95, linguini with clams $7.25, pacific snapper almondine $7.95, prime rib of beef $8.95 (extra-large cut $10.95), T-bone steak $10.55, double lamb chops with mint sauce $12.95, lobster tail $14.95, rack of lamb $14.95. ****(2)

WHITE HORSE TAVERNE, 637 Sutter (Mason/Taylor, in Beresford Hotel), 673-9900, 5:30-110:30pm Tues-Sat, closed Sun-Mon. A la carte. Bay shrimp cocktail $4.50, mixed salad $3.50. With vegetables & baked potato--T-bone steak, over 16 ozs, $13.95, filet mignon $11.95, prime rib $11.95, salmon, with vegetables & rice, $11.95. Elegant British-type atmosphere. ****(1)

SUSIE KATE'S, 2330 Taylor (Columbus), 776-5283, 5-10pm; also, 10am-2:30pm Sun. A la carte. 5-green salad or 3-pepper soup $2.95, sausage & biscuits $2.95. Entrees, with sour-cream cornbread biscuits, corn relish--southern fried chicken with mashed potatoes, blackeyed peas, & collard fribbles (sauteed collard greens with garlic & monterey jack cheese) $10.95; baked pork loin with mashed potatoes & vegetables $11.95; jambalaya (Cajun stew of shrimp, duck, 3 kinds of peppers & ham, over Louisiana Dirty Rice) $13.95. Vegetarian plate $9.95. Pecan pie, or chocolate-chocolate bourbon pie $3.50. Interesting bar-restaurant with a "taste of the South". ****(3)

GYPSY, 353 Columbus Ave, 781-6880. $20 dinner consists of soup, salad, choice of entree, dessert--choice of 8-oz entrecote with fries, grilled duck breast with orange sauce, filet mignon, salmon in puff pastry with asparagus sauce, or grilled tuna provencale. ****(3)

THE GALLEON, 718 14th St (Market), 431-0253, 6-11pm. Also, bar with piano music. With salad, rice or potatoes, vegetables-- salmon Wellington in puff pastry $12.75; steak with blue-cheese butter & steak fries $9.50; prime rib au jus with horseradish & red potatoes $13.25. ***(15)

SUNSET, 1241 Noriega (19 Av), 731-3669, 4:30-9pm, Fri-Sat to 10, closed Mon. Attractive neighborhood restaurant. With soup, salad, entree & dessert--calves liver $11.75, veal paprika $11.75, combination seafood $12.75, prawns $11.75, double French lamb chops $14.75. ***(20)

6. Big Splurge Restaurants ($15-$30+ Per Person)

This section is designed either for the very well-heeled, or for the economically-minded who want to celebrate a Big Occasion, such as a birthday, wedding, the day they met, etc. Of course, when spending $15-$30+ per person--plus tax, tip and drinks--one wants real value, right? Be assured I've chosen the Big Splurge restaurants with just that in mind.

Note: An asterisk (*) before a name means "especially recommended". I am putting those so noted at the top of the list in order to facilitate the choice. A tip on wines: Bottled wines are often marked up 300-400%, particularly in the "splurge" and "big splurge" restaurants. This puts some in the $15-30 range, although a few will have good choices in the $10-15 range. But almost all have a "house wine", usually of excellent quality, for $7-9 a liter (or a bit more than half that for a half-liter). Don't hesitate to ask for it. Another alternative is to drink 1 glass ($3-4).

*ZOLA'S (French), relocated from Sacramento Street to a stunningly simple location at 395 Hayes Street (Gough), 864-4824, 5:30-10:30m Mon-Sat. Menus change frequently. Here are excerpts from a recent one: Cream of Jerusalem artichoke & potato soup $5, arugula & radicchio salad with walnut oil dressing $5, charcuterie plate of duck rilletes & head cheese with pickled Chioggia beets $6.50. Entrees--cassoulet of red beans with duck, lamb & sausage $16, oven-steamed sturgeon with sundried tomato & basil vinagrette $18, cumin and coriander scented rack of lamb with artichoke $20. Desserts are elaborate, about $5-6. Some recent-vintage good wines in the $15-20 range ($4-6 a glass), plus older wines at higher prices but with practically no markup from retail, which is unusual. This is French haute cuisine which would cost much more in France for the same quality. In other words, good *value*--if you can afford it. ****(10)

*GOLDEN TURTLE (Vietnamese), 2211 Van Ness Ave

(Broadway/Vallejo), 441-4419, 5-11pm, closed Mon. Elegant. Possibly, the best Vietnamese restaurant in San Francisco (much better than their 5th Ave. branch). 8-course Special Banquet Dinner, plus rice & tea, for 4 or more, $18.95 per person, consists of: imperial rolls. shrimp & pork salad, crabmeat & asparagus soup, pan-fried whole crab or whole steamed fish, imperial beef, lemon-grass chicken, sizzling prawns, steamed rice, banana flambe', tea. The Seven Jewel Beef Dinner, for 2 or more, $18.95 per person, consists of 7 beef courses, including beef-ball soup, fondue, la lot etc. ****(10)

*L'ESCARGOT (French), 1809 Union (Octavia), 567-0222. 5:30-10:30pm. With soup *and* salad--sweetbreads with mushrooms & madeira $16.50, pork with apples and calvados sauce $16.75, roast rabbit with madeira & mustard sauce $15.75, duck with orange $17.50, poached salmon $17.50, rack of lamb $18.75. This elegant restaurant could also qualify for the cheaper Splurge Section ($10-$15) since the dinners include soup *and* salad (worth $7-8 in a restaurant of this caliber), but quality is definitely Big Splurge. ****(5)

NORTH INDIA (Indian), 3131 Webster (Lombard), 931-1556, 5-11pm. Traditional Feast $19.95 per person (minimum 2 persons) includes: assorted appetizers, soup, cucumber salad Indian-style, tandoori chicken (baked in special clay oven), minced lamb on skewers, lamb cubes in curry sauce, choice of dessert, coffee or tea. Tandoori Dinners--served with soup, vegetables, Indian bread, spicy basmatic rice, & condiments-- are $13.95 up. ****(6)

GOLD MIRROR, 800 Taraval (18 Av), 564-0401, 11am-3pm & 5-11pm. Dinner includes: assorted Italian appetizers, mixed green salad, ministrone, entree, and coffee--eggplant parmigiana $15, chicken cacciatore $15.50, veal piccata $18, jumbo prawns fried in butter & wine $19, prime rib of beef (Sat-Sun only) $19, 14-oz filet mignon $18. A la carte $5 less per entree. House Italian wine $4.75 1/2 liter, $7.50 liter. Elegant dining. ****(20)

GELCO (Yugoslav), 1450 Lombard (Van Ness Av), 928-1054, 5:30-11pm. Full dinners consist of hors d'oeuvres, green salad, entree with vegetables & pilaf, dessert & coffee--moussaka $17, filet of veal $20, lamb mixed grill (lamb chops, lamb sausage, ground patty) $20.50, rack of baby lamb $23. A la carte only, $5 less. If splurging, go for the whole meal. ***(6)

7. Bars With Free Hors d'Oeuvres

We all know "there's no free lunch", but how about buying 1 drink for $1-$2.50 and eating all the hot and/or cold hors d'oeuvres you want at no extra cost? In checking this out I was amazed at the number of bars that offer free hors d'oeuvres, usually during the cocktail hours and Mon-Fri only (but some on Saturday and a few even on Sunday). It's a pleasant way to pass the time, at little cost (one drink is enough, especially if you're driving). The hors d'oeuvres range from potato chips or cheese and crackers to hot & cold choices. Some resemble a small buffet supper. A word of caution: the price of drinks can be high, as much as $6 a drink at the posh hotels. I like the $1-$2.50 well-drinks range (even up to $4 in the plush-hotel bars), so watch the price. Here are a number to choose from:

Note: Bars are listed roughly in order of distance from Union Square.

DEWEY'S, Union Square (St. Francis Hotel), 397-7000, 4-7 Mon-Fri. (1)

MacARTHUR PARK, 607 Front St. (Jackson/Pacific), 398-5700. 5-7pm Mon-Fri. (8)

CADILLAC BAR, 1 Holland Court (Mason/Howard), 543-8226. 4-7pm Mon-Fri. (7)

MAYE'S, 1233 Polk (Sutter), 474-7674. 3-6pm Mon-Fri. (10)

PERRY'S, 1944 Union (Laguna/Buchanan), 922-9022. (5)

LA BARCA, 2036 Lombard (Fillmore/Webster), 921-2221. 4-6pm, Mon-Fri. (6)

VIAREGGIO, 1956-1/2 Lombard (Buchanan/Webster), 4-6:30pm, Tues-Sun. 921-1812.

ACHILLES HEEL, 1601 Haight (Clayton), 626-1800, 5-7pm Mon-Fri. (14)

8. Music, Film, Theater, Art, Cafe's

There is an abundance of free entertainment on the streets and in the parks of San Francisco. Each summer there are free concerts in Stern Grove and Golden Gate Park, classical, semi-classical, and jazz. There are also free concerts at the Hyatt Regency Hotel, at Levi Strauss Plaza, and in the patio of the State Compensation Insurance Fund at Market & Ninth Streets. There is a Brown Bag Opera, sponsored by the managers of One Market Plaza, in the plaza' atrium lobby, in July and August. The area around 5th and Market, Fisherman's Wharf, and Ghirardelli Square abound in streetside entertainment (jazz, pantomime, etc.), for donations. This is also a great city for "Little Theater" and dance groups (both classical and modern). Consult the pink section of the Sunday Examiner for details, as well as the Bay Guardian, and the free weekly programs of the Fort Mason Center and the public libraries.

Music

Classical (including operettas)

STERN GROVE CONCERTS, 666-7035, Stern Grove, 19th Ave. and Sloat Bvd. Free concerts of high caliber. The season begins in June and continues through August. Watch the newspapers (especially pink section of the *Sunday Examiner*) for details.

THE SAN FRANCISCO CONSERVATORY OF MUSIC, 1201 Ortega, 564-8086. Regular concerts, chamber and classical. They request a donation but will not turn away a poor student. Phone for details or watch the newspapers.

THE COMMUNITY MUSIC CENTER, 544 Capp St. (20-21st Sts), 647-6015. They have monthly programs. Prices are very low, phone for details.

OLD FIRST PRESBYTERIAN CHURCH, Sacramento and Van Ness, 776-5552. Concerts all year round. First-class performances of concert artists, trios and quartets, etc., & classical chamber music. Low prices, phone for details.

THE LAMPLIGHTERS, 361 Dolores, 752-7755. A popular music house for operettas, e.g., Gilbert & Sullivan's Pinafore, Die

Fledermaus.

Jazz Cafes & Discotheques

San Francisco is the home of well-known jazz groups, dozens of whom perform nightly, as well as many discotheques. Some are expensive, but some have no cover at all. To discover them yourself, stroll around North Beach, Union Street area, the Haight-Ashbury area, and Castro Street. Also, check the pink section of the *Sunday Examiner*, and the *Bay Guardian* for listings. Here are some choices:

CAFFE' TRIESTE, 601 Vallejo (Grant), 392-6739. This is also a coffee house where opera singers serenade on Saturdays.

KIMBALL'S, 300 Grove, 861-5585. Jazz jam sessions.

TOSCA CAFE', 242 Columbus (Broadway), 986-9651. Opera records on juke box.

CAFE' FLORE, 2298 Market (Noe), 621-8579. Bar and restaurant. Gay-oriented.

MEATMARKET COFFEEHOUSE, 4123 24th (Castro), 285-5598. Gay area.

PAUL'S SALOON, 3251 Scott (Lombard/Chestnut), 922-2456. Live bluegrass.

PLOWSHARES COFFEEHOUSE, Fort Mason, 441-8910. Live folk and other music, concerts.

LAST DAY SALOON, 406 Clement (5th Ave), 387-6344. Rock, blues, country, western.

FULL MOON SALOON, 1725 Haight (Cole), 668-6190. Reggae, world beat, Jamaican.

I-BEAM, 1748 Haight (Cole), 668-6006, 9pm-2am Mon-Sat and 6pm-2am Sun. New Wave disco with a program that changes weekly.

NIGHTBREAK, 1821 Haight, 221-9008. Modern dance music, DJ and live.

THE BOX, at the Kennel Club, 628 Divisadero, 931-1914. Frenetic dancing to black-oriented music. Popular with gays, lesbians, heterosexuals, blacks, whites. Dancing is the thing.

Opera, Symphony, Ballet

San Francisco is world-famous in these fields, hence prices tend to be high for budget travelers (but not compared to

Vienna and New York). The opera has stand-up tickets, while the symphony and ballet have afternoon performances with reduced prices for students and Seniors. The symphony has open rehearsals. You can also buy same-day half-price tickets at S.T.B.S. at Union Square (see below). Phone for details for Opera House 864-3330, and for Symphony 431-5400.

Ballet

SAN FRANCISCO BALLET, 864-3330 (Box Office, Opera House). The San Francisco Ballet is internationally acclaimed. It uses the Opera House from about the middle of December to the beginning of May each year. Students and seniors with proper ID get half off on subscriptions for "orchestra sides", also on day of performance 2 hours before curtain time. There is standing room for all performances at reduced price. Also, you can sometimes get half off through S.T.B.S. (see below) on the day of performance.

S.T.B.S. Pronounced "stubs". This is a 1/2-price ticket office at the Stockton Street entrance to the Union Square garage. They offer day-of-performance tickets at 1/2 price, when available, as well as regular-price tickets for some shows. Phone 433-7827 for details.

Film

SAN FRANCISCO PUBLIC LIBRARY, 558-3191 (Information). Free monthly program available on request, for weekly films in 8mm, as well as lectures and talks, *free*.

GOETHE INSTITUTE, 530 Bush (Grant), 391-0370. This institute is subsidized by the German Government and has a library of German publications for public perusal. Also puts on free lectures and films, in the German language. Phone for free printed program.

Theater

Of the little theaters (99-seat capacity), highly recommended are: *Magic Theater* (441-8822)--which is experimental and sometimes far-out--*Eureka* (558-9898), and *Theater Rhinoceros* (Gay, 861-5079). There are also ethnic theater groups, e.g., Chinese and Mexican. Most of these have previews at reduced prices, special offers, and sometimes free readings. Check the pink section of the Sunday Examiner for details.

The A.C.T. (American Conservatory Theater), which is pricey and tends to favor conservative classics, has half-price tickets for students. Phone for details, 673-6440.

Art

San Francisco has many private galleries. Some have permanent collections of important Impressionists and Grand Masters. Most have periodic shows of new artists, either individual or collective shows. Consult the pink section of the Sunday Examiner for a listing of private galleries and their current shows. Note: a number of galleries, some of the largest and most important, are located on Sutter Street, between Powell and Van Ness. A stroll along Sutter can provide a rewarding afternoon. For an interesting gallery for avant-garde modern ceramics, look at the Dorothy Weiss Gallery, 256 Sutter Street; for Impressionists, look into the Erika Meyerovich gallery on 231 Grant Avenue.

9. Museums

San Francisco has an abundance of Museums--art, science, ethnic (Chinese, Mexican, Italian, Jewish), Mint, wine, etc. Many are free while some are free on certain days of the week or month only. Most are listed in the pink section of the Sunday Examiner, with details of current shows.

SAN FRANCISCO MUSEUM OF MODERN ART, Van Ness and McAllister, 863-8800. 10am-5pm Tues, Wed & Fr, 10am-9pm Thurs, 11am-5pm Sat-Sun. *Free* all day Tuesdays, and reduced price 5-9pm Thursdays, under 12 free.

M.H.DeYOUNG MUSEUM, 8th Ave. and Kennedy Drive, Golden Gate Park, 750-3600, Open 10am-5pm Wed through Sun, except 1st Wed of the month when it is *free* and open until 8:45pm. Also *free* 10am-noon 1st Saturday of the month. Admission is also good for the Asian Art Museum which is in the same building but has a different entrance. $1 reduction to those who have bought a Muni fare, or have a Muni Pass. There is a permanent collection of the arts of Africa, Oceana and the Americas, as well as ancient and European art. *Free* docent tours.

ASIAN ART MUSEUM, same location and same hours as DeYoung, 668-8921, 1-5pm daily. Admission--which permits entrance to the DeYoung on days it is open--is the same as for DeYoung. *Free* 1st Wed of the month and 10am-noon on Sat.

PALACE OF THE LEGION OF HONOR, Lincoln Park, 750-3600. Open 10am-5pm Wed-Sun. *Free* First Wed of the month and 10am-noon on 1st Sat of month, otherwise same entrance charge as DeYoung. Permanent collection of French art; large Rodin sculpture collection.

ACADEMY OF SCIENCES, Golden Gate Park, 7507145, from 10am7pm every day of the year, except 1st Wed of each month to 8:45pm, on which day it is *free*, otherwise adults $4, students 1217 and Seniors $2, children 611 $1, under 6 *free*.

STEINHART AQUARIUM, California Academy of Sciences, Golden Gate Park, 7507145. The first Wednesday of the month is *free*. Open daily 10am-7pm. 14,500 live aquatic specimens. Dolphin feeding every 2 hours from 10:30am, penguin-feeding 11:30am and 4pm. Entrance fee included in Academy of Sciences ticket.

Morrison PLANETARIUM, in Academy of Sciences Building, but

extra admission fee, 750-7141: adults $2; ages 6-17, seniors, and students $1. Call 221-0168 for special shows.

EXPLORATORIUM, PALACE OF FINE ARTS, Lyon Street near Marina Blvd, 563-3200. A hands-on science, art and human perception museum. Open Wed from 10am-9:30pm, Thurs-Sun 10am-5pm. Admission *free* first Wed of each month and every Wed after 6pm.

AMERICAN CAROUSEL MUSEUM 633 Beach Street at Hyde, 928-0550. Finest examples of antique carousel art from 1880 to 1920. Daily 10am-6pm. Adults $2, Seniors $1, children under 12 free.

AMERICAN INDIAN CONTEMPORARY ARTS, 685 Market, Suite 250, 495-7600. Tues-Sat 10am-6pm, *free*.

CABLE CAR MUSEUM, 1201 Mason (Washington), 474-1887, 10am-5pm daily. *Free.*

CARTOON ART MUSEUM, 665 Third Street, 546-3922. Noon-6pm Thurs-Fri, noon-5pm Sat.

CHINESE CULTURE CENTER, 750 Kearny (3rd floor of the Holiday Inn in Chinatown), 986-1822. They also sponsor walking tours. Call for complete information. Open Tues-Sat, 10am-4pm. *Free.*

CHINESE HISTORICAL SOCIETY, 650 Commercial Street,, 391-1188. Open Tues-Sat 1-5pm. Traces the history of the Chinese in America. *Free.*

CRAFT AND FOLK ART MUSEUM OF SAN FRANCISCO, Fort Mason Center Bldg A, 775-0990. Open 11am-5pm Tues-Fri, 10am-noon Sat-Sun. *Free.*

FORT POINT NATIONAL HISTORICAL SITE, 556-1693. Open daily 10am-5pm. Civil War-era fortress beneath Golden Gate Bridge. Rangers are on hand to explain the fort's history. *Free.*

ITALIAN AMERICAN MUSEUM, 673-2200. Fort Mason Center Building C. Open noon-5pm Wed-Sun. Contemporary Italian or Italian-American artists. *Free.*

JEWISH COMMUNITY MUSEUM, 121 Steuart St., 543-8880. Phone for details. *Free.*

LIBERTY SHIP. The SS Jeremiah O'Brien, last unaltered ship in operating condition. At Pier 3 East, Fort Mason Center, Bay and Laguna Streets. 441-3101. Open daily 9am-3pm.

MARITIME MUSEUM, Beach St. at the foot of Polk, 929-0202. Open 10am-6 pm daily. Ranks as one of the great maritime museums of the U.S.

MEXICAN MUSEUM, Fort Mason Center, Bldg D, 441-0404, Wed-Sun noon-5pm, except 1st Wed of the month noon to 8pm, on which day it is *free*. The museum also offers walking tours of the Mission. $2, $1 seniors & students.

MISSION DOLORES, 16th & Dolores Sts, 621-8203. 9am-4:30pm, docent tours by appointment. Oldest buiding in San Francisco.

MODERN MYTHOLOGY, 693 Mission Street (3rd St, 9th floor), 546-0202. noon-5pm Wed through Sun. American folk art, story-telling. $1.50, students & seniors $1.

OLD MINT, 5th and Mission, 974-0788. Open Mon-Fri, except holidays, 10am-4pm. Gold rush exhibits, gold, old coins, minting equipment, vaults. *Free.*

PIONEER SOCIETY OF CALIFORNIA, 456 McAllister Street, 861-5278. Gold Rush, early San Francisco silver, 19th century paintings, research library, Wells Fargo stagecoach. Mon through Fri, 10am-4pm. *Free.*

PRESIDIO ARMY MUSEUM, Lincoln and Funston Ave., in the Presidio, 561-4115. Daily except Mon, 10am-4pm. Two hundred years of military and social history of the Presidio, including authentic uniforms and equipment. *Free.*

STRYBING ARBORETUM, next to Hall of Flowers, 9th Ave. at Lincoln Way, 661-0668. Seventy landscaped acres, with over 6,000 different plant species in seasonal bloom. Weekdays 8am-4:30pm, weekends and holidays 10am-5pm. Tours daily at 1:30pm. *Free.*

TATTOO ART MUSEUM, 30 7th St. (near Greyhound Depot), 864-9798. Open 12-6pm daily. *Free.*

TOY MUSEUM, INTERNATIONAL, 2801 Leavenworth (second level, The Cannery), 441-8697. 10am-5pm Tues-Sat, 11-5 Sun, closed Mon. Has thousands of toys from all over the world, mechanical & electrical. Also, an exhibit of antique toys. First hands-on (for new toys, naturally) toy museum in the world. Has play space for children. Admission for all, $1 (but no one is turned away if he/she doesn't have $1).

10. Seeing the City Walking Tours

San Francisco is best seen on foot. The city is divided into sections--geographical, historical, ethnic. There are many walking tours, some private, some city-run. The latter are free and are listed below. The private tours can be found in the pink section of the Sunday paper.

CITY GUIDE WALKS, 558-3981.

No reservations are required. The tours start at 2pm and last about one hour. Each tour covers one specific area, e.g., Market Street, North Beach, Nob Hill etc. Schedule can be had by sending stamped, self-addressed envelope to: City Guides, Main Library, Civic Center, San Francisco, CA 94102. *Free*.

GOLDEN GATE PARK WALKS, 221-1311. These tours begin on May 1st and run through October 31st, on Sat and Sun. Check by phone or look in the pink section of the Sunday paper. *Free*.

COMMUNITY COLLEGE WALKS. Two hours beginning 10am on Sat, 239-3070. *Free*.

11. Medical, Dental, Legal Aid

Travelers, as well as residents, often need medical or dental care on an emergency basis. Emergency care at most hospitals and clinics is prohibitive. There *are* alternatives, from moderate fees to free treatment. Also, San Francisco has a fair share of social medical services--for drug addiction, venereal disease, women's problems (including abortion), etc., at no-cost or low-cost. While there are drop-in hours at some clinics, it is always advisable to telephone and make an appointment.

Note: Some hospitals and clinics require local residence, but they will usually accept a local address without verification in an emergency.

Note: Listings are alphabetical.

ACUPUNTURE & HERBAL TREATMENT--QUAN YIN HEALING ARTS CENTER, 513 Valencia (Market), 861-1101. Alternative treatment for AIDS.

AIDS PROBLEMS. Because of the importance of this subject, information has been included in this book. See *Hospice* in this section below. See also the *AIDS* listings under Miscellaneous below (*S.F. Aids Foundation, Shanti Project, Aids Interfaith Network, Gay Switchboard Operation Concern*).

AMERICAN CANCER SOCIETY, 973 Market, 974-1592. Free counseling, information, tests.

BUENA VISTA WOMEN'S SERVICES, INC., 2000 Van Ness (Broadway), 771-5000. Counselling, abortions. Mon-Sat.

CALIFORNIA COLLEGE OF PODIATRIC MEDICINE, 1210 Scott, 563-8070. Free foot-screening examinations, 9 to 11am and 1:30-3:30pm Mon- Fri, 9-11am Sat.

CENTRAL AID STATION (Tom Waddel Clinic), Health Department, City of San Francisco, 50 Ivy St. (Civic Center), 554-2950. 24-hour service. Fees are   much less than those private physicians or most hospitals. For neighborhood Health Centers, check phone-book under City Government offices (at beginning of book), Health Department.

CLINICS. Most large hospitals have clinics which charge for services on a sliding scale. Usually, the scale is lower for San

Francisco residents, but they will probably accept a local address.

HAIGHT-ASHBURY FREE MEDICAL CLINIC, 558 Clayton (Haight), 431-1714. Phone for appointment. Includes VD testing. For drug-detoxification (529 Clayton), phone 621-2014. Women's Need Section (1825 Haight), 221-7371. For information and referral or general help, phone Haight-Ashbury Switchboard 621-6211.

HEARING-DIAL-A-TEST, sponsored by the Hearing Society of the Bay Area. Dial 863-4779 to test your hearing.

HOSPICE AIDS HOME HEALTH CARE, 1390 Market St. (Fox Plaza), 861-8705. This is a part of VNH (Visiting Nurses and Hospice of San Francisco). They provide 24-hour home health care for the terminally-ill AIDS patients. They also offer support to family members, relatives, lovers, friends. See also *S.F. Aids Foundation* and *Shanti Project* in *Miscellaneous* section below.

LYON MARTIN WOMEN'S HEALTH SERVICES, 2480 Mission (21 St), 641-0220. Health service for Bay area's lesbian community and women in general. Sliding scale, Medical & Medicare.

OPERATION CONCERN, 1853 Market (Guerrero), 626-7000. Provides counseling for gays; gives legal, medical and therapeutic referrals.

PLANETREE HEALTH RESOURCES CENTER, 2040 Webster (Buchanan), 923-3680. Non profit consumer health organization which provides public access to health & medical information. Has an information service, consumer health library, and a specialty health bookstore.

PLANNED PARENTHOOD, 815 Eddy (Van Ness/Franklin), 441-5454. Examination and counseling, abortion, on a sliding scale.

PREGNANCY CONSULTATION CENTER, 567-8757. Free pregnancy tests and counseling.

SAN FRANCISCO GENERAL HOSPITAL, 1001 Potrero (22nd St), Emergency 821-8111. This is a city hospital. No patient is turned away. If need is claimed, there is an eligibility interview *after* the treatment, on the basis of which the fee is determined. If a person is destitute, he or she will be charged nothing.

ST. LUKE'S NEIGHBORHOOD CLINIC, 1580 Valencia (Duncan), 641-6500. Mon-Fri, by appointment. Clinic is on sliding scale, according to need: $10-18 plus x-ray and lab fees.

SUTTER MEDICAL GROUP, 1154 Sutter (Polk/Larkin), 441-6930, 8am to 8pm Mon-Fri, until 6pm Sat. General medical only.

UNIVERSITY OF CALIFORNIA MEDICAL CENTER. By appointment only. Phone for location of clinics and services, 476-1000.

Dental

UNIVERSITY OF CALIFORNIA DENTAL CLINIC, Information 476-1891, or Emergency 476-5814. Fees are 1/3-1/2 of those charged by a private dentist.

UNIVERSITY OF THE PACIFIC SCHOOL OF DENTISTRY, 2155 Webster (Sacramento), 929-6500. Fees 1/3-1/2 that of private dentist.

Legal

Foreign visitors are advised to apply to their consulates for free legal advice, where available (see Yellow Pages of telephone book under Consulates for phone number). If a consulate recommends a lawyer, bear in mind that the consultation charge can be up to $200 an hour , so clarify in advance. An alternative would be to apply to a lawyer's guild or professional referral group, where a 1/2-hour consultation is $20-25.

NATIONAL LAWYER'S GUILD REFERENCE PANEL, 558 Capp (20-21 Sts), 647-5297. Charge for first half-hour $20.

S.F. BAR ASSOCIATION LAWYER REFERRAL SERVICE, 685 Market Street, 764-1615. $25 for first half-hour.

WOMEN AGAINST RAPE, 24-hour answering service, 647-7273.

LEGAL ASSISTANCE TO THE ELDERLY, 333 Valencia (14/15 Sts), 861-4444. Phone for information and referral.

AIDS LEGAL REFERRAL PANEL, 25 Hickory, 864-8186. Bay Area lawyers provide free simple wills & powers of attorney to persons with AIDS & ARC. More complicated legal matters--involving housing, employment discrimination, bankruptcy, insurance etc.--are handled on a sliding scale, according to ability to pay.

EMPLOYMENT LAW CENTER of the Legal Aid Society of San Francisco, 1663 Mission Street, 864-8848. Provides assistance to persons with AIDS or ARC in cases of employment or insurance discrimination, or in the field of public education.

NATIONAL GAY RIGHTS ADVOCATES, 540 Castro Street, 863-3624. Provides free legal assistance in certain AIDS-discrimination cases.

12. Miscellaneous A-Z

AIDS and ARC (AIDS Related Condition)

6TH INTERNATIONAL CONFERENCE ON AIDS, Moscone Center, San Francisco, June 20-24, 1990. About 15,000 delegates are expected to attend from all over the world--doctors, scientists, psychologists, AIDS activists, government officials, etc. If you plan to attend and need accommodations, start planning early.

Here are some of the more important organizations dealing with AIDS:

SAN FRANCISCO AIDS FOUNDATION, 864-4376. Initiates and coordinates AIDS prevention projects in the Bay Area for the general public and for people at high risk for AIDS. Also provides and coordinates direct social services, referrals, emergency housing, food-bank services for people with AIDS and ARC in San Francisco.

AIDS HOT-LINE (863-AIDS). This service of the S.F. AIDS Foundation operates 24 hours a day, and dispenses open and confidential information on AIDS problems in English & Spanish.

SHANTI PROJECT, 777-2273. Provides emotional support programs for persons with AIDS, their friends, lovers, and families, as well as non-counselling practical support such as transportation, shopping and housekeeping to persons with AIDS. Also, provides long-term low-cost group housing for persons with AIDS. *Note*: When the AIDS patient needs home health care, *Shanti* turns him/her over to Hospice for round-the-clock care.

AIDS INTERFAITH NETWORK, 928-HOPE. Provides spiritual support and counselling to persons with AIDS, their families, lovers and friends. Also, provides education and training to the religious community at large regarding AIDS.

CHURCH GROUPS. Practically all Church groups in San Francisco have special programs for AIDS-afflicted persons in their communities and provide, particularly, bereavement counselling and services. For information apply to the Church of interest. Special mention is made of the following:

CHURCH SERVICES & RESOURCES, KAIRO'S HOUSE, 114 Douglas Street (Market), 861-0877. Father John McGrann in residence, open daily. A spiritual resource center for care-givers and those with AIDS or ARC.

GAY CHURCH SERVICE, RADIANT LIGHT MINISTRIES. Every Sunday 10am, phone for location. Rev. Matt Garrigan. New Wave approach to love & God. Office: 3901 19th Street, San Francisco, CA 94114. Write for Radiant Light Newsletter, or phone 861-1667. Counsellors are available by phone 24 hours, 626-2636.

AIDS AND ARC PROGRAMS OF THE CATHOLIC CHURCH, 1049 Market Street, 864-7400 ext. 26. Emergency help and referral for persons with AIDS or ARC, their families and loved ones.

THE HOPE/HELP CENTER OF THE PARSONAGE, Episcopal Diocese of California, 555-A Castro, 861-HOPE or 800-AID-TALK. This is a church or spiritual resource center for persons with AIDS or ARC, their families, lovers, friends. It is part of a national spiritual network. They work closely with other AIDS groups for exchange and referral.

HOSPICE. Hospice provides 24-hour home health care for the terminally ill. See also under Medical, Dental, Legal Aid section above.

OPERATION CONCERN. See below under Gay Switchboard.

Books, New

Here are some stores offering discounts or bargains:

A WRITER'S BOOK STORE, 2848 Webster (Union) 921-2620.

BOOKS INC, 140 Powell Street (Tro Harper's), 397-1555 & 3515 California (Laurel Village), 221-3666.

CITY LIGHTS, 261 Columbus Ave. (Broadway), 362-8193. A literary meeting place.

COLUMBUS BOOKS, 540 Broadway (Columbus), 986-3872; 84 4th St. (Moscone Center), 896-0611.

CROWN BOOKS, 5198 Castro (18 St), 552-5213, 740 Clement (8/9 Avs), 221-5840, 1245 Sutter (Polk/Van Ness), 441-7479. All books discounted.

DALTON B., 200 Kearny (Sutter), 956-2850 and 2 Embarcadero Center, 982-4278. Especially art books and best-sellers.

DOUBLEDAY, 265 Sutter (Grant/Kearny), 989-3420.

EUROPEAN BOOK STORE, 500 Sutter, (Powell), 362-4812 and

925 Larkin (Geary/Post), 474-0626.

FOLEY BOOK STORE, 119 Sacramento (Drumm), 982-7766. All books discounted.

HUNTER'S BARGAIN BOOKSTORE, 151 Powell Street (O'Farrell), 397-5955. sells thousands of art & and other books at large discount.

KINOKUNIYA BOOKSTORE OF AMERICA, 1581 Webster (Japantown), 567-7625. Complete collection of Japanese, Asian and American books.

PAPERBACK TRAFFIC, 1501 Polk (California), 771-8848. Large selection of gay themes.

RAND MC NALLY, 595 Market Street (2 St), 777-3131. Travel books & maps.

STACEY'S, 581 Market (2nd St), 421-4687. Large economic section.

WALDENBOOKS, see phone book for stores.

Car-Rentals to and from Europe, Asia etc.

For those going to the States, order in your own country and ask for unlimited mileage; you'll get a better rate. The same is true if you are leaving the States for Europe, Asia etc.--order in the States for a better rate. The large companies like Hertz & Avis have an international booking service.

Credit Cards

Many shops, restaurants and department stores will not take *American Express* cards but will take *Visa* or *Mastercard* (in Europe, *Eurocard*). Many gas stations will not accept credit cards, only cash. Those who do, sometimes charge more than for cash.

Daily Events in Five Languages

THE SAN FRANCISCO CONVENTION AND VISITORS BUREAU gives you tips on daily events and sightseeing in French (391-2003), German (391-2004), Spanish (391-2122), English (391-2001), and Japanese (391-2101).

Dial

Note: See phone-book for complete listings.

DIAL-A-PRAYER, 664-7729. Prayers and readings from the Bible.

DIAL-THE-CORRECT TIME, 767-8900.

DIAL-THE-WEATHER REPORT, 936-3212.

DIAL-AN-ATHEIST, 668-8085.

DIAL-A-FRIEND, 976-1221.

Foreign Newspapers and Magazines

HAROLD'S, 599 Post Street (Taylor), 474-2937.

EASTERN NEWSSTAND CORP., 3 Embarcadero Center, 982-4425; 101 California, 989-8986; 1 Market Plaza, 546-1488. European newspapers & magazines.

WASHINGTON'S NEWSTAND, 344 Mason (Geary St), 434-4560.

EUROPEAN BOOK CO., 925 Larkin (Geary/Post), 474-0626.

NAKED EYE, 533 Haight (Fillmore), 864-2985. European newspapers, magazines, and a selection of videos.

MAGAZINE IMPORTS KIOSK, 1504 Haight, 626-2436; 548 Castro, 431-3323; 544 Clement, 221-3556.

CAVALLI BOOKSTORE, 1441 Stockton. European newspapers.

KINOKUNIYA bookstores, 1581 Webster (Japantown), 567-7625. Japanese newspapers & books.

Haight-Ashbury Switchboard

SWITCHBOARD, 1338 Haight (Masonic/Central), 621-6211. This switchboard handles all problems of survival: medical, legal, drugs & cheap transportation (share-rides), etc.

Hairdressers, Barbers

Most everyone needs a haircut now and then. Prices are high in San Francisco, as elsewhere, but if you wash your own hair (the same day), you can get a good, styled haircut for $6–$8 at the following:

GREAT HAIRCUTS, $8. See phone book for listings.

SUPERCUTS, $8, See phone book for listings.

VIEN UON, 657 Geary Street (Leavenworth/Jones), 771-0885. $6.

UNDERHILL'S NOB HILL, 879 Bush (Taylor/Mason), 441-4855, $6, $4 for Seniors.

YICK SAN, 1335 Grant (Green/Vallejo), 433-4990, $4.

AMERICUTS, 5548 Geary Blvd (20 Av), 752-4020 & 297 West Portal Ave, 665-4020, $6.

FANTASTIC SAM'S, 5824 Geary Blvd (22/23 Sts), 221-2777. Adult cut & finish (shampoo, cut) $5.95, kid style & finish $4.95, shampoo & set $6, perm plus (shampoo, cut, perm) $21.95.

VIDAL SASOON, 130 Post Street, 989-0744. The Vidal Education Center is a haircutting school. They advertise 50%-off deals and the like for "individual cuts". A student cuts while a supervisor watches and corrects. Phone for details.

Money Exchange

To avoid charges, it is best to cash traveller's checks at bank of issue. If not possible, exchange at other banks, not hotels. You'll usually get a better rate.

Photocopies

There are machines at Woolworth's, post offices, and drug stores at 10-15 cents a copy. But there are also a number of copying centers in various parts of the city where copies are only 5 cents. These centers also offer a variety of quick-printing services. Here are a few:

COPY CIRCLE, 1701 Polk (Clay), 474-5757.

CARBON ALTERNATIVE. See phone book for locations.

KWIK KOPY, see phone book for locations.

PHOTO DAY, 3512 Geary Blvd, 387-4779.

Post Office

All branch post offices are open from 9am-5:30pm weekdays, and some are open on Saturday 9am-3pm. Rincon Annex, 99 Mission at Spear, is open on weekdays from 8am to 10pm and on Saturday 9am-5pm. Conveniently, the post office in MACY'S on Union Square is open on Sundays from 11am-5pm.

Radio

CLASSICAL MUSIC STATIONS. The following two stations play classical music all day, interspersed with low-key advertising: KDFC, 102.1 FM and KKHI, 95.7 FM.

KGO, AM 81, interesting talk shows and frequent news, weather, and traffic reports.

KQED, FM 88.5, a public radio station of high quality. No advertising. News reported 5-9am and 4-7pm.

NATIONAL PUBLIC RADIO. Station KALW, 91.7 FM. This station is free of advertising and presents high-caliber news reporting

(7-10am and 5-6pm), symphonies, opera etc. Of particular interest to foreign travelers, since it reports extensively on foreign events in the morning, switching to BBC at 9am. A free quarterly program can be obtained by phoning 648-1177.

COUNTRY MUSIC RADIO, KSAN, 94.7 FM.

JAZZ RADIO, KFAZ, 92.7 FM; KPFA, 94.1 FM.

ROCK RADIO, KMEL,106 FM; KOME, 98.5 FM; KTIM, 100.9 FM; KQAK, 98.9 FM; KFOG, 194.5 FM.

Restaurant Talk Show

Russ Riera talk show, "Restaurants in the Bay Area", Sundays at 12:10pm, on KGO, AM 81. Emphasis on good dining at reasonable prices.

Senior Citizens

SENIOR CITIZENS' INFORMATION, 1182 Market, 626-1033, 24 hours. For all kinds of information, for lists of discounts on goods and services, for reduced-price fares (a driver's licence with photo on it, showing age 65 and over, is required). Information can also be obtained from the following: Catholic Office on Aging, 864-4044; Lutheran Care for Aging, 441-7777; Jewish Center, 346-6040. See phone book white pages and yellow pages under Senior Citizens for further references.

Shoe Repair

Actually, you can buy a pair of shoes for what some ask to repair full soles and heels--up to $35. Here are some shoe repair shops where the prices are less than the general run:

VETERAN SHOE SERVICE, 2138 Irving (22nd Ave), 664-3046. Men's heels $7, half soles and heels $21, full soles and heels from $25. Women's heels from $3.50, soles from $10.

STAN'S SHOE REPAIR, 1056 Fillmore, (Golden Gate), 346-2124. Heels--women's $4.50, men's $6.95; 1/2 soles--women's $12.50, men's $17.50; full soles and heels--women's $16.50, men's $24.95. 10% discount for seniors and students. Very good workmanship.

Telegrams, Cablegrams, Night Letters

GRAPHNET, 1-800-336-3729 (8:30am-7pm), or 1-800-631-1581 (24 hours), accepts major credit card. They send Night Letters-- which usually arrive overnight, and are cheaper than direct cablegrams--to most countries, as well as cables which are faster. worldwide.

WESTERN UNION, 1-800-325-6000. Accepts major credit cards for cablegrams to most countries. Will also charge to a U.S. phone. You can also go to their local office in San Francisco, 201 3rd Street (near Howard), tel. 495-7301, from 8am-10pm (9am-6pm Sundays & holidays), and pay cash or via credit card for cablegrams

Traveler's Aid

TRAVELER'S AID SOCIETY OF SAN FRANCISCO, 38 Mason (near Market), 781-6738. Helps travelers in need.

Telephoning Long Distance or Overseas

You cannot phone (or send cablegrams) from post-offices (as is common in most of Europe). If you have access to a private phone, you can direct-dial to most parts of the world or ask the operator for person-to-person calls. Phoning from a hotel is usually much more expensive. If you have to telephone from a hotel, ask what the service charge is. Calls to most overseas locations are cheaper from 6pm to 7am. Check the telephone book for details and rates or call the operator. The same holds true for long-distance calls within the United States. Lower evening rates are from 5pm-11pm and lowest night rates are from 11pm-8am, Mon-Fri and all day Sat-Sun. Before making the call, be sure to determine *the exact time* in the area you are calling, otherwise you may be waking someone at 3am....The Operator can tell you, if you do not know it yourself.

Glossary of Asian & Mexican Cuisines

San Francisco has over 4,000 restaurants. The Chinese restaurants are by far the largest group, followed by Italian, Central-American, Vietnamese, Thai & Japanese. Most of us like to explore new cuisines but often lack the elementary knowledge which is required if the visit to a new (to us) ethnic restaurant is to be a success. Even experienced travelers who are used to new culinary adventures often have embarrassing experiences. Not long ago sophisticated European friends of mine visited a Chinese restaurant for the first time. They wanted to try various dishes, beginning with an exotic-sounding soup. Since they were 3, they ordered 3 soups and were promptly served with 3 huge bowls, each enough for 4 persons! Another problem is that many ethnic menus assume the diner knows the nomenclature. Often the curious diner is not even aware of the *kind* of food he might be getting. For example, not everyone likes tripe soup (menudo), snails (escargots), or frog legs (grenouilles); others consider them delicacies. Perhaps this modest beginning of a Glossary for Asian and Central-American cuisines will help.

Chinese

The Chinese cuisine ranks among the best in the world. Some place it even above the French & Italian. Since China is such a large country, there are regional differences in climate and foods, hence different cuisines have developed. One can divide the cuisines into four major types: *Cantonese, Mandarin, Szechuan* and *Mongolian. Cantonese* is endemic to southern China. Here the food is lightly-seasoned, and quickly stir-fried. Thus, the crispness in the vegetables is preserved and the meats remain tender and tasty. *Mandarin* dishes are spicier, more seasonings are used, including an abundance of garlic and onions. *Szechuan* food is noted for its full-flavor and many dishes are considered "hot", i.e., prepared with chilies. *Mongolian* cuisine uses lamb a good deal, which is often prepared over indoor barbecue devices. There are other sub-categories, e.g., *Hakka* cuisine which derives from a mountain tribe near Canton. This cuisine uses wine in the preparation of some dishes. Another cuisine is *Hunan* which is similar to *Szechuan*, i.e., "hot".

As we all know, the Chinese use chopsticks instead of cutlery in eating their food. As a result, all Chinese food is prepared in "small bites", so that it can be handled by chopsticks. Another characteristic of Chinese food is that it is prepared in such manner that a small group can have a number of dishes, often 5-6 or more, on special occasions. A Chinese meal contains no bread, butter or salad. It usually begins with an appetizer--egg rolls, BBQ ribs etc.--then soup and the main dishes, with rice or noodles. The only recommended cold beverage to drink is beer (although Americans and Europeans often drink wine with the meal). The Chinese drink tea at the end of the meal but in the U.S., the Chinese restaurants serve tea throughout the meal, which I find good.

Some popular Chinese dishes (beginning with appetizers) are-- *potstickers,* chinese ravioli, *chungun,* spring or egg rolls made of pancakes with pork-shrimp or chicken filling; *won ton,* Chinese ravioli with various fillings; *chow mein,* noodles either fried crisply or boiled, with various meats or fish; *egg drop soup;* egg-flower soup; braised fish; shrimp in black bean sauce; chicken with almonds or walnuts; fried or roast duck; sweet and sour pork, beef, shrimp or fish; stir-fried vegetables; rice or noodles with pork, shrimp, fish etc. Most food in Chinese restaurants is prepared *after* it is ordered, in woks (cone-shaped pans which store enormous heat and permit very fast cooking, which is the secret of Chinese cooking).

A "Chinese" way of ordering for a group of 4 or more is to order 1 soup or appetizer, and 1 main dish for each person, plus rice. Tea usually comes with the meal automatically, at no extra cost. This will be ample, even too much for some.

Mexican, Central-American

San Francisco has many Central-American restaurants, mostly Mexican. The other cuisines--e.g., Salvadoran, Nicaraguan, Cuban--are similar to Mexican and use similar ingredients. Here is a listing of the more popular dishes: *Tacos*--crisp corn tortillas folded & filled with beef, chicken or pork, lettuce, tomatoes & grated cheese. *Tostados*--open-face, crisp corn tortillas covered with chicken, beef or pork, lettuce, tomatoes & grated cheese. *Burritos*--flour tortilla rolled & filled with beef, pork or chicken. *Enchiladas*--soft corn tortillas dipped in a mild red sauce and stuffed with cheese, chicken, beef or pork and topped with sour cream, lettuce & grated cheese. *Chile relleno*--large Mexican green pepper (not hot), stuffed with

Monterey Jack cheese and topped with salsa. *Carnitas*–seasoned chunks of pork deep-fried and topped with tomatoes and onions. *Flautas*–rolled crisp tortillas stuffed with beef or chicken and topped with sour cream and guacamole (avocado dip). *Steak ranchero*–sauteed beef with bell peppers, onions, tomatoes and mild salsa. *Machaca*–chunks of beef, scrambled with eggs. *Spanish omelette*–made with mild salsa, bell pepper, onions and tomatoes. *Birria*–stew, lamb or goat. *Menudo*–tripe.

Thai (Siamese)

Thai dishes are among the spiciest in the world. The dominant spices used are coriander, lemon grass, citrus juice, tamarind, garlic, basil and chilies. Staples are fresh vegetables, fish and rice. They also use peanuts, coconut milk and curries, as does the cuisine of India. The green curries are the hottest. But they also have mild dishes, particularly the noodle salads with carmelized sauce and shrimp, or the egg rolls filled with rice and shrimp or crab. They also have mild soups, light salads and steamed dishes for the more timid. The Thais do not use chop sticks but eat with fork and spoon (no knife). They drink tea or beer during or after the meal. Desserts are novel, e.g., the liquid desserts of pureed fruits or the puddings made with sago (tapioca) or rice flour.

Cambodian, Laotian, Burmese foods are similar to Thai and Chinese, some a bit milder than Thai.

Japanese

A typical Japanese meal begins with *sake* (rice wine) served warm. Japanese observe a great deal of ceremony in serving and drinking the sake, as they do in setting the table and in serving and drinking tea. Food is regarded as an esthetic experience, hence a typical Japanese meal will contain much artistic detail. For example, a tiny but perfect sliver of carrot is placed in clear consomme and meat is arranged with mathematical precision. Soups are clear (suimono) or in a base of fermented beans and malt (*miso-shiru*). *Tempura* is deep-fried food. *Sukiyaki* is chicken or beef with soy sauce, pan-fried with vegetables and Japanese noodles. The Japanese like to finish a meal with a bite of pickle (*konomon* or *daikon*) made from the giant white radish which is about 3-feet long. Some everyday Japanese dishes are *udon* (a wheat-flour noodle), *tofu* (a soybean curd), *soba* (buckwheat noodles), *gohan* (boiled rice), *nimame* (boiled beans), *yosenabe* (a soup containing fish, meat, vegetables). Japanese green tea is the favorite beverage.

Vietnamese

This cuisine is similar to Thai but milder. Chilies are used a lot, however, in southern Vietnam). There is a similarity to Chinese cooking as well, especially in the spring rolls (*cha gio*) which are made from bean sprouts, bean threads, pork & crabmeat wrapped in transparent rice paper and fried. The cuisine uses coriander, lemon grass, mint and basil, like the Thai. The most important ingredient is a pungent flavoring made from fermented anchovies, other small fish and salt, called *nuoc mam*. The Vietnamese use this in almost every dish, together with garlic, shallots, sugar and chiles as a dipping sauce which is called *nuoc sham*. The Vietnamese use chopsticks and eat family-style, like the Chinese. A typical meal would consist of one or two appetizers, soup, and 4-5 main dishes, for 4 or more persons. Some favorite Vietnamese dishes are–*chao tom*, ground seasoned shrimp served on skewers. *Sup man cua*, a creamy asparagus and crabmeat soup flavored with *nuoc mam* and pepper; *Ga xao sa ot* is chicken sauteed with lemon grass, chile and fish sauce; also known as "singing chicken"; *ca chien*, deep-fried fish; *ca hap*, steamed fish garnished with pork, ginger, scallions, pickled cabbage and tomatoes; *nem nuong*, barbecued pork balls, served with peanut sauce; *tom rim*, shrimp in a sauce of carmelized sugar and seasoned with pepper. There is also a fondue dish, *thit bo nhung dam*, which consists of raw slices of beef dipped in a flavored beef stock and often eaten with scallions and vegetables wrapped in rice paper. Due to the French influence, the Vietnamese often drink wine with their meals but tea, beer, and coffee are also popular.

List of Ethnic Restaurants

* Especially recommended

Index

Notes

Notes